For Bernice,

with thanks,

George
1/30/92

NIKOLAI F. FEDOROV: AN INTRODUCTION

George M. Young, Jr.

Nikolai F. Fedorov: An Introduction

NORDLAND PUBLISHING COMPANY
BELMONT, MASSACHUSETTS 02178
1979

This book is dedicated to my parents and to the memory of William Blackburn, 1899-1974

Library of Congress Catalog Card Number LC 78119
ISBN 0-913124-31-1

© Copyright 1979
by
NORDLAND PUBLISHING COMPANY, INC.
ALL RIGHTS RESERVED

This publication may not be reproduced, stored in a retrieval system, or transmitted in whole or in part, in any form or by any means, electronic, mechanical, photocopying, recording, or otherwise, without the prior written permission of Nordland Publishing Co.

PRINTED IN THE UNITED STATES OF AMERICA
BY
ATHENS PRINTING COMPANY
NEW YORK, N.Y.

CONTENTS

PREFACE 7

CHAPTER I
FEDOROV IN LIFE 13
  The Idea 13
  Origins and Early Life 17
  Fedorov and Dostoevskii 37
  Fedorov and Solov'ev 52
  Fedorov and Tolstoi 60
  Last Years 71

CHAPTER II
THE COMMON TASK 77
  The Philosophy of the Common Task 77
  Resurrecting the Dead 93
  Regulating Nature 113
  Integrating Knowledge and Action 119
  The Role of the Autocrat 126
  Christ as the Icon of Sonship 145

CHAPTER III
FEDOROV IN CONTEXT 151
  Fedorov and His Times 151
  Fedorov and Russian Thought 168
  Fedorov and the Twentieth Century 180

NOTES   201
  Notes to Preface   201
  Notes Chapter   I   206
  Notes Chapter II   216
  Notes Chapter III   219

APPENDIX I   227
  Contents of *The Philosophy of the Common Task* 228

APPENDIX II   237
  Fedorov in Askhabad   237

BIBLIOGRAPHY   247

INDEX OF NAMES   269

PREFACE

The purpose of this book is to introduce readers of English to the eccentric life and remarkable thought of Nikolai Fedorovich Fedorov (pronounced and sometimes spelled Fyodorov), a major, neglected Russian thinker who was born probably in 1828, died in 1903, worked most of his life as an obscure Moscow librarian, and believed that the only solution to every problem now known to man was for all men now living to join what Fedorov called "the common task" of resurrecting all the dead.

As startling—even as absurd—as his idea may sound at first, Fedorov's "project" of universal, physical resurrection is, I would submit, one of the most profound, comprehensive, and original ideas in the history of Russian speculation. As I hope to demonstrate in the course of this study, Fedorov's "common task" is both a synthesis of the entire tradition of Russian thought and a unique system unlike anything conceived before or since. Fedorov is at once both the most traditional and the most original of Russian thinkers. His idea both includes and goes beyond all ideas traditionally labeled "Russian."

Partly because of his predilection for obscurity, and partly because he feared that his ideas were too radical to be understood by most of his contemporaries, Fedorov published almost nothing during his lifetime. And his one, lifelong work, *The Philosophy of the Common Task*,[1] would not even have been published posthumously had not three disciples, V. A. Kozhevnikov[2], N. P. Peterson[3], and N. A. Setnitskii[4], taken upon themselves the formidable tasks of collecting, editing, printing, and reprinting the disorganized piles of manuscripts that Fedorov had been writing and rewriting for most of his life.

That Fedorov has had probably only a few dozen serious readers in the last hundred years matters little when one considers who some of those few dozen readers were and what they said about Fedorov's idea. Dostoevskii wrote of Fedorov: "He has aroused my interest more than enough... I am essentially in complete agreement with these ideas. I have read them as if they were my own." Vladimir Solov'ev wrote: "I accept your 'project' completely and without any discussion. Since the time of the appearance of Christianity your 'project' is the first forward movement of the human spirit along the path of Christ. For my part I can only regard you as my teacher and spiritual father." And the poet Fet tells us that Tolstoi once remarked of Fedorov: "I am proud to have lived at the same time as such a man." And Fet added: "One must have considerable spiritual capital to be deserving of such opinions, but I do not know one person who is acquainted with you who would not have said the same about you. If I did not consider it too awkward then I too would dare to include myself among such people." [5]

In this century, the first to write about Fedorov were his disciples. Kozhevnikov begins his study of Fedorov: "A wonderful, rare, exceptional man has passed away. Those who knew him at all do not have to be reminded of Nikolai Fedorovich Fedorov's exalted mind, of his conscientiousness as a worker, and of his ideal moral purity; without any prompting, they will say: 'he was a wise and righteous man;' and those closer to him will add: 'he was one of the small number of saints who hold the world together.' " [6]

As might be expected of disciples, Kozhevnikov, Peterson, and Setnitskii more often treat Fedorov's ideas as doctrine to be propounded than as thoughts to be analyzed or criticized, and treat his life as a subject more nearly fit for hagiography than biography. But, as N. V. Ustrialov writes: "One does not have to be a 'Fedorovian' to sense in this original system something uncommon and compelling. Its unparalleled, head-spinning optimism is apt to intoxicate one's soul." [7]

One who was not a "Fedorovian," the literary critic D. S. Mirskii, considered Fedorov "the greatest of Russian religious thinkers." [8] And another literary critic well known in his day, A. L. Volynskii, wrote: "Fedorov is a unique, unaccountable, and incomparable phenomenon in the intellectual history of mankind.... The thousand year existence of Russia has been justified by the birth and life of Fedorov. No one anywhere on earth can now reproach us for having failed to offer up to the ages a fruitful thought or a labor begun by genius.... In Fedorov in and of himself lies the atonement for all sins and crimes of the Russian people."[9]

The religious philosopher, Father Sergei Bulgakov, wrote of Fedorov: "A most original mind and a most original man speaks to you from these pages, so variegated in theme, but imbued throughout with a unity of thought. An extraordinary feeling takes hold of you at once—a reverence and awe before a greatness that is genuine and unassertive in our vain, clamorous age."[10] And Nikolai Berdiaev, who is probably still the best known of the remarkable group of religious philosophers who left Russia in the 1920's, and who has written frequently and extensively about Fedorov, tells us: "Nikolai Fedorovich Fedorov was a man of genius. Fedorov was Russian to the core, one who epitomized the particularities of Russian thought and Russian soul-searching."[11]

And, finally, Konstantin Tsiolkovskii, the once-ridiculed genius who is now venerated as the father of the Soviet space program, said in an interview: "it is no exaggeration to say that for me he took the place of university professors.... I bow down before Fedorov."[12]

Fedorov's influence, and "Fedorovian tendencies" have been detected by one commentator or another in works of many of the leading poets, novelists, artists, scientists, and political figures of the Soviet period: Valerii Briusov, Andrei Belyi, Vladimir Maiakovskii, Velimir Khlebnikov, Boris Pasternak, Nikolai Zabolotskii, Anna Akhmatova, V. I. Vernadskii, Aleksandr Scriabin, even Iosif Stalin.[13] And, most recently, one could perhaps even add Solzhenitsyn, whose letter to the leaders of Russia may have shocked western intellectuals, but should seem quite understandable (and familiar) to anyone who has read Fedorov.[14]

Clearly, then, Fedorov is a figure of major stature. Yet both the man and his work have received relatively little attention from students of Russian literature and thought. One reason for this neglect is that until recently Fedorov's own works and the major commentaries on him have been extremely difficult to lay hands on. Nearly all the most important items are great bibliographic rarities, few are available in one place, and most are too fragile to be duplicated or allowed out on interlibrary loan. The unavailability of essential materials, and the need to travel to most of the major research libraries of America and Europe, has greatly inhibited serious study of Fedorov.[15] Another reason for the general neglect is that many of the earliest and most vocal Fedorovians were zealots and enthusiasts who made such outrageous claims that serious academic commentators have not wanted to be associated with them For a while, in the late twenties and early thirties, serious commentators had to spend a great deal of time explaining who they were not and what they did not think before they could begin to state what they thought. And to a certain extent, Fedorov's reputation still suffers from the distorted versions of his idea propagated by early, evangelistic "Fedorovians."[16] Third, the religious side of Fedorov's thought made him unfit for the official Soviet pantheon of major precursors of dialectical materialism, while the scientific side of his thought repelled many of the *émigré* religious philosophers. The question of which side Fedorov's thought was on, "ours" or "theirs", made objective discussion difficult for both Soviet and *émigré* thinkers.

So for these, and probably other reasons as well, Fedorov's work has not received the attention it deserves. Much of what has been written about him, not only in Western languages, but even in Russian, is based on the most readily available, rather than on the most valuable, primary and secondary sources. In reading the secondary literature on Fedorov, one comes across any number of variations of the same, basic five to eight page summary. Each new author adds a few observations or generalizations of his own, but the essential picture remains the same. The same details are always included, and the same equally important details and facts from the less readily available sources are always left out.

In this book I have attempted to present more information

about Fedorov's life and to discuss more sides of his "project" in fuller detail than has previously been possible. Nevertheless, my study remains only a general introduction. Fedorov is such a vast topic, so much about him and his thought remains unknown or uninvestigated, so many individual points need to be treated in greater detail, that "the definitive work" on Fedorov must remain a project for the future.

The literature on Fedorov, incomplete, tentative, and scanty as it is, bristles with controversy. In addition to those who consider him "the atonement for all sins and crimes of the Russian people" there are those who consider him "half crazy," a dreamer, a mystic, a "reactionary," and those who consider his project "an imaginary project," a call for sorcery and magic, a "nightmare." [17]

From the start, I would like to make my personal attitude toward Fedorov and his project clear. I am not a Fedorovian, and for reasons that I present in the course of this study, I do not accept his project of resurrection. But I am convinced that Fedorov is one of the two or three greatest thinkers that Russia has produced, that his ideas are worth the most serious consideration, and that despite his present obscurity his "place" in the Russian pantheon of intellects is neither above nor below, but on a level with, that of even his greatest contemporaries, Tolstoi, Solov'ev, and Dostoevskii. I would not attempt to argue that Fedorov is the "justification" of the "thousand year history of Russia," but I would submit that *The Philosophy of the Common Task* is one of the great Russian books, the equivalent in philosophy of the "loose and baggy monsters" that seemed something less and more than novels to the fastidious Henry James. Fedorov's book is not philosophy in the strict sense, nor is it poetry or fiction in the strict sense—but like *War and Peace*, *The Gulag Archipelago*, and *Notes from Underground*, it creates the need for a new taxonomy, it makes its own genre for itself, and stands colossal, isolated, and imperfect, an inspiration to the generalist, a snare for the imitator, an annoyance to the purist.

My emphasis throughout is on the complexity and scope of Fedorov's idea, on the many sides of his idea of resurrection, and on the points of similarity and difference between

Fedorov's idea and the ideas of his compatriots and contemporaries. I touch on a number of points that deserve fuller discussion than is possible in a study of this kind. Fortunately, other students of Fedorov and his thought have either recently completed or are presently at work on discussions of separate topics, such as Fedorov's relationship to Western philosophy, and the idea of physical resurrection as a philosophical concept, which I have not attempted to discuss in detail here.[18] My purpose is more nearly to present a general overview of Fedorov's life and thought than to offer an exhaustive analysis of any single aspect of his biography or project.

This study, an earlier version of which was presented as a doctoral dissertation for the department of Slavic languages and literatures at Yale University, has benefitted from suggestions, criticisms, and comments by a number of people. Among those whom I would especially like to thank are my teachers at Yale, Robert Louis Jackson and Victor Erlich; my Dartmouth colleagues Jeffrey Hart, and Charles Stinson; George L. Kline, Taras Zakydalsky, and Alexey Kiselev, who have offered especially valuable suggestions; Dorothy Beck, Anselm Parlatore, and Evelyn Marcus for "nonspecialist" observations; Maurice Hanrahan of Gregg International; Richard Haugh of Tuskegee Institute; Barbara Brown, Lois Krieger, Patricia Carter, Virginia Close, Teresa Blake, and Ralph Cryesky of Baker Library; Barbara Lönnqvist and Michael Winn, for special help in obtaining rare materials; Elisabeth Koutaissoff and Professor N. Zernov for sharing their information and research with me; Nellie Plummer for help in preparing sections of the manuscript; Patricia Vaughan, for personal sacrifices; and the many staff members at Harvard, Columbia, and Helsinki university libraries, the New York Public Library, the Lenin Library in Moscow, and the Saltykov-Shchedrin and Academy of Sciences libraries in Leningrad. Finally, I am especially grateful to Dean Fred Berthold and to the Faculty Research Committee at Dartmouth College for grants which helped to make the publication of this book possible.

CHAPTER I

FEDOROV IN LIFE

The Idea

"Now there's a saintly man" said Lev Nikolaevich. "He owns nothing; any book that he buys or that is given him he at once donates to the library. At home he sleeps on a trunk on newspapers in a tiny little room he rents from some old woman. He is, of course, a vegetarian, but is bashful and doesn't like to talk about it. But do you know, he has his own theory!"

And Tolstoi began to tell us something strange: Fedorov can in no way reconcile himself with the thought that men are dying and that people now very dear to us will vanish without a trace, and he has developed a theory that science, by a giant step forward, will discover a means to extract from the earth the remains—the particles—of our forefathers, in order then to restore them again to living form.

—from the notebook
of V. F. Lazurskii, July 13, 1894.[1]

Fedorov was a thinker with one vast idea. He believed that all problems known to man have a single root in the problem of death, and that no solution to any social, economic, political, or philosophical problem will prove adequate until men have solved the problem of death. But if a solution to the problem of death can be found, then solutions to any and all other problems will follow.

Fedorov believed, and throughout his works attempted to demonstrate, that any question, no matter how apparently trivial, is at root a question of life and death. A consideration of the development of handwriting,[2] or of the history of the human race,[3] will lead to one and the same conclusion: that disintegration is the universal rule, and that redintegration is the human task. Everywhere that Fedorov looks he sees manifestations of the natural principle of disintegration and death, and yet, with unfailing optimism, he views every instance of disintegration as a fresh opportunity for men to begin their common task. In grief for the world as it presently exists, Fedorov finds that nothing now operates free of death's power: even in the smile of a beautiful woman, in the sublime cantos of Dante's *Paradiso*, and in the cry of a newborn infant,[4] Fedorov sees death. And yet so profound is Fedorov's faith in man's potential creativity that even in long forgotten graveyards and in regions too desolate to support human life at present, Fedorov finds grand opportunities to restore death to life.

Fedorov speaks of two kinds of death. The one he gives most attention to is death as a disintegration. Particle is separated from particle, the inner ties dissolve, the whole is shattered. Fedorov finds disintegration everywhere—in the physical universe, in society, in the family, even within the individual. Wholeness is no longer to be found anywhere. The task of man here is to restore to wholeness and life all that nature would disaggregate and drive to death. The opposite of disintegration, in the world as it presently exists, is not wholeness, but fusion. This also is a kind of death. Each unit loses its individuality and particularity, and all discrete parts are amalgamated into a lifeless mass. Fedorov finds death by fusion, like death by disintegration, present everywhere: in mass movements, in blind allegiance to calls to war, and in the swallowing of the lives of individual rural villages by cities. The task here is to decentralize, to turn the lifeless, shapeless mass back into living units. The world "as it is" operates under the principles of disintegration and fusion, everything is either disaggregated into unconnected particles or amalgamated into huge, lifeless, corporate entities. The common task is to reverse the natural flow of life toward the two opposite poles of death, and to restore everywhere a wholeness that insures both the integrity of the unit and the unity of the whole. The model—or icon—for the universe "as it should be" is the Holy Trinity, perfect as both three and one.

In today's terms, Fedorov's project might be described as an attempt to turn the universe of the "big bang" into one of a "steady state." In Fedorov's utopia (which he did not consider a utopia, but the world "as it ought to be"), there will be neither birth nor death, but a gradual restoration of life to all who have ever lived. The life in unity of all mankind must include the dead. For men to stop the task of unification after only the living had been united would, Fedorov insisted, be an act of selfishness and immaturity. Maturity requires that sons and daughters not only take life from their parents, but return it.

By uniting all people alive in a task to overcome the only true enemy of all people alive, namely death, the project of resurrection would represent a great step toward the solution of many other problems which seem insoluble today. Energies and resources now directed toward war would be directed toward resurrection. Historical enemies would find mutual assistance not only possible but necessary. Unbelievers, who in theory might find Christianity unacceptable, would, by resurrecting the dead, become in practice followers of Christ.

The resurrection of the dead would be a long and gradual, but, ultimately, universal project. The first steps might consist of little more than the brief, temporary resuscitation of a person who had just died. But, as all scientific technology, socio-political organization,—indeed all human knowledge and action—gradually became directed toward the goal of resurrection, more than brief and temporary resuscitation would soon be possible. Eventually, the synthesizing of bodies should be possible, and ultimately, Fedorov believed, whole persons could be re-created from the least trace recovered. To recover particles of disintegrated ancestors, Fedorov imagined, research teams would have to travel to the moon, the planets, and to distant points throughout the universe. Eventually these outer points of the cosmos would be inhabited by the resurrected ancestors, whose bodies might be synthesized so as to live under conditions that could not now support human life as it is known.

These, and other details of Fedorov's project, will be discussed at some length in the second part of the present study. For now, it is perhaps sufficient to say that while Fedorov may be considered a thinker with one idea, his single idea was extremely complex. He includes any number of individual projects within his one grand project of resurrection. Some of these subsidiary projects, such as the gathering of all nations into one political unit governed by a Russian autocrat, constitute in themselves vast and complex undertakings. Other projects, such as the establishing of small, local museums, are less grandiose in scale. But an important point to be made, even from the start, is that all of Fedorov's projects are interrelated, and all are directed toward the ultimate goal of resurrecting all the dead. Fedorov's scientific projects cannot be understood in isolation from his religious, political, artistic, and economic projects. He clearly understood that technological advance, if pursued independently from advances in morality, the arts, government, and spirituality, and if pursued for its own sake or for purposes other than the resurrection of the ancestors, could end only in disaster. And further, he understood that spiritual development alone, without scientific technology, could also lead only to a dead end. Many thinkers before and since Fedorov have proposed one or more of the ideas that Fedorov puts forward. But only Fedorov puts them all into one project.

Fedorov was convinced that his project was realizable. He insists throughout that his ideas are not utopian fantasies but are part of a realistic, workable task. He does not himself claim to know how, for instance, future biologists will create synthetic bodies. But he does insist that if, as they should, future biologists take the creation of synthetic bodies as their task they can and will find the solution. Fedorov believes that man's creative potential is unlimited. In the long run, people can accomplish whatever they set out to accomplish. Fedorov argues that we are now at work on our own destruction, and that the only way that we can not destroy ourselves is by radically altering our goal of unconsious self-annihilation to the goal of conscious self-perfection. And the only way to do this is to stop doing everything that we are doing now and to start trying to resurrect the dead.

One of the most important parts of Fedorov's idea has to do with the need to redintegrate life and thought. People now are divided into two classes: those who live thoughtless lives, and those who think lifeless thoughts. What most impressed

Tolstoi about Fedorov was his apparent ability to live exactly in accordance with his own teachings—something that Tolstoi had found all but impossible to do. And in many ways, Fedorov's own life can be understood as a simple, unforced, unadvertised attempt to incarnate the essence of his thought. It would be wrong to attempt to reduce Fedorov's entire philosophy to an obssession easily explained by a few choice bits of available biographical information. But it can be said with some truth that what is known of Fedorov's life is not as irrelevant to our understanding of his thought as may be the case with other philosophers.

Origins and Early Life

Fedorov was the illegitimate son of a Russian prince and a woman whose identity remains unknown. The father, Prince Pavel Ivanovich Gagarin, was an undistinguished member of one of Russia's oldest and most illustrious families. From Fedorov's father, the line has been traced back as far as Riurik, the legendary founder of Russia.[5] Fedorov's grandfather, Ivan Alekseevich Gagarin, was a dignitary and a leading freemason of Catherine's time. This Gagarin's second wife was the noted actress, Katerina Semenova,[6] considered by Pushkin to have been the greatest tragic actress of her time. Through marriage, the Gagarin family was related to the Kropotkin family, and thus Fedorov was the unacknowledged second cousin of the famous anarchist, P. A. Kropotkin. Another, closer relative of Fedorov's was Ivan Sergeevich Gagarin, a leading Slavophile of the 30's and 40's who later converted to Roman Catholicism and became a Jesuit. Of the Gagarin family in general, P. A. Kropotkin once wrote that it was after the infusion of Gagarin blood that the Kropotkin family first began to display literary talent and social concern.[7]

Fedorov's mother could claim no such pedigree. According to one source, she was a simple peasant woman, according to another, a captive Circassian girl.[8] All that can now be said of her is that she remains one of the nameless masses, one of those whose accomplishments and sufferings remain unrecorded, whose full or empty lives pass without general notice, who are swallowed by the earth, forgotten by history, and replaced by those whose fate will be the same. From first to last, Fedorov was the issue of two very different Russias.

Fedorov was born somewhere in central south Russia, probably near Tambov, and probably between January and April of 1828, the same year in which Tolstoi was born.[9] There is some evidence that he had at least one brother and one, possibly two sisters. Together with his mother and the other children, Fedorov probably lived the first few years of his life in the luxury of the Gagarin household.

A few things are known about Fedorov's father. P. I. Gagarin was born in 1798, was educated at home, was further schooled in the Tsar's *corps des pages*, and apparently took the entrance examinations for, but did not enter, Moscow University. He was discharged from military service in 1822 for unknown reasons, and after a brief stint in the Ministry of Foreign Affairs, in which he was assigned for a short time to Philadelphia, Pennsylvania, he resigned "for reasons of health" at the age of twenty-eight, and did not work again for the remaining six years of his life. It was probably during his "retirement" that Pavel Ivanovich Gagarin began his liaison with Fedorov's mother. That Fedorov was not an only child suggests that the liaison was not simply a brief affair between a master and a servant. After the death of Pavel Ivanovich in 1832, Fedorov, his mother, and the other children were forced to leave the Gagarin household. Nothing is known of the further lives of Fedorov's mother and brother and sisters.

Among Fedorov's papers, the editors of his posthumous works found only one torn sheet of autobiographical material. It reads: "From the years of childhood three memories remain clear to me: I saw black, very black bread, on which (I heard people say) the peasants fed in what was probably some year of famine. From childhood I heard an explanation of war (to my question about it) that put me into terrible confusion: 'in war people shoot *each other*.' And, finally, I learned that some people are not one's kin but strangers, and even one's kin are not kin but strangers."[10]

These three childhood memories, recalled nead the end

of a long life of activity and thought, point to three of Fedorov's abiding concerns: the problems of hunger, war, and the absence of feelings of kinship among men. His project of resurrection would eventually include proposals that men regulate nature to provide adequate harvests, that implements of war be turned into instruments of salvation, and that Christianity become a project of universal sonship and a labor to restore life to the fathers. The memory that "even one's kin are not kin but strangers" is Fedorov's only recorded reference to his own illegitimate birth. But Fedorov's entire work can, in part, be understood as an attempt to deal, on a universal scale, with a problem that he first had to confront when he became fully aware of the circumstances of his birth. In a sense, Fedorov views all people as illegitimate children: the issue of blind natural force; offspring who have no true knowledge of even their mortal fathers—much less the divine Father; brothers and sisters unaware, or unwilling to acknowledge, that they are of one family. Fedorov's reaction to the problem of illegitimacy is opposite that of Shakespeare's Edmund, whose secret thought is: "legitimate Edgar, I must have your land" (*King Lear*, I, ii), and whose first concern is for sons ignored by their fathers. In Fedorov, all children are born illegitimate, and the task of all is to win legitimacy together by restoring life to the fathers they have ignored.

And although Fedorov never uses the word "illegitimate," the role that he always assumes for himself in his writings is that of the outsider looking in, the unlearned man addressing an audience of learned men, the practical man talking to philosophers. As a nobleman without a title, an educated man without a degree, and a teacher without an academic appointment, Fedorov was able to discuss "learned" questions from an unusual perspective. His ideas, he believed, were not particularly original, but were simply ideas that have long been common among the people. By giving these ideas philosophical expression, Fedorov was merely making them accessible to intellectuals. As an "unlearned" man addressing "the learned," Fedorov insisted that he was merely pointing out problems which those who lacked privilege and comfort could not afford to ignore.

The patronymic and surname, Fedorovich Fedorov, probably came from the child's godfather.[11] Other than that the mother and children were evicted from the Gagarin household, nothing is known of Fedorov's life between the death of his father in 1832 and his graduation from the gymnasium in Tambov in 1848. He then attended the Richelieu Lyceum in Odessa until March of 1854, when, for undetermined reasons, he left the school without taking his degree. According to his later friend and disciple, N. P. Peterson, Fedorov left the Lyceum just before graduation, when, during an oral examination, he fell into a heated dispute with one of his instructors and refused to stand for further examination. Later, to a colleague at the Rumiantsev Museum, Fedorov mentioned that he had not obtained his degree because of an act of insubordination.[12]

Although he did not attend a university, Fedorov's education was a good one for a young man of the time. That he studied at the respected Richelieu Lyceum indicates that his father or some other member of the Gagarin family had provided him with the encouragement and the means to receive a sound education. That he left before receiving his degree suggests that quite early in life he had acquired some of the stubbornness, self-assurance, and intellectual independence that characterize his later writings and that seems to have been a trait of the Gagarin line.

After the Lyceum, Fedorov began his years of wandering through southern and central Russia. From 1854 to 1868, he moved from one provincial village to another, serving as a teacher of elementary history and geography in such places as Lipetsk, Bogorodsk, Uglich, Odoeva, Bogoroditsk, Borovsk, and Podolsk. As a teacher, Fedorov seems to have been loved by his pupils and regarded by his superiors as a nuisance and a crank. Kozhevnikov tells us that Fedorov's frequent removals were due to his unwillingness to limit his work to prescribed activities. Apparently he caused constant friction by going beyond the duties officially assigned to teachers. In later years, Kozhevnikov tells us, Fedorov's former pupils continued to seek his advice on major decisions and his answers to questions that troubled them in life. Fedorov believed that a teacher should treat his pupils like sons. Love, not discipline, should be the rule. This did not mean letting children run wild or encouraging them to follow their "natural" i.e. self-destructive—inclinations. Fedorov's idea was, rather, that a teacher show his paternal love by letting students join him in common tasks. Students should learn about nature, for example, by participating in some project of study or regulation organized and supervised by a mature scientist. As a teacher, Fedorov did not want to take the place of the student's father, but rather to serve as a paternal model in situations that would let children see how to work with their elders. Fedorov believed that the entire family should take part in the children's education, and he encouraged his pupils to undertake projects which could only be accomplished with help from home.

One of the stories that Kozhevnikov tells of Fedorov indicates the depth of Fedorov's love for his pupils. Like other provincial school teachers in Russia at that time, Fedorov received a salary that only a saint could live well on. Nevertheless, Fedorov's greatest concern seems to have been not how to increase his income but how to give the largest part of his meager income away. Once when a pupil's father fell ill and could not pay for a doctor, Fedorov gave the boy all his money to defray the father's medical expenses. When the pupil's father died, Fedorov sold his only teacher's uniform and gave the proceeds to the orphan to pay for the burial. When Fedorov appeared in school without his uniform, wearing the only other shabby clothes he owned, a school inspector severely reprimanded him for having dared appear in class in dress not befitting the station of teacher, and demanded an immediate explanation. Fedorov stubbornly refused to offer any explanation and apparently indicated that he would rather resign than say a word in his own defense. Fortunately, on this occasion, the principal evidently learned the whole story and persuaded Fedorov not to resign. But from this incident one can perhaps begin to understand why Fedorov seldom stayed at any school for more than one year.

The years that Fedorov spent as a village teacher were critical years in the life of Russia. The Crimean War, the Emancipation of serfs, the decline of village life and the growth of cities, and the emergence of a radical intelligentsia all combined to make this period one of the most decisive in the history of the country. The Russia that Fedorov knew during these years of enormous change was not the Russia of Moscow and Petersburg, but the Russia of Lipetsk, Bogorodsk, Uglich, and Podolsk. The people he knew were not those who were making decisions for all, but those who had to live with whatever decisions were made. In the villages where Fedorov lived, war meant peasants returning without arms or legs and families without fathers or sons. Emancipation meant being uprooted. Education meant learning to remove oneself from the common people and the common life.

Fedorov would later write that the most serious division between men was not between rich and poor but between the learned and the unlearned. Those of the learned class, he argued, had separated themselves from the unlearned masses, from the soil, from their origins, from their fathers, and, ultimately, from nature, God, and life. The learned, who had the knowledge to control the blind, destructive forces of nature, did not feel the need to do so. Living in cities, insensible to nature's brute power, the learned viewed nature merely from an aesthetic standpoint. The unlearned, on the other hand, who knew and daily had to bear the brunt of nature's blind force, had the desire but lacked the knowledge to exercise control. To the learned, nature was a matter of beauty or ugliness; to the unlearned, a matter of life and death.

Moreover, by pursuing knowledge for its own sake and scorning all practical application of knowledge, Fedorov argued, the learned merely aided those who would wage war. "At the present time everything serves war. There is not one discovery which the military could not apply toward war, not one invention which they could not attempt to turn toward military aims." (1, 4) The learned contribute to the waging of war either directly, by discoveries which can be turned into weapons, or indirectly, by allowing their discoveries to be turned into commercial articles which result in competition which eventually leads to war. The only solution was for the learned to turn themselves into a temporary task force whose assignment would be to find practical means to regulate nature.

In the war against nature, all armies of the world would collaborate to liberate mankind from blind force, and all military weapons would be turned into instruments for the benefit of man. As an indication of how this might be done, Fedorov pointed to a discovery by American scientists that cannons fired into clouds could sometimes bring rain.[13] If in war, "people shoot each other", in the task of regulation people would shoot their cannons not at each other but at the natural forces they wished to control. This simple, but radical shift in direction seemed to Fedorov the first step toward the solution of the problem of how to keep people from killing each other and how to attain everlasting life for all. By shifting his orientation from horizontal to vertical,[14] in the aiming of cannons and in every other way, man could begin the task of his own resurrection.

In the early 1860's, the book that all young Russian intellectuals were talking about was Chernyshevskii's long, turgid, didactic novel, *What Is To Be Done?* In his hero, Rakhmetov, and his heroine, Vera, Chernyshevskii attempted to create positive models to be emulated by Russian youth. In deliberate contrast to the line of talented but ineffectual "superfluous men" notorious to all students of Russian literature, Rakhmetov is an upright, faultless, unwavering "new man" selflessly dedicated to his "cause", the establishing of utopian communes and the eventual revolutionary transformation of Russian society. Vera, the model of the new Russian woman, launches, as her part in the transformation of Russia, a sewing cooperative in which three young girls gradually become aware of the benefits of communal life and labor.

This book, and the writings of Chernyshevskii's two younger fellow "nihilists", Nikolai Dobroliubov (1836-1861) and Dmitrii Pisarev (1840-1868), had an enormous impact on the student generation of the 1860's. Living in tiny, filthy, book-cluttered rooms, underlining pages of Mill, Comte, Darwin, and Büchner's *Kraft und Stoff*, calling themselves "socialists," "scientists," "determinists," "nihilists," or simply "new people," thousands of sometime students all over Russia were discussing, planning, and sporadically attempting to take actual steps toward the radical transformation of Russia into a vaguely socialist, materialist, utopian society.[15] Some of these young revolutionaries and would-be revolutionaries met in more or less secret groups to discuss ideas, exchange literature, and lay plans for future action. Early in 1864, Nikolai Peterson, then twenty years old and a member of a Moscow based group which would later be known a "The Organization," came to Bogorodsk, ostensibly to teach mathematics, but chiefly to spread revolutionary propaganda. He writes:

> One of my fellow-members in the circle informed me that in Bogorodsk there was a teacher at the district school, a certain Nikolai Fedorovich Fedorov, a selfless man who by his life reminded one of Rakhmetov, a man of unusual intelligence and honesty; and at that time we thought that an intelligent and honest man could not help but be on our side. And so, arriving in Bogorodsk on March 15th, 1864, I went at once to see Nikolai Fedorovich, who turned out to be a man about forty years old, i.e. about four years older than Lev Nikolaevich [Tolstoi]; he was a bachelor and lived as an ascetic: he not only did without a bed, but without even a pillow; he ate whatever his landlords, simple merchants, put out for him, the healthful, but simple food that they themselves ate; during Lent, N. F. ate Lenten dishes, and on Wednesdays, Fridays, and other days of fasting, he fasted. N. F. never made any special demands and was always content with whatever he was given. In my first meeting with N. F. I immediately laid out everything about myself, and explained the purpose for which I had become a teacher at the district school. To this I heard: "I don't understand," N. F. said, "what you're troubling yourself about. After all, you won't be able to give those for whom you're troubling yourself anything except material well-being, since you don't admit to any other well-being; but meanwhile, working to obtain material well-being for others, you renounce it for yourself and indeed are prepared even to sacrifice your life for the sake of this. But what if material well-being is no more important to those for whom

you're troubling yourself than it is for you? To what end is all your bother!" In the course of our conversation I heard from N. F. that the so-called great principles of the great French Revolution—*freedom, equality, and brotherhood*—are the product of extremely flippant thought, or even of thoughtlessness, since *brotherhood cannot result from freedom to fulfil one's whims or from the envious desire for equality*; only brotherhood leads to freedom, for brothers who love one another will not envy one brother who is elevated above others, and will not try to lower him to their own level; and the brother who has raised himself above the others will try to bring all his brothers up to his level. For that reason, we must seek brotherhood first and not put it at the tail, after freedom and equality, as did the proponents of freedom, equality, and brotherhood—we must seek brotherhood first, and the rest will follow. But there cannot be brotherhood without fatherhood and a fatherland [*otechestvo*]—for only by fathers are we brothers, and therefore filial and paternal love must be placed at the head, and from this fraternal love will issue. Conversing in this manner, N. F. gradually unfolded an entire world outlook which was perfectly new to me, and which called for the unification of all people in a labor of universal resurrection. I was committed at once, and, already, forever. Nikolai Fedorovich did not stay long in Bogorodsk while I was there, no more than about three months; but these three months enriched me more than my entire life had before and gave me a firm base for the remainder of my life.[16]

A young revolutionary thus became Fedorov's first disciple.

As Peterson's account indicates, Fedorov had already worked out the main lines of his entire project by 1864. But he may not have begun to develop his ideas in writing until Peterson joined him and began to take down Fedorov's dictation. Although work kept them apart for most of the year, Fedorov and Peterson would meet on vacations and during the summers, and, it was during these periods, over many years, that Fedorov's ideas were committed to writing. As Peterson acknowledges, it was he who first brought Fedorov's ideas to the attention of Dostoevskii and Tolstoi. But what neither Peterson nor any of Fedorov's other previous biographers have mentioned, is that it was also through Peterson that Fedorov's ideas came to the attention of a revolutionary group called "The Organization", and through them, to the attention of the Tsar's police.

On April 4, 1866, Dmitri Karakozov, a former student and a member of "Hell" (the assassination squad of "The Organization") waited for the Tsar outside the Petersburg Summer Garden, and when the Tsar and his company appeared, fired a shot that hit no one. This attempt was the first of a number of attempted assassinations and acts of terror that various revolutionary groups conducted over a period of some fifteen years, culminating in the 1881 assassination of Alexander II by a group that called itself "The People's Will."

A few weeks after the Karakozov episode, Peterson was arrested and questioned about his former close ties with the group. Soon, Fedorov was also brought in for questioning. In the trial, Ermolov, one of the revolutionaries, testified that through Peterson he and two other revolutionaries, Iurasov and Zagibalov, had met and discussed philosophical questions with Fedorov, and that on each of these occasions, Fedorov had tried his best to persuade them to abandon their revolutionary ideals. Fedorov was released soon after being questioned, and was cleared of all suspicion of collusion. But Peterson was found guilty of not having reported his knowledge of the group's illegal activities, and was sentenced to a six month prison term.[17]

In 1868 Fedorov ended his career as a peripatetic village teacher and began his work as a Moscow librarian. His first position was as an assistant, with Peterson, to P. I. Bartenev at the Chertkov Library. From there he moved to a position at the Rumiantsev Museum, where he worked for twenty-five years, first as a call clerk in the reading room and later as a cataloguer. After his retirement from the Rumiantsev Museum, he lived for a while on his minimal pension, and then took a position as desk clerk in the hall of the Moscow archives of the Ministry of Foreign Affairs, where he worked until the end of his life. During these last years, Fedorov spent his summers and vacations in such places as Voronezh, near Russia's Ukrainian border, and Askhabad, now the capital of Turkmenia, where he wrote articles for local newspapers and worked on his major essays with Peterson, who had to move from one city to another as an official in the district court system. According to Ostromirov, Fedorov also spent at least two summers in monasteries not far from Moscow, Sergeev-Holy Trinity, and New Jerusalem.

The Rumiantsev Museum, where Fedorov worked for twenty-fiive years, was Moscow's leading public library. Founded in 1862, and named after the former Ambassador to Germany, N. P. Rumiantsev (1754-1826) who had spent his life collecting books about Russia, the Museum contained in Fedorov's time some 85,000 books and pamphlets, and some 18,000 broadsides, maps, and other unbound materials. And Fedorov was said not only to have known the title and location, but also to have been familiar with the contents of every single item in the entire library. The system then in use was essentially the one still used in Russian libraries. From the catalogue file, the reader would draw up a list of books he needed, which he would present to the desk clerk, and a few hours later, or perhaps the next day, he could get the books at the desk and read them at one of the tables in the reading room. After that, the books would be kept for him at the desk each day until he had no further use for them, at which time they would be returned to the stacks. But whenever a reader gave Fedorov a list of books, he was usually surprised to find, on returning, many more books than he had ordered, some of which he had never heard of, but all of which would prove extremely useful, sometimes even essential, for his study When asked where the extra books had come from, the reader was told simply that Nikolai Fedorovich had sent them. And sometimes, after receiving repeated "extras" from Nikolai Fedorovich, the reader would be delivered an invitation to visit Fedorov in his office. Then, it was said, the reader's real education would begin.

The Rumiantsev Museum now forms one wing of the massive Lenin Library, and the books housed there in Fedorov's time have been incorporated into the collection that is now claimed to be not only the largest but also the one serving the greatest number of readers in the world. In Fedorov's day, the Museum could boast of only 50,000 or so visitors per year (in 1961 more than 2,300,000 visits were recorded), but regular visitors and users included such luminaries as Tolstoi, Dostoevskii, Solov'ev, Chekhov, D. I. Mendeleev, K. A. Timiriazev, V. O. Kliuchevskii, D. N. Mamin-Sibiriak, V. V. Veresaev, V. Ia. Briusov, and even Lenin himself, who used the library whenever he was in Moscow, and even, in 1897, on his way to serve a sentence in Siberia: "arrived in Moscow February 19 ... and immediately upon arriving, hardly having had time to embrace his wife and sisters, set off for the reading room of what was then the Rumiantsev Museum. In this reading room Vladimir Il'ich spent all three days of his stay in Moscow, working on his historico-economic study, 'The Development of Capitalism in Russia.' " [18] Whether Vladimir Il'ich was one of the readers to whom Fedorov gave extra assistance remains one of the few trivial bits of Lenin lore that no Soviet scholar has yet seen fit to investigate.

But in his work, first as call clerk, and then as cataloguer, Fedorov was soon a familiar figure to the writers, scholars, and scientists who used the library regularly. His biographers tell us that even those who did not know his name or know of his strange ideas were invariably struck by Fedorov's unusual manner and appearance. Hump-backed and dressed in old, torn clothes, he was a tall, thin man whose eyes, even in advanced age, were said to burn with ferocious passion. At first sight, many were intimidated by his apparent severity. His short, graying beard was said to twitch strangely when he became excited, and the muscles and veins on his enormous brow would bunch into protuberant lumps whenever some original thought struck him and he began to speak.

But, as Ostromirov writes: "If you asked him for several books, he would unerringly define the subject of your research, knowing beforehand, in all details, the entire contents of every book you ordered, and there was not one question or problem which was not of profound interest to him. He was, literally, ahead of recognized authorities and specialists in many fields, and there was literally no question, even, at first glance, the most trivial, to which he did not attend with the same interest and same warmth with which he attended to the fundamental problems of all knowledge and belief." [19]

Among the more famous legends of Fedorov's erudition is the story told of a party of engineers who in the early nineties visited the library on their way through Moscow to do research for the Siberian railway. They came, it is said, not suspecting that they might learn something new, but chiefly to be able to say that they had made use of all available resources prior to their expedition. When they gave Fedorov their request for materials, he, as usual, brought back many items they had never heard of, including several very useful descriptions of the parts of Siberia they were to travel through. And when they showed him their projected route, he at once pointed out two mistakes on their maps: in one instance the elevation of a mountain had been incorrectly stated, and in another the map had neglected to include a large stream. The engineers maintained that their maps were correct, but two years later they sent one of their party to Fedorov to confirm that he, not the maps, had been correct.

Another story tells that Fedorov argued about the contents of a scientific book with the very author of that book, and in the course of the argument demonstrated a much better grasp of the book's details than the author himself was able to show. Fedorov was never heard reading or speaking a language other than Russian, but one scholar who worked with him, Professor I. A. Linnichenko, tells us that when Fedorov opened a book in English, French, or German he could translate it at sight, and read it aloud in Russian as if it were not written in a foreign language. He was fascinated by Chinese characters, and started to learn the language, but probably didn't learn it well enough to use it.[20]

Kozhevnikov tells us that Fedorov read with almost equal interest every book and pamphlet that happened to fall before his eyes. He would read through a list of residents of such and such a village in such and such a year with as much interest and care as he would a new book of philosophy, theology, history, or science. He liked especially to read about the history, customs, and legends of small, isolated localities. During his stays in the country, he helped local residents establish small, regional museums containing documents and artifacts pertaining to the locality. When he returned to Moscow after his vacations, he would continue to gather whatever material he could find there that could best be kept in regional museums.[21] In his later writings, he assigned the local museum an important role in the resurrection project. Museums, he argued, offered better opportunities for education than universities could. Whereas in universities human activities are divided into separate topics and subtopics for study, in museums, knowledge is used to recreate whole representations of many sides of life. A university education gives one knowledge of a special field and leads eventually to the isolation of the scholar's knowledge from the knowledge of all other men, including other scholars. University education suffers from and contributes to the separation of knowledge from action. Museum education, on the other hand, depends on and contributes to the redintegration of knowledge. To assemble, for instance, a museum display on village life in a past era, one must put together knowledge of history, botany, animal husbandry, anatomy, architecture—all the separate branches of knowledge that university education would further separate. And if, at present, museums can display only collections of lifeless objects and inanimate representations of past life, in the future museums will become the centers for the actual re-creation of past life. Museum-temple-schools will replace the individual present equivalent institutions as active centers for the study and practice of the sacred-scientific art of resurrection. And in the meantime, local museums must begin to serve as repositories for every bit of information that can be gathered about people who now live and have lived in the locality. Thus a list of residents in a particular town in a particular year, which may now seem to be a worthless scrap of paper, may in the future prove to be a vital source of information essential to the project of resurrection.[22]

As a librarian, Fedorov held to the principle that nothing printed should be discarded. Room must be found for everything, for, as he often said to Kozhevnikov and others, "Behind the book a man is hidden."

On Sundays, after library hours, and on library holidays, Fedorov often returned to the reading room to work. When scholars and other regular library users learned of this, they began to visit Fedorov there, and gradually the reading room became a center for after-hours discussions, informal seminars and scholarly debates. For a short time a few of the library officials objected to this infraction of regulations, but when several eminent scholars made it known that they would look with extreme disfavor upon any attempt to curtail these informal sessions, the objections were quietly withdrawn.

Several times Fedorov was offered raises and promotions, but each time he refused the offer. He seemed to prize his poverty and wished to receive no more than five hundred rubles a year.[23] Even the greater part of that meager sum he managed to give away: to the doormen who stayed to let him work after hours, to impecunious young people whom he hired as "assistants" to keep an eye on frequently used books that he kept in special places for the convenience of users, to "the poor", and to a special group of ragged young scholars whom he liked to call his "stipendiates."

Among this latter group was Konstantin Eduardovich Tsiolkovskii (1857-1935), the visionary scientist whose ideas eventually found embodiment in 1957 when the world was shocked by the first Sputnik.

Tsiolkovskii was sixteen years old in 1873 when he arrived in Moscow from a provincial village. He had no money, no friends, and only a minimal education. But he had come to Moscow to learn, and in Fedorov he found an ideal teacher. He once told an interviewer how he made Fedorov's acquaintance at the library.

"It happened on one of my first visits. I dropped in and here's what I saw: a dozen or so people, mostly students, were crowding around the librarian. I was shy. I stood there waiting for the librarian to get free. I had time to look him over: a bald head, around it white curls sprinkled with gray, coal-black eyebrows and surprisingly young eyes. He looked about fifty, but he had youthful movements—quick and sharp.

When the last student had left, the librarian noticed me and motioned for me to come to him. Apparently I looked nervous, because he smiled encouragingly. If you could only have seen his smile! It changed him and brightened him up at once. It was so affable and open, the way a father smiles at a son, or one brother at another. But this was the first time he had seen me. I was immediately filled with affection for him, and, having forgotten my earlier shyness, walked up to him. He cheerfully asked:

'What do you want to read?'

'Give me, if you can, *The History of the Peasant War*.'

'That book is forbidden.'

'Please speak a little louder—I don't hear well.'

'The book is for-bid-den!'

The words sounded so harsh, as if to say: 'See here, now, with the kinds of readers we have—give out forbidden books indeed!' But his eyes were merry and smiling. Still, I hadn't been around people much and didn't know what to say. He went off somewhere, quickly returned, and handed me a book. I asked:

'What's this?'

'*The History of the Peasant War*.'

'But isn't this book forbidden?'

'Take it!' [24]

Tsiolkovskii tells us that he was soon visiting Fedorov every day and joined the "enchanted" group of young people under Feodorov's spell.[25] Each day, Fedorov brought the young Tsiolkovskii a fresh stack of books, and often spent hours with him discussing his studies. And once, noticing that Tsiolkovskii's coat was too light for the cold weather, he said: "Let's go to the store and get you a new overcoat—I suddenly have some spare money."[26] Tsiolkovskii tells us: "The library was my university." And adds: "Understanding my inclination toward mathematics, physics, and, in part, chemistry, he selected literature for me and directed my self-education. He taught me to use the catalogue, to draw up a conspectus, and to extract from books what was foremost and basic. It is no exaggeration to say that for me he took the place of university professors, with whom I had no association."[27]

Oddly enough, however, in the interview, Tsiolkovskii says that he and Fedorov never discussed the idea of space travel. Even as a child, Tsiolkovskii had dreamed of "a medium without weight, where movement on all sides was perfectly free and where everyone felt lighter than a bird in air."[28] And, according to Peterson, as early as 1864 Fedorov had incorporated the idea of space travel into his resurrection project. How strange, then, that between 1873 and 1876, two of the few people in Russia who were able to take the idea of space travel seriously met almost every day and discussed ideas of all kinds but did not once touch on the subject that set them apart from almost all of their contemporaries. But when asked directly if they had discussed space travel, Tsiolkovskii answered:

> "No. And I very much regret it. How could this have happened? At that time I had youthful dreams about exploring interplanetary space, and tormented myself looking for a path to the stars, but didn't meet even one like-minded person. In the person of Fedorov, fate had sent me a person who thought, as I did, that people would certainly master the cosmos. But by an irony of that same fate, I absolutely didn't know about Fedorov's views. We had many discussions on various topics, but somehow we avoided space. Probably our difference in age accounted for this. He apparently found that conversations about space with me would have been premature."[29]

But Viktor Shklovskii, who apparently asked Tsiolkovskii the same question, has written just the opposite. Both in his memoirs, *Once Upon a Time*, and in an article on cosmonautics for *Literaturnaia gazeta*, Shklovskii tells us that it was Fedorov who first encouraged Tsiolkovskii to develop his serious interest in space travel. Writing, even for the official press, in his own, aphoristic manner, Shklovskii says:

> There was a man by the name of Fedorov, a philosopher, respected by Lev Tolstoi. He said that mankind would soon find earth too crowded. He said this in the last century. He's the one who was Tsiolkovskii's teacher.
>
> Tsiolkovskii was deaf. He was deaf and he was studying in school. He was sitting in the then Chertkov Library, over books of mathematics. The old man Fedorov walked up behind him and started speaking. The mathematician didn't turn around—he was deaf. Then Fedorov wrote on paper: "I'm going to do mathematics with you, and you'll help mankind build rockets so that we will finally be able to know more than earth and so that we can see our earth." People need a distant look, because only those people who are thinking about the future are real and present.[30]

But whether he did nor did not discuss space travel with Fedorov, Tsiolkovskii returned to his village after three years in Moscow, began to teach school, and devoted most of his spare time to thinking about space travel. In 1879, at the age of twenty-two, he became the first known person in the world to work out a feasible plan for an artificial earth satellite.[31] Though unacknowledged as such, Tsiolkovskii remains the most illustrious alumnus of "Fedorov University."

Apparently Fedorov never did marry. And since his only known friends were men, and since his works contain many references to "feminine caprice", "the feminine demand for comfort" (as opposed to duty) and usually describe woman-as-she-is as "the painted harlot", some readers may jump to the immediate conclusion that Fedorov was probably a homosexual and certainly a woman-hater. But his love was directed not so much toward members of the male sex as toward all humanity, and his argument is not so much against women as against the sex drive itself. Fedorov believed that all men and women should be sisters and brothers, sons and daughters, and should resist any force that would draw them from total devotion to their parents, sisters, and brothers. The sex drive, Fedorov believed, drives all people into the vicious cycle of competition and war, and represents not the force of life but the force of death. Our task is not to bring new children into the world to swallow us and in time be swallowed by their children. The task is to reverse the apparently natural but eternally unnatural cycle of birth, growth, decay, and death, and to devote all possible creative energy to the task of resurrecting the dead. (I, 9-10)

For most of his long life in Moscow, Fedorov lived alone in a small room the size of a closet which he rented for six rubles a month, and he always slept on a humpback trunk, sometimes bare, sometimes covered with newspapers, placing under his head not a pillow but some hard object, usually a book. The only coat he wore was more rag than coat, and strangers easily mistook him for a beggar on the streets. He had no furniture, and each time he moved to new quarters he gave away whatever objects the room had accumulated. He spent nothing on entertainment, diversion, or any conveniences, and he refused to take cabs even in the coldest winter months. He drank only tea, ate hard rolls, sometimes accompanied by a piece of old cheese or salt fish, and lived for months without hot food. One of Fedorov's landlords asked visitors if Fedorov ate with them, for he had never taken the board that was included in the price for the rent of the room. Sometimes, almost by force, friends would settle him in decent, comfortable quarters, arrange with the landlord for a daily meal with at least two courses, and furnish the room with at least a bed and pillow. If the friends returned in a week, however, they would find that the room again was bare, that Fedorov had already given away the bed and pillow, and that, on Fedorov's insistence, the landlord would again be serving him only bread and tea.

According to Kozhevnikov, Fedorov had a fear of money and considered it poisonous, infectious, and vile. If he found any change in his pockets at night he would curse himself for not having managed to give it away. He was obsessed with the fear that someday he might be found dead with two or three kopecks left in his pocket.

Fedorov lived a spare, ascetic life, but he was certainly not a gloomy recluse. He carried candy in his pockets for children, sought out the company of others, and seems never to have passed up an opportunity to engage in some lively—even heated—dispute. His energy, and, most of all, his fiery eyes, made a strong impression on all who met him. N. N. Chernogub, who was then director of the Tretiakov Gallery, wrote that whenever Fedorov appeared at his door the maid would say: "Here comes that old man with the dreadful eyes again!" [32] Chernogub goes on to say that when Fedorov spoke he became so agitated that it was difficult to imagine how he wrote.

But Fedorov did write. At first, apparently, he expressed his ideas only orally, leaving it to Peterson to put the ideas into written form. Perhaps after Peterson had prepared a draft, Fedorov would go over it and suggest changes. Only after Dostoevskii had responded enthusiastically to the outline of Fedorov's thought that Peterson had sent him, did Fedorov seriously begin to try to write a complete exposition of his project. During his years as a librarian Fedorov spent so much time and energy on the job that he was able to devote only a small portion of his day to writing. But during vacations, and after his retirement, he turned most of his attention to the problem of getting all his ideas onto paper. Hence the only people, besides Peterson and Kozhevnikov, who had a fuller idea of Fedorov's project than could be obtained through conversations were the few to whom Peterson sent manuscripts that he had written from Fedorov's dictation. How much of Fedorov's work Dostoevskii saw remains unknown. But Peterson has reported exactly how much of Fedorov's work he showed to Solov'ev and Tolstoi. That the interest and even enthusiasm accorded his ideas by his greatest contemporaries proved a great stimulus to Fedorov is beyond question. That Fedorov's ideas also had some influence on the work of his greatest contemporaries has often been suggested; but the nature and magnitude of that influence is one of the topics to which we shall now turn our attention.

Fedorov and Dostoevskii

Although Dostoevskii encountered Fedorov's ideas more than once, he probably never met Fedorov personally,[33] and did not even know the name of the man whose ideas he had endorsed "as if they were my own."

Dostoevskii's first, indirect encounter with Fedorov's ideas came in 1876, when, in his capacity as editor of *Diary of a Writer*, he received a manuscript from Peterson. For years, Peterson had been trying without success to persuade Fedorov to submit some of their joint writings for publication. Finally, without Fedorov's knowledge, Peterson decided to take matters into his own hands. Apparently early in 1876 he sent Dostoevskii a manuscript of his own that contained a number of ideas that he could only have gotten from Fedorov. In the issue of *Diary of a Writer* for March, 1876, Dostoevskii, without mentioning Peterson's name, published some extracts from the manuscript and offered the following explanatory postscript.

> The history of the manuscript from which I took the above excerpt is as follows: its distinguished author (only I don't know if he is a young man or one of those young old men) published a short sketch in some provincial periodical, the editor of which—having given space to that sketch—also printed with it a note of reservation, partly disagreeing with the author. Thereupon, when the author in refutation of the editor's note, wrote a whole article—not too long, however— the editor's office refused to print it, under the pretext that "it is more sermon than article". The author then wrote me a letter, and mailed the manuscript and asked me to read it, think it over and express my opinion of it in my *Diary*. First, I wish to thank him for his confidence in my opinion, and second—for the article, since it gave me great pleasure: rarely have I

read anything more *logical*. And even though I am unable to print the entire article itself, nevertheless I made the above excerpt with an intent which I shall not conceal: the point is that in the author, who advocates a genuine communion of men, I also detected something extraordinarily "isolated"—specifically, in those parts of the manuscript which I do not risk quoting; it is so "isolated" that one seldom finds anything like it. Thus, not only the article but the author himself, as it were, corroborates my idea about the "isolation" of units and the extreme, so to speak, chemical decomposition of our society into its component parts, which has occurred suddenly in our time.[34]

From an entry in his notebook of 1876, it is clear that the person from whom Dostoevskii received the manuscript was Peterson. From both the contents and the style of the excerpts that Dostoevskii printed it is clear that the article was Peterson's restatement of ideas dictated to him by Fedorov. It is interesting, then, that in 1876, Dostoevskii found Fedorov's ideas "isolated." A year later, when Peterson sent him another manuscript, which apparently contained a more detailed presentation of Fedorov's idea, again composed from Fedorov's dictation, Dostoevskii wrote back:

.... The first matter is a question: who is this thinker whose thoughts you have sent me? If possible, let me know his real name. He has aroused my interest more than enough. By all means do tell me something more detailed about him as a person—all this if you can.

Let me tell you that essentially I am in complete agreement with these ideas. I have read them as if they were my own. Today I read them (anonymously) to Vladimir Sergeevich Solov'ev, our young philosopher who is now delivering lectures on religion, lectures that nearly a thousand attend. I waited for him on purpose to read him your account of your thinker's ideas, since I found in his view much that is similar. We spent a beautiful two hours at this. He finds your thinker's ideas much to his liking and had wished to say almost the same things in his next lecture (of twelve lectures he still has four to give.) But now I have a friendly, if difficult question, one that I've wanted to put to you since December.

In your account of this thinker, the most essential thing, without a doubt, is the duty to resurrect the ancestors who lived before. If this duty were fulfilled, then childbirth would cease, and what the Gospels and the Apocalypse have designated as the first resurrection would begin. But what you have not stated at all in your account is just how you understand this resurrection of ancestors—in just what form you envision and believe in it. That is, do you understand it somehow mentally or allegorically, like, for example, Renan, who understands it to be something like a total illumination of human consciousness at the end of the life of man, an illumination of such intensity that it will be clear to the mind of those future people how great was, for example, one of their ancestor's influence on mankind, how and in what manner his influence was exerted, and so forth, and of such intensity that the role of every man who lived before will be seen with perfect clarity, his contribution will be divined..., so intense that we shall even recognize the influence that all those who have lived before have exerted on us and the extent to which they are reincarnated in us; and will all this come to pass among those last people, who will know everything and be in utter harmony, those last people in whom humanity will reach its conclusion—

or:

does your thinker intend this to be taken directly and literally, as religion implies, and that the resurrection will be real, that the abyss that divides us from the spirits of our ancestors will be filled, will be vanquished by vanquished death, and that the dead will be resurrected not only in our minds, not allegorically, but in fact, in person, actually, in bodies (N. B. not of course in their present bodies, for when immortality begins, marriage and the birth of children will end, and that alone is testimony that in the first resurrection, designated to be on earth, the bodies will perhaps be like Christ's body in the fifty days between his resurrection and ascension?).

An answer to this question is essential—otherwise it will all be impossible to understand. I warn you that we here, that is, Solov'ev and I at least, believe in a real, literal, personal resurrection, and one that will come to pass on earth.

Do let me know, then, if you can and will, esteemed N. P., what your thinker thinks about this, and, if possible, let me know in more detail...[35]

Since the manuscript that Peterson sent to Dostoevskii has never been published, we do not know how much of Fedorov's project it outlines, or how closely it concurs with material later published in *The Philosophy of the Common Task.* Perhaps at this time, Fedorov had not yet formulated precisely how the resurrection would be accomplished. But from his later writings we know that he, like Dostoevskii and Solov'ev, envisioned a resurrection that would be "real, literal, personal," and that people would be resurrected whole and perfect, with bodies resynthesized from particles that had belonged to them before death. But where Dostoevskii and Solov'ev are content to believe that the resurrection will in some way and at some indefinite point in the future "come to pass', Fedorov insists that people on earth, after long joint labor, will begin to resurrect their ancestors, who in turn will resurrect *their* ancestors until all people who ever lived on earth will be resurrected.[36]

We are not told Fedorov's initial reaction to having been "discovered" by Dostoevskii. He may have been elated, he may have been upset, or he may simply have taken this remarkable letter in stride. All that Peterson tells us is: "I sent Dostoevskii's letter to Nikolai Fedorovich, and he decided that it was necessary to answer it, and an answer was begun in the summer of 1878, when Nikolai Fedorovich came to spend two weeks with me in Kerensk, Penzensk Province."[37] They continued to work on the letter off and on during the next two years, but before they could prepare a response that they considered adequate, Dostoveskii had died.

What began as an answer to Dostoevskii's questions eventually turned into Fedorov's longest and most important essay, "The Question of brotherhood, or kinship, of the reasons for the unbrotherly, unkindred, i.e. unpeaceful state of the world, and of the means for the restoration of kinship. A note from the unlearned to the learned: clergy and laity, believers and unbelievers" (I, 1-352, hereafter called "Brotherhood"). The twenty or so pages from this essay (beginning at I.64) that were written in the summer of 1878, as a start toward a response to Dostoevskii, were shown to Tolstoi later that year, and, eventually, almost three hundred pages were shown to Solov'ev. So, while Dostoevskii did not see Fedorov's answers to his questions, the answers prepared for him served to introduce Fedorov's project to Tolstoi and reintroduce it to Solov'ev.

That Fedorov's ideas had some impact on Dostoevskii is unquestionable. Everyone who has written on the matter has agreed on this point. What remains controversial is the question of how much influence and what kind of influence Fedorov exerted on Dostoevskii. At one extreme, Gornostaev claims that Fedorov's ideas provided Dostoevskii with the idea that he had been searching for all his life, that *The Brothers Karamazov* represents Dostoevskii's first attempt to present Fedorov's ideas in novelistic form, and that had Dostoveskii lived longer he would have given full artistic embodiment to Fedorov's project of resurrection. At the other extreme, Pletnev finds that Fedorov's ideas interested Dostoevskii but had no significant influence on his work. While not claiming as much as Gornostaev, Komarovich and Lord conclude that Fedorov's influence on Dostoevskii was significant; the Soviet critic Bursov and the Canadian Zakydalsky have more recently taken positions similar to Pletnev's.[38] My own view on the question is that "influence" is too simple a term to describe the complex interactions that take place when one great mind, in maturity, encounters another. Fedorov and Dostoevskii had read many of the same books, had been sensitive to many of the same issues, had given years of thought to many of the same problems, and had independently reached a number of similar conclusions. In reading Dostoevskii, Fedorov had no doubt found many ideas similar to his own, some better formulated and more fully developed, others not as well formulated or as fully developed as his own. In reading Dostoevskii, as well as other thinkers and writers, Fedorov probably took whole ideas, parts of ideas, and developed lines of thought of his own in reaction to ideas formulated by the person he was reading. Similarly, in reading Fedorov, Dostoevskii found much that he had previously thought and written about: in some places, Fedorov had gone farther than he had, in other places not so far. His general feeling was that he was reading something that he could have written himself. He was probably not so much "influenced" as stimulated and inspired. He may have found in the manuscript confirmation of some ideas that he had entertained but not yet firmly committed himself to, and full, bold assertions of positions that he himself had been moving toward but had not yet reached. In Fedorov, he may have found clear statements of ideas that he himself had always had only fuzzy notions of, and, on other questions, cursory or incomplete thoughts that forced him to think out for himself problems that might not have occurred to him previously. In general, Fedorov's manuscript focused Dostoevskii's attention on problems to which he had already given some thought, forced him to rethink some of his earlier conclusions, stimulated him to develop his own ideas to new lengths and in new directions, and startled him with a few new ideas and conclusions that might otherwise never have occurred to him. Dostoevskii probably found Fedorov's ideas as stimulating and as inspiring as anything he had read since Schiller. From his letter, it is clear that after reading Fedorov ideas raced through Dostoevskii's head for days. As these ideas developed, some remained reconginzably Fedorovian, while others continued to change until their connection to Fedorov could no longer be detected. Lord and others who have found specific traces of Fedorov's idea throughout *The Brothers Karamazov* are right in claiming that Fedorov's idea had a great impact on Dostoevskii, just as Pletnev and others are right in claiming that in *The Brothers Karamazov* there is little clear, whole, direct evidence of Fedorov's "influence" on Dostoevskii. The obvious, if overlooked, fact is that the impact that one mind has upon another is usually more complex a matter than that of mere "influence," and that a creative writer can absorb and use other people's ideas without necessarily regurgitating them whole.

One idea which Dostoevskii came upon in the Fedorov manuscript, an idea which he read "as if it were my own' and yet which he had not yet formulated for himself, is that the task of living sons is to resurrect their dead fathers. In his first draft for *The Brothers Karamazov* Dostoevskii planned for his characters to discuss the resurrection of the dead in the first scene, set in Zosima's cell. In his notebook for this chapter, we find such entries as: "resurrection of (our) ancestors depends on us," and the character who eventually becomes Fedor Karamazov remarks of the character who becomes Dmitrii, "this (one) will not resurrect his parents." [39] In the final version of the novel there is not one direct statement of or reference to Fedorov's idea. Whether between the first and last drafts of the novel he had decided to reject outright the idea that sons are responsible for the resurrection of their fathers, or had merely decided not to try to work it into this particular novel (which was to nave been only the first part of a larger work entitled *The Life of a Great Sinner*) remains a matter for mere speculation. But probably, in writing the novel, Dostoevskii realized that the responsibility of sons to resurrect their fathers was no longer an idea that he could present as his own. Fedorov had stimulated him to think seriously about the problem of resurrection, but in the end Dostoevskii probably felt more comfortable with the Solov'evian idea of a transcendent resurrection, to be accomplished through men but by God in ways now unknowable to men, than with Fedorov's immanent resurrection, to be accomplished by human knowledge and effort. Had he lived longer, I think Dostoevskii would not have drawn closer to Fedorov but further from him.

Throughout the novel, Lord and others find statements

that may or may not be understood as Fedorovian statements: Markel's "Do not weep, mother, life is heaven, and we are all in heaven... we do not wish to know it even, but if we did, we should have heaven on earth the very next day"; Dmitrii's "Brother, during the past two years I have felt a new man within myself, in me a new man has risen again! He was in me all the time, but had never appeared before... An awesome thing!"; Zosima's insistence, diluted in the final version, that "Your flesh will be changed.... Life is paradise, the keys are with us."; and, especially, Alesha's entire speech beside Iliushechka's grave, which includes such statements as "People talk to you a good deal about your education, but some good, sacred memory, preserved from childhood, is perhaps the best education.... let us never forget one another! .... I'll never forget one of you.... May his memory live in our hearts from this time forth! .... Let us remember his face and his clothes and his tiny boots, his coffin" and which concludes, "Certainly we shall all rise again, of course we shall see each other and tell each other with joy and gladness all that has happened!"[40] But as Lord himself acknowledges, and as Pletnev emphasizes, all that Dostoevskii calls for, to change earth to heaven and to see that all the dead will be resurrected, is a change in attitude, a change internal and individual to each person. Fedorov calls for a project, a universal task, action to realize the ideas of paradise and resurrection. In his novel, Dostoevskii leaves the "Fedorovian" statements as conclusions that can only be understood and accepted by faith. Fedorov uses the same statements as starting points for his projects of implementation.

Since *Notes From the House of the Dead*, in which the narrator, on leaving the camp, feels resurrected from death, the theme of resurrection had been a central one in Dostoevskii's works. But in both the characters like Raskol'nikov, who are marked for future resurrection, and the characters like Markel and Zosima, who are already filled with the joy of resurrection, "resurrection" is understood as a shift in consciousness. When one no longer views the world as hell, one no longer lives in hell, and when one begins to view the world as paradise, one has already begun to live in paradise. The shift is internal, and individual. In Fedorov, internal and individual shifts are necessary but not sufficient to bring about the general transformation of the world.

In viewing what Fedorov called "the world as it is" Dostoevskii and Fedorov are so close together that it is almost impossible to tell where one's ideas end and the other's begin. Implicit in *The Brothers Karamazov* is the idea that sons are responsible for the death of their fathers. Ivan, Dmitri, and even Alesha must all share the guilt with Smerdiakov for the murder of Fedor Karamazov. This idea of the collective responsibility of sons for the life and death of their fathers had been hinted at in *The Raw Youth* and *The Possessed*, but Fedorov's manuscript probably contributed to the clarity, intensity, and central position that this theme obtains in *The Brothers Karamazov*.

Pletnev finds that Fedorov and Dostoevskii have nine points in common: "1) a quest for a worldwide task and goal for life that is not only personal, but general for mankind; 2) coloration of this "all-human" task as a feat of service; 3) faith that the Russian people have a great mission to preserve the true faith and holy traditions; both thinkers saw chiefly in the peasantry the expression of the true personality and idea of the people; 4) faith that bliss was possible for all on earth, in 'God's kingdom,'; 5) a conviction that when mankind is affected by a unifying force, i.e. a death-bearing force, and is not affected by a disunifying force, then we find in mankind 'the purest childlike feeling' and a feeling of mutual love and kinship; 6) a faith in a general resurrection in the flesh and the possibility that this can be worked for; 7) both were sharply tormented by the question of fatherhood, of the family, of the father, a thread running through the work of Dostoevskii and Fedorov; 8) the exceptional sensitivity of both to the spirit of the age and a struggle to *synthesize* all thoughts and impressions *into an original* doctrine; 9) faith in their calling, as prophets of a new teaching and of the restoration of Christ's task." [41]

It should be observed that many of Pletnev's nine points were common not only to Dostoevskii and Fedorov but to most neoslavophiles in the second half of the nineteenth century. And in almost every one of these shared points, Dostoevskii stood for something general and unspecified ("a goal", "a mission", "a task"), whereas Fedorov insisted on the specifics: *the* task, *the* goal, *the* mission, *the* solution.

In his ten-point list of differences, Pletnev offers a number of interesting insights into the work of each thinker. Some of these differences have already been discussed or will be discussed below. To summarize his points, rather than quote them directly; 1) Fedorov is closer to sectarianism, Dostoevskii to the mainstream of Russian Orthodoxy; 2) Dostoevskii sees Christ as an expiator who offers man free choice of the good, Fedorov sees Christ as a teacher of resurrection; 3) Dostoevskii emphasizes the salutary, cleansing function of suffering, and that by suffering man comes closer to Christ; Fedorov wants to rid us of suffering ,and believes that we suffer only because we live unreasonably—by enlightening our lives and by acting in accordance with our reason we shall eliminate suffering from the earth; 4) Dostoevskii emphasizes the guilt and torment of the individual, brought on by the "sleepless" conscience; Fedorov's idea of guilt is naturalistic and, strangely, positivistic; 5) Fedorov's attitude to art is cold—he does not care or try to understand beauty and believes that art is only the creation of dead likenesses, whereas Dostoevskii believed that beauty can save the world; 6) Fedorov opposes active "resurrecting" [*voskreshenie*] to Dostoevskii's passive "resurrection" [*voskresenie*]; 7) Fedorov's tone is declarative, postulatory, and attempts to be incontrovertible, whereas Dostoevskii's work is always searching, and considers the complexities of experience; 8) Fedorov did not understand the problem of sex; Dostoevskii did; 9) Fedorov had a poor understanding of man's sinfulness; 10) Fedorov is a utopian fantast, Dostoevskii a mystic; Fedorov's rationalism is foreign to Dostoevskii.

I would question several of Pletnev's assertions, especially that Fedorov is closer to sectarianism than to the mainstream of Russian Orthodoxy, that his attitude toward art was cold, that he did not understand sex, and that he poorly understood man's sinfulness. But these matters can best be treated when we turn to a fuller discussion of Fedorov's ideas. For now, it is perhaps sufficient to point out that many of the differences which Pletnev finds between Fedorov and Dostoevskii are supported by Fedorov's own criticisms of Dostoveskii. In general, despite their many shared convictions, Fedorov found much to criticize in Dostoevskii's view of resurrection.

Most of Fedorov's significant remarks on Dostoevskii are to be found in two places: in an anonymous preface he wrote to accompany the publication of Dostoevskii's letter to Peterson in an 1897 issue of the periodical *Don*, and in a section of his essay *Supramoralism* subheaded, "*Supramoralism*, or unification for resurrecting by the path of knowledge and action, by means which are natural, real, and not mystical, *in opposition to mysticism*, in general, and to the mysticism of Dostoevskii and Solov'ev in particular" (I, 439-442). From internal evidence, it is clear that the *Don* preface was written in 1897, the year in which it was published. Although we do not know exactly when the section in *Supramoralism* was written, it is probably safe to assume that it, like most of Fedorov's work, was put into final form sometime after Fedorov's retirement from the Rumiantsev Museum, i.e. sometime between 1897 and 1903. Since the *Don* preface is referred to in the *Supramoralism* essay (though the reference may have been inserted by one of the editors) it seems clear that the article was written after the preface. What is interesting about the two articles, and why it would be useful to know exactly when each was composed, is that in the *Don* preface Fedorov exalts Dostoevskii and paints him as a spokesman for the right approach to resurrection, whereas in the *Supramoralism* article he points out flaws in Dostoevskii's idea that he must have been aware of even when writing the most laudatory passages of the *Don* preface. He begins this preface:

> We have by chance come upon a letter of F. M. Dostoevskii's, one which is very important for the characterization of his religious convictions. And we have decided to publish this letter in the newspaper which you edit, with minor deletions of passages not relevant to the expression of the, to us, startling thoughts of Fedor Dostoevskii.

In the letter there is discussion of some unknown thinker or other, of whom there are now so many in Russia and who need not concern us here—what is important to us is the thought of Fedor Dostoevskii himself—thought of amazing greatness—this thought gives a meaning and goal to life, which is precisely what is lacking in our time, when due to the loss of a goal and a meaning, life has lost all value.

Dostoevskii says in his letter that: *"the most essential thing is the duty to resurrect the ancestors who lived before,"* i.e. our duty, our obligation, our task consists, consequently, in the resurrection of all that has died, all that has been lost by us, as sons, as descendents of our fathers and ancestors. [42]

Here, Fedorov's attempt to dismiss himself as "some unknown thinker or other" seems something other than an act of saintly self-effacement. By neglecting to include Dostoevskii's words, "in your account of this thinker" Fedorov gives the reader the impression that the idea of the sons' responsibility to resurrect their ancestors originated with Dostoevskii rather than himself. And throughout the preface, Fedorov continues to imply that Dostoevskii was more nearly a spokesman for the project of resurrection than in fact Dostoveskii was. Since, without access to the issue of *Don* in which the letter first appeared, we do not know just how much of Dostoevskii's letter was printed, we cannot be certain that the reader had the opportunity to correct Fedorov's slight misrepresentations of Dostoevskii's remarks. That Fedorov attributed to Dostoevskii an even fuller endorsement of his ideas than Dostoevskii himself was able to give might be understood as an innocent lapse of perceptivity had not Fedorov so sharply attacked Dostoevskii only a few years later for having failed to propound the very ideas that Fedorov attributes to him in the *Don* preface. In the *Supramoralism* article, Fedorov is at his best: battling openly, concealing nothing, disregarding his opponent's fame, seeking only to expose what he considered to be false ideas and to defend ideas that he considered true. But in the preface to the *Don* article we get a glimpse of a side of Fedorov never acknowledged by his biographers, a man who was capable of slightly misrepresenting facts to allow his own theories to appear in what may have seemed the best possible light.⁴³

In the *Supramoralism* article, Fedorov again quotes Dostoevskii's letter, this time finding that neither in the letter "in which he speaks *about the duty of resurrection,* as the most essential thing, nor in any of his other works, does he make even the slightest reference to the way, to the course of the task, by which this duty is to be fulfilled, i.e. *the task of resurrecting.* In his letter it is said that it, the resurrection 'will come to pass on earth;'—but the only thing that this *"will come to pass"* shows is that according to Dostoevskii's thoughts the resurrection will somehow as it were accomplish itself, that it is not the task of the human race." (I, 439).

As Fedorov himself points out, Dostoevskii believed in "resurrection" [*voskresenie*], but the task of men is to engage in "resurrecting" [*voskreshenie*], the activity of resuscitating the dead. Furthermore: "Dostoevskii does not say that no other obligations can stand in comparison with this duty, that this duty is higher than all other obligations and contains all others in it—and since this is the case, then only those obligations are true which enter into the duty of resurrecting, whereas those which do not enter into this duty are to be excluded as untrue. Neither does Dostoevskii say that the duty of resurrecting is a duty of sons, *first of all,* to their fathers, and not to remote ancestors, because this duty—if it is to be fulfilled not supernaturally—will be fulfilled gradually, beginning with the nearest and proceeding to the most remote. If love exists between sons and fathers, then survival is possible only in terms of resurrecting;—without fathers, sons cannot live, hence they may live *only* for the sake of resurrecting their fathers—and in this *only,* everything is contained." (I, 339-40).

Fedorov criticizes Dostoevskii for even having dared to suggest that an abyss divides us from the souls of our ancestors. In Fedorov, there can be no abyss between the present and the past or between the living and the dead. That what is gone is forgotten does not mean that what is gone no longer exists. The only abyss is in our minds.

Fedorov is wrong, I think, to lump Dostoevskii and Solov'ev together as "mystics." Dostoevskii was able to create characters whose visions of the world are essentially mystical, such as Markel, and, to a certain extent, Zosima, in *The Brothers Karamazov*. But it is too simple to equate the mind of a writer with the minds of his characters. Certainly it is clear from his letters that Dostoevskii created Zosima to express his positive beliefs, just as he created Ivan to represent his doubts. But if Dostoevskii had wanted to express only positive beliefs he would have written sermons instead of novels—or, like Gogol', or even Tolstoi, he would have renounced his art in the name of some higher teaching. But to the end, Dostoevskii remained an artist who could most effectively and most fully express his own thought in novels containing a dialectic of ideas. Dostoevskii puts all his mind neither into the doubts of Ivan nor into the preachings of Zosima but into the dialectic between the two.

One basic difference between Dostoevskii and Fedorov is that Dostoveskii emphasizes the act of choosing between the path toward heaven and the path toward hell—both of which are internal and individual. Dostoveskii's characters always retain, and sometimes even to their own torment insist on retaining, a free choice between alternatives. Dostoevskii often leads his main characters through some kind of inner hell, plunges them toward self-destruction, then leaves them just before or just after they have begun the long path toward regeneration. Dostoevskii's great theme is man's potential for good and evil. His characters, like the Underground Man, are sometimes most conscious of their potential good at the very moment they are committing some despicable act, and, conversely, like Myshkin, are also sometimes most conscious of their potential for evil just when performing their noblest deeds. Those who have known hell are often left just after they have taken (Raskol'nikov) or have given signs that they may take (Ivan) their first step toward heaven, while the "saintly" heroes are often left either just before (Alesha—The Great Sinner) or just after (Myshkin) they have begun to fall. As a novelist, Dostoevskii is not so much interested in showing where good and evil are distinct as he is in showing where they overlap. Even Zosima has his bad memories, and even Svidrigailov has his love of beauty. Dostoevskii does not want to make the choice for his characters and his readers easier and clearer—he wants to show how difficult and murky free choice can be.

But where Dostoevskii emphasizes the free choice between alternatives and the potential for movement in either direction, Fedorov emphasizes what must be done after the choice has been made. Dostoevskii insists that man retain his freedom to choose, Fedorov that man give up the life of pure freedom (the gratification of whims) for the greater freedom (from death) that he will find in the life of duty. Fedorov believes that we have no real choice: either we will allow nature to destroy us or we will control nature and thereby win eternal life. The only alternatives, Fedorov insists, are life and death. Once we have chosen life we cannot turn back. Since salvation is not simply an internal or an individual matter in Fedorov, but can only be achieved by all for all, individual liberty must be sacrificed to collective obligation. This does not mean that we must all become slaves, but that we must all freely choose to join the task—otherwise the task will fail and individual liberty will remain only an illusion. At the heart of Fedorov's teaching is a variation on the ancient paradox: pursue freedom and you will have none; give up your freedom and you will find it. The Underground Man's cry for "one's own free and unfettered choice, one's own whims, however wild, one's own fancy...."[44] would represent, in Fedorov's view, a determination to remain a slave to nature and death.

Dostoevskii understood that the Underground Man's way was a dead end, and in later works he tried to discover among existing paths one that might lead to something better. Dostoevskii writes of Raskol'nikov's spiritual rebirth at the end of *Crime and Punishment*: "But that is the beginning of a new story, the story of the gradual renewal of a man, the story of his gradual regeneration, of his gradual transition from one world to another, of his learning about a new, hitherto utterly unknown reality. That might be the subject of a new story—but our present story is ended."

Fedorov begins where Dostoevskii ends.

Fedorov and Solov'ev

As we know from Dostoevskii's letter to Peterson,[45] Solov'ev first learned of Fedorov's ideas early in 1878. At this time Solov'ev was delivering his famous *Lectures on Godmanhood*,[46] which, Dostoevskii told us, "nearly a thousand attend." Dostoevskii apparently waited for Solov'ev after the eighth of the twelve lectures to read him Peterson's account of Fedorov's ideas, for Dostoevskii had found in their ideas "much that is similar." Dostoevskii and Solov'ev spent "a beautiful two hours at this. He finds [Fedorov's] ideas much to his liking and had wished to say almost the same things in his next lecture."

Students of Fedorov and students of Solov'ev have drawn opposite conclusions from the evidence provided in Dostoevskii's letter.[47] Peterson and Gornostaev use Dostoevskii's letter to support their claims that Fedorov's influence on Solov'ev began in the 1870's. But Prince Evgenii Trubetskoi, author of one of the first and best works on Solov'ev, argues more persuasively that Dostoevskii's letter proves that by the late 1870's Solov'ev had already independently developed ideas similar to Fedorov's. Trubetskoi finds that Fedorov's influence was important, but places that influence on the middle, rather than on the early, period of Solov'ev's development, that is, roughly from 1885-95, rather than from the late seventies. But here again, as in our discussion of Fedorov and Dostoevskii, "influence" is too simple a term to describe the relationship between the two thinkers.

When he first encountered Fedorov's ideas, through Dostoevskii, Solov'ev did not even know whose ideas he was hearing, but he knew immediately that he had found a likeminded thinker. As he learned more of Fedorov's thought, Solov'ev found much that he could incorporate into his own system, enlarging, but not essentially altering or violating his original tenets. For a brief time, in the early nineties, Solov'ev found that he and Fedorov shared so many ideas that they could together issue one call to the task of resurrecting—their separate systems, he believed, were one. But their essential differences soon became all too apparent. Their basic assumptions about the means of resurrection were incompatible, and each had to reject the most important and original parts of the other's thought. They certainly stimulated each other, and probably each had an "influence" on the other. But Solov'ev, at least twenty-five years younger, and at least fifty times more flexible than Fedorov, was able and willing to incorporate into his own growth much more of Fedorov than Fedorov incorporated of Solov'ev. But, most important, each helped the other attain a clearer understanding of what he did and did not mean by resurrection. Each served the other as the respected, worthy opponent that every thinker needs when it is time to sharpen the arguments and nail down the positions.

When and how Solov'ev and Fedorov first became personally acquainted is not known. But Peterson does tell us that he personally wrote down, from Fedorov's dictation, the manuscript to which Solov'ev responded in his first, undated letter to Fedorov. The manuscript, later printed with some changes as pp. 64-346 of the first volume of Fedorov's works, must have been the one that was begun in 1878 as an answer to Dostoevskii's letter. Twenty or so pages of this manuscript were shown to Tolstoi in the autumn of 1878; but, according to Peterson, Tolstoi was not impressed. When the manuscript was finished, then, Peterson must have decided that since Dostoevskii was dead and Tolstoi seemed uninterested, the best person to send it to was Solov'ev. In his letter, writter probably between 1882 and 1885, Solov'ev endorses Fedorov's project even more enthusiastically than had Dostoevskii:

> I read your manuscript avidly and with a delight of spirit, devoting all night and part of a morning to the reading, and for the next two days, Saturday and Sunday, thought much about what I had read. I accept your 'project' *completely* and without any discussion; what

must be talked about is not the project itself, but several of the underlying theoretical assumptions or suppositions, and also the first practical steps toward its realization. On Wednesday I'll bring the manuscript to you at the museum, and at the end of the week we will somehow have to get together in the evening. I have a great deal to tell you. But in the meantime, I will say only that from the time of the appearance of Christianity, your 'project' is the first forward movement of the human spirit along the way of Christ, For my part, I can only recognize you as my teacher and spiritual father. Your goal is not to proselytize, however, or to found a sect, but to save all mankind by a common task, and for the sake of that it is necessary, first of all, that your project be made known and be recognized by all. The means by which this might be accomplished —that is the main thing I would like to talk about with you when we meet.

Be well, dear teacher and comforter! [48]

Apparently they did meet, and continued to meet regularly for several years. The closest they came, however, to attempting to make Fedorov's project known and "recognized by all" was in 1891, when Solov'ev was preparing an address to be delivered at an October 19th meeting of the Moscow Psychological Society. Peterson writes: "Solov'ev attempted to persuade Nikolai Fedorovich to present the call to the common task jointly with him, and for this reason proposed to write down what Fedorov would dictate to him. When he refused, Solov'ev said to him: 'What's the matter, do you think that Peterson can present your thoughts better than I can?' Finally, Fedorov agreed to Solov'ev's proposition—a time was set, but Solov'ev did not come...." [49]

The paper that Solov'ev read to the Psychological society was "The Collapse of the Medieval World-Conception", which, as S. L. Frank tells us "produced the impression of a bombshell" [50] in religious and conservative circles. Essentially, the paper is Solov'ev's variation on ideas outlined by Fedorov in his essay, "What History Is" (I, 128-247). But if the paper seemed too radical for the religious conservatives of the day, it did not seem radical enough to Fedorov. In a special critique of Solov'ev's paper, (I, 479-491), a critique almost as long as the paper itself, Fedorow gives a point by point account of what Solov'ev failed to say. That Solov'ev had defined Christianity as the task of resurrection, and that he had argued that the medieval world-conception had collapsed precisely because medieval Christianity had not understood and adopted that task did not satisfy Fedorov. He laments that Solov'ev said nothing about precisely how that task was to be fulfilled. He blames what he call Solov'ev's "vagueness" about the means of resurrection on Solov'ev's inability to understand the true implications of the task. But here Fedorov is clearly wrong. Solov'ev did have a clear understanding of both the idea of resurrection and the means by which the resurrection would be achieved. But his understanding was altogether different from Fedorov's. Even in his first, enthusiastic letter to Fedorov, Solov'ev had mentioned that "several of the underlying theoretical assumptions or suppositions" had to be discussed. In his second letter to Fedorov, also undated, Solov'ev touches directly on one of the points on which they ultimately had to disagree.

> ... The task of resurrection not only as a process, but even *in the goal* itself is something conditional. The simple, physical resurrection of the dead cannot, in its own self, be the goal. The resurrection of people in the same state in which they strive to devour each other— to resurrect man in a stage of cannibalism would be both impossible and utterly undesirable. This means that the goal is not the simple resurrection of man in *his personal organic structure*, but the resurrection of man in the form he *ought to take*, namely, in that state in which all his parts and separate units do not exclude and change each other, but, on the contrary, preserve and fulfil each other. You, of course, perfectly agree with this: if the form that man ought to take (what he will be in the resurrection of the dead and in the life of the age to come) is still only desired, and

not actual, then actual man may in no way be discussed in terms of the form he ought to have, because if man as he ought to be (in which God is all in all) brings about the Father's will in full, so that here in human actions God himself acts directly and inseparably, so that there is no necessity for any special acts on the part of God, then this is not at all the case in actual man, who does not at all carry out the will of the Father and who is in no way a direct expression and form of the Divinity; insofar as our actions do not correspond to God's will, this will accomplishes for us its own particular action, which for us takes the appearance of something external. If man by his own action were to conceal Divinity (as in your future psychocracy), then God would actually not be visible behind people; but at present this is not the case, we do not conceal God, and for this reason Divine action (beneficence) peeps out from behind our actuality and hence the more this happens in strange (miraculous) forms, the less we ourselves correspond to our God. If a grown son enters into inner solidarity with his beloved father to such a degree that in all his actions he carries out his will, needing no external instructions, then necessarily for a young child the will of the father appears to a certain degree to be an external force, to be unfathomable wisdom, from which he expects instruction and guidance. We are all still children, and for this reason we need the child-guidance of external religion. Consequently, in positive religion and in the church we have not only elements and a prototype of the resurrection and the future Kingdom of God, but also a present (practical) path and actual means toward this end. Therefore, our task must have a religious, and not scientific character, and it must rely on the believing masses, and not on disputatious intellectuals. So there is a short explanation for you of the feelings that I was trying to express to you my last time in Moscow.

Until we meet again, dear teacher. God keep you. Take more care for your physical health—the rest you have in surplus. Are you collecting your manuscripts? It would be good to have them ready for the lithographer by autumn.[51]

In their personal relations, we see that Solov'ev still felt an almost filial respect and affection for Fedorov, and that he, perhaps like others, was trying to get Fedorov to publish his writings. But as a thinker, Solov'ev raises a crucial problem: how can we be certain that we will not resurrect death?

On reading this part of the letter, Fedorov wrote in the margin: "To resurrect cannibalism, i.e. to resurrect death! What absurdity! It's impossible to understand against whom you're writing!"[52]

From various places in his works (e.g. I, 447; II, 103, note 2; and II, 77), we know that Fedorov believed that people would be resurrected as they were at the end of life, and yet, at the same time, that they would be whole and perfect. How perfection can be reconciled with the form of a person near the end of life is a problem to be considered later in this study. For now, suffice it to say that Solov'ev took this problem more seriously than Fedorov did, and that the solution that Solov'ev offers reveals a fundamental difference between his and Fedorov's ideas of the resurrection.

In the letter quoted above, in several published articles,[53] and, especially, in a letter written to Tolstoi in the summer of 1894,[54] Solov'ev clearly states his reasons for believing that resurrection must be a religious and not a scientific task. His chief argument is that we are not yet fully developed. We are now only at a certain stage in our organic evolution. Just as signs of rationality sometimes appear in the animal kingdom, so signs of immortality sometimes appear in the human world. Christ, the perfect God-man, is to us as the first human being was to the apes, as the first animal was to plants, and as the first organic cell was to the primordial universe of inorganic matter.. At present our spirits are weak and are easily destroyed by the physical world and by the mortality of the body—our spirits, which are marked for immortality, are nevertheless still dominated by death. Our task is to develop our spirits (through prayer, fasting, meditation, and other religious practices which have been given to us precisely for the purpose of spiritual development) until we have attained spiritual immortality. Our immortal spirits will then resurrect our bodies. Spiritual immortality will create physical immortality. Our immortal bodies will not be exact material replicas of our present bodies, but will be our present bodies spiritually transfigured. Solov'ev's project of resurrection calls for the full realization of the mystic oneness of God and man. To Fedorov, Solov'ev's resurrection seemed a project of "magic" and "sorcery." But Solov'ev was simply calling on all men to develop the spiritual qualities now hidden within them, qualities which have always been recognized by poets and seers throughout human history, and which have been partially manifest in saints and prophets, but fully manifest only in Christ.

The second major point of difference between Fedorov and Solov'ev is on the question of the unification of churches. Both believed in a theocratic state, and in Christianity as a task of resurrection. But where Fedorov held that only the Russian Orthodox church could lead the task, Solov'ev looked for leadership to the Pope in Rome. As part of his argument, Solov'ev turned the idea of returning to the fathers back on Fedorov, pointing out that the first father of Christendom was not the Russian Metropolitan but the Holy Father in Rome. In an entire article written in response to Solov'ev's call for church unity (I, 469-491) Fedorov argues that the special virtue of Orthodoxy is that its emphasis is not on theological doctrine but on liturgy, i.e. on the embodiment of doctrine. Only in Orthodoxy is faith regarded as a living task.

In general, Fedorov criticizes Solov'ev for being a spokesman not for a particular nationality or people, but for being a spokesman for an international class, a privileged, intellectual elite who believe that all problems and the solutions to all problems are matters of the mind. Fedorov, on the other hand, wishes to speak for those who know from daily experience rather than from reflection that the problems of the physical, material world are real and must be solved by physical and material means. Mental and spiritual effort, Fedorov insists, cannot alter the material world, and in the end it is the material world that must be changed.

Solov'ev is usually regarded as the culmination of nineteenth century Russian philosophy. Questions raised by Chaadaev at the beginning of the century find resolution in Solov'ev at the end. His philosophy is generally regarded as the first great system in Russian thought, and is considered to provide a grand and original synthesis of all previous Russian philosophy. Without demeaning Solov'ev's achievement, I would suggest that both as a synthesizer and as an original thinker, Fedorov is Solov'ev's equal. Just as Solov'ev unites any number of previous tendencies of Russian thought into his vision of the world's organic wholeness and the mystical oneness of God and man, so Fedorov, as we shall see in a later discussion of his relationship to previous Russian thinkers, unites many of the same earlier Russian intellectual tendencies into his project for resurrection. And by including technology in his project, Fedorov brings into his system at least one whole side of Russian thought that Solov'ev leaves out of his.

As a writer, Solov'ev was much clearer, and much more precise and orderly than Fedorov. His writing has a grace, a conciseness—a purity— unequaled in Russian philosophical literature before or since. But, as we shall also see later in this study, Fedorov was not at all the inept writer than many have considered him to be. Fedorov's writing is full of energy, inspiration, and strong feeling. He does not lead the reader gently and courteously through his arguments, but hammers at the reader with his arguments until the idea sinks in. Brilliant aphorisms suddenly pop out in the middle of what seem to be interminable and belabored formulations. His best ideas seem bolder and more radical than anything in Solov'ev. But Solov'ev has a consistent depth that Fedorov cannot match.

Psychologically, the two were polar opposites. If Solov'ev's philosophy can be seen in part as an exaltation of "the eternal feminine", then Fedorov's must be called the exaltation of "the eternal masculine." Solov'ev celebrates the mysteries of Divine Sophia and abandons the path of strict rationality to open himself to holy wisdom. In Solov'ev, true knowledge is received: an illumination that cannot be achieved merely by human effort. Fedorov, on the other hand, celebrates the Father of fathers. He stands, stern at the crossroads, waving mankind onto the path of duty, urging: work, struggle, control nature! For Solov'ev, death and sexuality are ultimately holy mysteries. One passes through them and emerges whole. For Fedorov, death and sexuality are two faces of a Nature that man must control. Love, for Solov'ev, offers us access to the unity of heaven and earth. For Fedorov, love is brotherly, sisterly, filial affection, and devotion to the task. Fedorov and Solov'ev stand together on the centrality of the task of resurrection, but the means that they propose for the realization of the task—Fedorov's scientific projectivism, and Solov'ev's mystical development of Godmanhood—set them very far apart.

In 1875, at the age of twenty two, Solov'ev was sitting in the reading room of the British Museum when he experienced a mystical vision of Holy Sophia. She instructed him to leave the reading room and go to Egypt, which he promptly did. And one morning not long after, there he stood: at the edge of the desert, just before dawn, dressed in a long black European coat and a stovepipe hat, waiting for Sophia to appear. And probably at the same time, still before the opening hour, Fedorov was already at the library which he had been reluctant to leave the night before, scurrying around, gathering up books, waiting for Tsiolkovskii and the other young men to arrive so that they could resume the common task they had already begun.

And even after Fedorov and Solov'ev met, they would always remain that far apart.

Fedorov and Tolstoi

Dostoevskii and Solov'ev were attracted to Fedorov's ideas before they knew anything at all about the man. But Tolstoi, characteristically, had to find out what kind of life Fedorov lived before becoming interested in his ideas. And even after he had long known both Fedorov and his thought, Tolstoi seemed to remain more impressed by the idea that Fedorov slept on a trunk than by the idea of universal resurrection. Peterson tells us how Tolstoi first learned of Fedorov.

> I cannot but relate here that in the summer of 1878 Nikolai Fedorovich spent only two weeks at my house. In the same summer I came to see him in Moscow, and of the Syzrano-Morshansk railroad, on the half between Penza and Moransk, I met L. N. Tolstoi; he was returning with all his family from the Samarstok estate to Iasnaia Poliana, and I rode with him as far as Riazsk. On the way I told him about Nikolai Fedorovich and my communications with Dostoevskii. I read him Dostoevskii's letter and what I had written from Nikolai Fedorovich's dictation in reply to that letter during the two weeks that Nikolai Fedorovich had just spent with me. After he had heard me through, Lev Nikolaevich told me that he didn't find the idea very attractive. Nevertheless, that same autumn Lev Nikolaevich went to see Nikolai Fedorovich at the Museum and told him that he knew me, and from that time they began their acquaintanceship.[55]

N. N. Gusev, Tolstoi's friend, secretary, and, later editor, tells us that Tolstoi first met Fedorov in the Museum in the fall of 1878 while doing research on the Decembrists.[56] They may have met a few more times during the next two or three years, but the first indication of the impression that Fedorov made on Tolstoi is found in a notebook entry for October, 1881: "Nikolai Fedorovich—a saint. A closet. To carry it out!—It's self-evident.—Doesn't want a salary. No linen, no bed."[57] And a month later, Tolstoi wrote to his friend V. Alekseev:

> It is very difficult for me in Moscow.... But there are some people here. And God has granted me to get together with two.
> One is V. F. Orlov. The other, N. F. Fedorov.
> He's the librarian at the Rumiantsev Museum—you remember I told you about him. He has put together

a plan for a common task involving all mankind, which has as its goal the resurrection of all people in the flesh. In the first place, this is not so crazy as it sounds. (Don't worry, I don't share his views, but I understand them so well that I feel myself able to defend these views before any other creeds that have some goal outside themselves.) In the second place, and most important, thanks to that creed, he is, in his life, a pure Christian. When I talk to him about Christ's teachings, he says: yes, that's right, and I know that he himself is carrying out those teachings. He is sixty years old, is poor, gives everything away, and is always cheerful and meek.[58]

During the next several years, Tolstoi frequently refers to Fedorov in his letters and notebooks: "I am at peace with him"; "N. F. kind and good"; "N. F. kind as ever to me". For Tolstoi, these were years of spiritual unrest. Never a complacent person unaware of his own self-development, Tolstoi, in the late seventies and early eighties, was passing through a stage of especially intense spiritual torment and especially ruthless elf-examination. His earlier religious faith, never terribly strong, had collapsed utterly, and he was seeking a new faith to live by. Family life, an earlier ideal, had become odious to him. He had always detected a certain amount of hypocrisy and emptiness in the life of people of his class— now he saw in that life only hypocrisy and emptiness. His diaries, letters, and notebooks indicate that he woke up almost every morning convinced that everything that he had done the previous day was false. A few years before he had seriously considered suicide, and, in a lucid moment, had even removed a rope from his study lest he be tempted in one of his increasingly frequent spells of despondency. In many notebook entries throught the eighties, we find expressions of the recurrent feeling that death would be better than this life. His plans to write a sequel to *War and Peace*, set in the period of the Decembrist uprising, were finally abandoned. He no longer believed in the truths that had been central to his art. He was no longer the Tolstoi of *War and Peace*, and he was not yet the Tolstoi of the late moral tales. He was trying to formulate a new affirmation of life, but he found that he could think only of death.

That he could not live a life strictly consistent with his deeply felt (and widely published) principles had always troubled him, and now tormented him. Intellectually, he had rejected the ideal of family life and was moving toward an ideal of individual asceticism, but he still lived as—and at times very much enjoyed being—a family man. Theoretically he had turned against his own social class and against all art that did not illustrate some simple moral truth—and yet one of his biographers [59] gives us a charming picture of Tolstoi at age fifty, and his old enemy, Turgenev, age sixty, sitting at opposite ends of a child's teeter-totter, seesawing up and down as children from the neighborhood laugh and applaud. Even during his famous "peasant" phase, in which he allowed himself to be portrayed by the artist Repin *à la moujik* behind a plow, he had, we learn from his wife's Diary, under his peasant smock always worn silk underwear.

In the early 1880's, then, he was searching for, among other things, a person whose life was in full accordance with whatever principles he espoused. One of the persons he especially revered at this time was a shepherd named Siuteev, who preached brotherly love, refused to pay taxes, married his children off without priests, and believed that everything should be shared. Tolstoi viewed this man as a great teacher and prophet. Another person he admired was V. F. Orlov, a poor teacher at a school for the children of railroad workers. Orlov had once been arrested for revolutionary activities, but now he lived a simple life, supported a large family, and followed the teachings of the Gospels. Tolstoi often visited this wise and good man and wrote about him in many letters. Tolstoi, then, met Fedorov at a time when he felt very much in need of a model for the life of simplicity and consistency to which he himself now aspired.

But Tolstoi's attitude toward Fedorov and his teachings is interesting and complex. He admired Fedorov's unforced integrity, and, almost always, in recorded conversations with Fedorov, treated him with unusual deference. He seemed to view Fedorov as his moral superior, and in his behavior with

Fedorov, sometimes acted more like a son in the presence of his stern father, than like a contemporary and an equal. Professor I. A. Linnichenko, who observed Tolstoi and Fedorov together many times, tells us that Tolstoi "not only highly valued N. F.'s moral qualities, even openly bowed down before him, seeing in him one of the best personifications of his theory about loving what is close at hand and living life simply." [60] The director of the Tretiakov Gallery, Chernogub, tells us that he once heard Tolstoi say: "if I didn't have my own teaching, I would become a follower of Nikolai Fedorovich's teaching." [61] People who often observed them talking together tell us that when Fedorov spoke Tolstoi would listen respectfully and nod his agreement, but when Tolstoi spoke Fedorov would usually scowl sternly and shake his head in strong objection. In one of their conversations, described by I. M. Ivakin, a longtime acquaintance of both men, we are given a clear look at how they behaved in each other's presence. On this particular afternoon, in 1887, Tolstoi had gone to Fedorov's house, and, not finding him at home, had decided to look for him at the library, even though it was after the closing hour. On the way to the library, Tolstoi was met and joined by Ivakin, and together they intercepted Fedorov not far from the library on his way home. " 'Let's walk back—may I come to your place' [Tolstoi] asked Nikolai Fedorovich, seeing that N. F. had met him as though without any special pleasure. 'But perhaps you're tired—do you need to rest?' he said in a somewhat fallen voice, just like a man in love, waiting for an answer." As they walked back, Tolstoi tried to converse in a friendly manner, but Fedorov rejected almost everything he said. When, for instance, Tolstoi said that he didn't mind illness, because it was meant to be, Fedorov replied sternly: "Illness is not *meant to be*." And when Tolstoi began to praise a young writer whose works he had recently read, saying that as a writer himself he had found in the young man's work such "negative merits" as a sense of measure, the absence of anything false, a sense of independence and a willingness to ignore contemporary trends, Fedorov replied: "Well that can't be said about him—he listens to what's being said." Agreeing, and yet not agreeing, Tolstoi said: "Yes, like an intelligent person, he listens to them all in order to digest it later himself. He's very seriously studying aeronautics." But not even aeronautics was enough to earn Fedorov's approval of Tolstoi's "fine young man." Ivakin tells us: "But Nikolai Fedorovich said that all this tends not toward the joining but toward the separation of people, toward isolation. And that isolation was already so great." And, to Ivakin's slight amusement: "Tolstoi suddenly fell into the tone of Nikolai Fedorovich and began to say that when gunpowder was invented it was as if people thought that would bring an end to wars—but nothing had come of it, everything was as before. Then they invented dynamite, roborite, melinite, and nothing had come of that either!" [62]

Fedorov was apparently one of the few people who dared to tell Tolstoi to his face that he was an utter fool. Gusev tells us that once while walking with Fedorov through the stacks, Tolstoi looked at the books piled everywhere, and remarked: "Ech, they ought to dynamite here!" Fedorov apparently never forgave him for this remark. In another version of what may have been the same incident, Tolstoi said: "So many stupid things are written; it all ought to be burned!" Fedorov, as if stung, seized his head. "I've seen many stupid men in the world, but never one like you!" The witness reports that the author of *War and Peace* looked shocked, embarrassed, and confused.[63] Linnichenko tells of another rift between them.

> ...Once, when I was sitting in the office of the librarian, Nikolai Ivanovich Storzhenko, Lev Nikolaevich walked in to see him. "I've come to you for help. I don't know what's the matter with Nikolai Fedorovich. You know how deeply I respect the old man but he's not speaking to me—and I have no idea why." Nikolai Ivanovich, well acquainted with the old man's peculiar nature, promised to have a talk with him. Wondering what had upset him so, I went to Nikolai Fedorovich the following day and asked what he had held against Tolstoi and just what had been said in their recent encounter. To get a candid reply out of Nikolai Fedorovich was not easy. I was able to understand only that

he and Tolstoi had discussed some philosophical matters and that Nikolai Fedorovich had been perturbed by Tolstoi's views. When Tolstoi had begun to refer to what he had written earlier on the matter under discussion, Nikolai Fedorovich had replied: "Very well, but at that time you, Lev Nikolaevich, were not only a distinguished writer, you were an intelligent person as well." [64]

In talking about Fedorov to third persons, Tolstoi seems to have been half amused by, and half seriously drawn to, his ideas. As we have seen, in his letter to Alekseev, Tolstoi wanted people to know that the ideas were not as crazy as they sounded, that Tolstoi didn't share them but could defend them, and that he considered Fedorov the man to be a saint. His mixed feelings are further revealed in a collection of reminiscences by V. F. Lazurskii, who writes, after hearing Tolstoi's account of Fedorov and his ideas:

> I could not keep from smiling, even though I was trying to listen seriously. Lev Nikolaevich had warned that to a fresh listener this theory would seem the product of a deranged mind, but in fact it was not devoid of sense.
> "Yes, if you had tried to smile in his presence he would have let you have it. Once I happened to catch sight of a little book in the Rumiantsev Museum—a list of colonels for some certain number of years—and I smiled. Did he scold me! 'All this is needed: all these are reminiscences of our ancestors.' Now he can't abide me: in the first place, because I don't share his theory; in the second place, because I love death." [65]

In a letter to Kozhevnikov, Fedorov tells of a number of attempts on the part of Tolstoi to bring Fedorov's ideas to the attention of serious thinkers. He even went so far as to propose Fedorov for membership in the prestigious Moscow Psychological Society. But when Professor Troitskii, a leading member of the society, asked how place would be made for all those to be resurrected on earth, Tolstoi is said to have replied with a smile that even *that* had been taken into account, that the kingdom of knowledge and regulation was not limited to this earth, and all present, presumably including Tolstoi, broke into loud laughter.[66]

Although Tolstoi continued to have great respect and affection for Fedorov for the rest of his life, Fedorov grew more and more incensed at what he considered Tolstoi's "immoral" teachings. Especially repugnant to Fedorov was Tolstoi's "love of death." Once, on a visit to Fedorov, Tolstoi picked up a skull lying on the desk, and instead of: "Alas, poor Yorick—I knew him, Horatio," apparently said: "I love this snubnosed fellow!"[67] This, plus a remark he made to Peterson: "here I am standing with one foot in the grave, and all the same I'll say that death is not a bad thing"[68]—offered Fedorov reason enough to break off all personal relations. But according to Gusev, the final break came in 1892 when an article of Tolstoi's on the famine, which because of the censorship had first appeared in the London *Daily Telegraph,* was quoted from and commented on in the Moscow papers. When Tolstoi next came to the library, Fedorov refused to shake hands with him and moved around the room so that Tolstoi could not even come close. "Nikolai Fedorovich!" Tolstoi protested. "We're old men—why can't we forgive each other?"[69] But Fedorov apparently never did speak to him again. In the article, Tolstoi had sharply criticized the governmen's policy of famine relief, and had called for a vague, radical redistribution of wealth, which was interpreted by radicals and conservatives alike (and apparently by Fedorov) as a call for a socialist revolution.

But long after their break, Tolstoi contined to speak highly of Fedorov. In 1895, when a colleague of Fedorov's asked Tolstoi to sign a petition to Fedorov requesting him not to retire from his post, Tolstoi wrote back: "I will joyfully sign any petition which you write to Nikolai Fedorovich. And no matter how highly you appraise both the person and the deeds of Nikolai Fedorovich in your petition, you will still not express the profound respect which I hold for his person, or my opinion of the good which he has done and is doing for people by his selfless activities. I am grateful to you for having turned to me." [70]

And even in his last years, when he was plagued by Peterson with reproaches for not having made Fedorov's task his own, Tolstoi repeatedly affirmed his love for the memory of his sharpest critic.[71]

Although both upheld many of the same ideals, such as brotherhood, chastity, the superiority of the rural life over the urban, and the task of carrying out Christ's commandments, Tolstoi and Fedorov understood these ideas in such opposite ways that they actually shared few convictions. In a section of *Supramoralism* entitled: "Supramoralism, or Unity for the Activity of Resurrecting, in Opposition to Tolstoi's Immoralism, i.e. to His Doctrine of Disunity, to which his Invitation to Non-Thought and Non-Action Leads," Fedorov calls Tolstoi's idea of non-resistance "a most spiteful mockery of Christianity and of wholesome thought." By advocating disobedience to laws that he considers unjust, Tolstoi becomes a champion of all immoral activity. Furthermore: "Tolstoi recognizes only himself, his own *I*;—he is above the law, above everything." "The worthlessness of life is the first principle of Tolstoi's philosophy, and hypocrisy is the second principle." (II, 437-438) Fedorov attacks Tolstoi for advocating a brotherhood that includes only the living and not the dead, and for demanding absolute chastity (and therefore the end of the human race) without first calling for an end to death and a beginning of the task of resurrection. To Fedorov, Tolstoi's Christianity is not Christianity at all but a modern version of Buddhism. And Fedorov finds that to advocate inaction, as Tolstoi does, is to advocate death, for nature continues to act even when man does not.

Tolstoi received a copy of the first volume of Fedorov's works, but probably did not read it.[72] He thought that he understood Fedorov's idea perfectly, and perhaps he wanted to retain his picture of the man and his ideas as he remembered them.

In a letter to Tolstoi, the critic and thinker N. N. Strakhov draws an accurate contrast between the two thinkers. Fedorov is a healthy, cheerful, natural saint; Tolstoi is a man at war with himself.⁷³ Fedorov certainly felt much more comfortable living within his idea than Tolstoi did trying to live up to his. Tolstoi's life and work tell us as much as can be told by one man about the world as it is, but Fedorov was trying to tell Tolstoi and us about the world "as it ought to be."

Gornostaev's claim that Tolstoi's entire life and work after 1880 can be understood only as a response to Fedorov is, of course, highly exaggerated. All that can be said, I think, of Fedorov's "influence" on Tolstoi, is that Tolstoi did seem to view Fedorov's life as an ideal, and that some of Tolstoi's efforts at asceticism may have been inspired by Fedorov's example. In *What Is Art*, which he showed to Fedorov and discussed with him, Tolstoi articulates a number of convictions that bear some resemblance to Fedorov's: art should be a means of uniting men and of joining them in the same feeling; the inaccessible art most highly valued by the upper classes separates the elite from the rest of humanity, whereas true art should be accessible to all and should make us all aware that we are of one family; art should not be pursued and prized for its own sake but for the good effects it can produce; the best art is that which embodies Christ's teachings. But Fedorov goes much farther and is much more specific: art should now begin to provide men with representations of the idea of resurrection, and should, eventually, in collaboration with science and theology, become the activity of reordering the cosmos. Art then will not only be an act of representation, but of transformation.

The only other major work in which Tolstoi's views come close to Fedorov's is *The Kreutzer Sonata* (1890). Here, through Pozdnyshev, Tolstoi proposes that sex is: 1) disgusting; 2) a force not of life but of death; and 3) counter to man's true life purpose. Fedorov nowhere says that sex is disgusting, but the other two ideas are central to his philosophy. The idea that people should live in absolute chastity (after the task of resurrection has begun) is an idea that has a natural and logical place in Fedorov's system. But the idea of perfect chastity has always seemed a strange and sudden departure in the development of Tolstoi's thoughts on the subject. To condemn extra-marital sex was one thing—to preach abstinence for married couples was another. The idea behind *The Kreutzer Sonata* has always seemed too extreme to have been a natural consequence of the ideas that lay behind *Anna Karenina*. And after *The Kreutzer Sonata* Tolstoi does not return to the idea. Pozdnyshev's ideas are usually interpreted as extreme, radical views which Tolstoi shared partly but not fully. Perhaps Tolstoi released Pozdnyshev's views as a sort of trial balloon, as a position to which he was drawn but to which he did not want to be committed. As sources for Pozdnyshev's ideas, scholars have pointed to materials that Tolstoi may have read about the Shakers, and to a book called *Tocology: A Book for Every Woman* by Dr. Alice B. Stokham, as well as to Tolstoi's own earlier expressions of moderately negative feelings about sex even as far back as in *War and Peace*.[74] But in Fedorov, Tolstoi knew a living proponent of an idea of chastity far more consistent and radical than that proposed by Stokham, the Shakers, or even by Pozdnyshev. In Fedorov, asexual love and control of the sex drive are not ends in themselves but integral parts of the larger tasks of resurrecting the dead. People will have learned to re-create life, so sex will no longer be necessary to perpetuate the human race. But to Pozdnyshev, and perhaps to Tolstoi himself, the idea of the end of sex seemed in itself such a vast and far-reaching idea that nothing beyond it was considered. When asked how the race can perpetuate itself without sex, Pozdnyshev does not give Fedorov's answer (by resurrecting), but replies that if life has no aim, then there will no longer be any reason for man to go on living, and if life does have an aim, then by living in a state of chastity man will have reached that aim and again there will be no need to go on living. So even in *The Kreutzer Sonata*, where Tolstoi takes up an idea central to Fedorov, Tolstoi's treatment of that idea is, in the end, contrary to both the spirit and letter of Fedorov.

One major difference between Fedorov and Tolstoi is in their very attitude toward their disagreements. Fedorov, in the end, could neither forget nor forgive the differences between Tolstoy's ideas and his own. Tolstoi, on the other hand, even in his semi-fanatic old age, continued to separate his feelings for the man from his attitude toward the man's ideas. This split view was Tolstoi's strength, even though he sometimes considered it his weakness. But no matter how Tolstoi struggled, he could never view the world with a single eye. He remained, in Sir Isaiah Berlin's ingenious formulation, a "fox" trying to turn himself into a "hedgehog." [75] It was precisely Fedorov's difference from him that attracted Tolstoi to Fedorov: the hedgehog in Fedorov that drew the ever restless fox. But the very quality that made Fedorov so attractive and interesting to Tolstoi, the inseparability of his life and his thought, was the quality that made it impossible for Fedorov to continue warm personal relations with him. Tolstoi could forget ideological differences long enough to enjoy a few happy moments with a Turgenev, but Fedorov was not the kind to forget a quarrel long enough to sit even for a moment on one teeter-totter with a Tolstoi.

Last Years

During Fedorov's last years, his daily working schedule remained essentially the same as always. He would arrive at the library an hour or so before it opened, to make certain that books ordered late the previous day would be ready when the reader called. He would stay at the library after the closing hour to take care of any jobs that he had not been able to complete during business hours. He had no sympathy for those who were demanding an eight-hour workday, which he called "sixteen-hour idleness." At home, he would have a light meal and talk with any friends who dropped by. He would sleep for two or three hours, until about midnight, then he would read and write until almost dawn. Then, after another short sleep of about two or three hours, he would set off for the library to start a new day.

In addition to his regular work at the library, he had two special projects on which he worked overtime. One was to collect folk legends from among the people. Anonymously, he edited and published at least two of these legends.[76] Another project, to which he devoted considerable energy, was a plan to enlarge the library catalogue to include not only the author, title, and call number of each book, but a brief summary of its contents written by the author himself. Another library project that Fedorov proposed was an exchange of scientific literature between the Rumiantsev Museum and the Bibliothèque Nationale in Paris.[77]

In 1899, Peterson was appointed a member of the District Court in Askhabad, Turkestan, and in the summer of that year Fedorov visited him there to continue their long joint project of writing. This visit to Turkestan brought a new theme into Fedorov's thought: the task of uniting east and west, Asia and Europe. The question of Asia's future role in the world was one of much popular speculation at the time. In different ways and on different intellectual levels, Madame Blavatsky's theosophical writings proclaiming "new light from Asia," Solov'ev's apocalyptic visions of "Panmongolism," and journalists who wrote of the "yellow peril" all contributed to the commonly shared *fin de siècle* assumption that in Russia as well as in Europe the time of Western dominance was coming to an end and a period of Asian dominance was about to begin. But Fedorov took quite a different view. Turkestan, the vast territory both joining and separating Russia and China, a wasteland dominated by the Pamir mountain range and the surrounding desert, became in Fedorov's thought a major focal point for the task of regulating nature and resurrecting the dead. Formerly, Fedorov learned, the wasteland had been inhabited, and, according to local legend, was even the site of the original Eden. Only man's failure to regulate nature had permitted the former paradise to become an uninhabitable wasteland. The bones of Adam, the first father, were buried somewhere in the mountains. And, as Fedorov once wrote in a letter to Kozhevnikov, the landscape of the Pamir region reminded him of "a pyramid of skulls."[78] At that time, also, the Pamir region was one of the most likely candidates for the hypothetical original homeland of the hypothetical Aryan race. From here the first fathers of the white races had supposedly dispersed to India, Persia, and Europe. In later times, the Pamir region had been the center from which the mongol hordes had overrun Russia and Europe. Pamir, then, represented to Fedorov, the world's center of repulsion. Adam, the Aryans, and the Mongols had all fled from this lost paradise. On either side of the Pamir region now lived representatives of the major races and religions of the world: Turan and Aryan, Buddhist, Hindu, Islamic, and Christian. The region had, by a recent treaty between Russia and England, fallen under the jurisdiction of the Tsar, the father of the Russian people. The task of the father-autocrat, and of all Russians, was to turn this natural center of repulsion into a center of attraction. By bringing rain to the desert and warm winds to the mountains, the wasteland of snow and sand could be transformed back into the garden spot of the world. Russia, lying between east and west, combining the principles of Europe and Asia, could, by restoring life to the "pyramid of skulls" under which the first father of all men lay buried, show the way to unite the entire divided world. (I, 134, 218, 247).

One of the ideas that Fedorov retained through life was that even the most menial and mundane job could become a sacred task. In the library and museum, he had treated even the most trivial assignments as opportunities to resurrect dead knowledge. In his last position, as desk clerk in the hall of archives for the Ministry of Foreign Affairs, he transformed his actual humble duties into the projected duties of caretaker of the record of present worldwide disunity, and future, Russian-directed, worldwide unity. In the records of Russia's foreign relations, he found innumerable confirmations of his conviction than Russia had a special destiny in the world. His late writings show that he had done considerable research on the historical meaning of the title "Tsar," and that he had looked carefully at the wording of treaties under which Russia had acquired new territories. He found, essentially, that Russia's territorial growth had resulted from a series of acts that had sacred, as well as worldly, significance. The Russian Tsar was intended to be the father of all living peoples, and to represent the interests of the dead among the living. The true task of the Tsar was to gather all lands into one land and to make all peoples one people. Subscribing to the medieval doctrine of "Moscow—The Third Rome," Fedorov was convinced that in the archives of the foreign affairs Ministry lay documents of paramount importance for the history of mankind. Russia's history was the world's history: dividing all in history as fact, uniting all in history as project.

In letters to Kozhevnikov, written during the last five years of his life, Fedorov often expressed his doubt that his lifelong project would find immediate acceptance and recognition. "I have no hope that in our age of unthought and inaction the problem of the universal task, of the regulation of nature by human reason and will, can possibly attract attention to itself." Fedorov wrote, he confessed, "under the influence of complete hopelessness," and "knowing that no one has any use for these writings," and that "the teaching on the active relationship to nature, with all its consequences, will be rejected by some as a diatribe from the age of ignorance, and by others as unbelief." But, he also wrote: "my certainty and boldness grow together with the negative reactions and non-recognition accorded my convictions." [79] As Kozhevnikov writes: "He knew that it is not the grain that appears before all others that grows longest and bears the most abundant crop; he was even convinced that a doctrine too far advanced over the general level of its time, would be condemned to temporary failure, that it would have to be buried, perhaps for a long time, but that in time it was also certain to be resurrected, and that it would be recognized and accepted in the very place where once it had elicited only mockery or a smile of doubt." [80]

The only portrait that we have of Fedorov was done in stealth by the well-known painter, Leonid Pasternak (father of the poet Boris Pasternak.) Pasternak tells us that once while working in the Rumiantsev Museum, he became intrigued by the appearance and manner of the old man who served in the reading room. He began to make a sketch, but noticed that the old man suspected what Pasternak was doing and obviously did not like the idea of being drawn. So, for several days in a row, Pasternak sat behind a huge stack of books and tried to appear to be busy reading them. He would look up only infrequently, so not to arouse the old man's suspicion. He kept his sketches, and only later learned that the old man was Fedorov. He later used these sketches as the basis for his portrait of Fedorov, Tolstoi, and Solov'ev together. In it, Fedorov is an old man with a full, white beard, and a high, bare brow. He is sitting at his desk with his hands crossed before him inside the large, loose sleeves of his shirt. Behind him is a shelf full of books. Although he is looking in Tolstoi's direction, his eyes seem to be staring intently at something behind the portrait's frame. In the death mask, also done by Pasternak, and printed in the journal *Vesy*, the face carries the same intense but meditative expression, but now the eyes are closed.[81]

Fedorov died in December of 1903. As Ostromirov tells us, Fedorov had been healthy in even the harshest Moscow winters of previous years, but in this particularly severe winter friends persuaded him to wear a warm coat instead of the light outer rag he had always worn summer and winter, and got him to start taking a cab instead of walking to work. Not long after he had begun to follow this well meant advice, he contracted pneumonia and died.

Kozhevnikov, who was at Fedorov's deathbed, tells us that during the last, painful hours, Fedorov said nothing of himself or of his pain, or even of death itself, but continued to talk as long as he had strength about the contents of the last two articles he had written, and that even after he could no longer speak, his lips continued to tremble as if he were trying to express the unuttered thoughts that were still burning in his eyes. He was buried in the Skorbiashchenskii Zhenskii Monastery where, when Ostromirov wrote in 1928, his grave could still be found, marked by a cross engraved with the words: "Christ is Risen."

CHAPTER II

THE COMMON TASK

"The Philosophy of the Common Task"

The Philosophy of the Common Task, the posthumous collection containing almost all that we now have of Fedorov's thought, is a massive, two volume, 1200 page miscellany of long and short essays, articles for newspapers, "letters to the editor," finished and unfinished works, drafts, fragments, variations on arguments developed more fully elsewhere, notes of books read, and inspired jottings.[1] The whole reads like a first draft, an ambitious plan for a work that neither Fedorov nor his disciples tried to complete.

Although the ideas, and the articles and essays themselves, are attributed to Fedorov, the book cannot be considered the work of one individual, but must be viewed as a product of the collective efforts of three men: Fedorov, Peterson, and Kozhevnikov. From the reminiscences of Peterson and Kozhevnikov, we can put together a general picture of how the works were composed. Fedorov would either dictate his thoughts to Peterson, or, when alone, would write down fresh ideas on whatever scraps of paper were at hand. Peterson and Kozhevnikov would then put Fedorov's ideas into written form, and then Fedorov would either make revisions to what they had written or begin a different version of the same work. As Peterson once wrote, in a letter to Kozhevnikov: ". . . his thought works on without cease; for that reason, it seems to me, he may never bring all that he has written into order. As soon as he begins to rework something he has written it begins to turn into something new, a fresh attempt at something whole and complete; and that's the way it goes—without end. . . ."²

After Fedorov's death Peterson and Kozhevnikov had to work with more bits and pieces than wholes. Some of the works published as single, complete essays were not written as such, but were put together from many drafts, each of which appears to have been a fresh attempt to present the entire project. Thus, in reading Fedorov, one encounters any number of repetitions, variations on a single argument, and one has a constantly reinforced sense of *déjà vu*. And just as the editors had to put together essays, and a whole book, from bits and scraps of paper on which Fedorov had hastily scribbled various of his ideas, so the student of Fedorov has to put together a systematic outline of the entire idea from arguments scattered throughout the book. In an article ostensibly devoted to one topic, one may find points absolutely essential to a discussion of a topic treated under some other, entirely different title. As an example, two of the clearest statements of what Fedorov means by physical resurrection are found not in articles with "resurrection" in the title, but in articles on the mysticism of Dostoevskii and Solov'ev, and in an article entitled "The Question of Sanitation." Moreover, Fedorov's ideas even on topics to which he devotes comparatively little attention, such as the significance of the Pamirs, cannot be found in one single place, but are scattered throughout the two volumes. Consequently, a reader can obtain a general idea of Fedorov's project by reading almost any twenty or thirty pages in either volume of his works. But to learn his entire thought on any single question, whether that question be the role of women in the task or the significance of the ideas of the early nineteenth century meteorologist V. N. Karazin, one may well have to read the entire 1200 pages.

Part of the unsystematic character of *The Philosophy of the Common Task* may indeed be due to what many critics have regarded as Fedorov's ineptitude as a writer. As Zenkovskii notes, Fedorov's writing style is "often very difficult and awkward."³ Bulgakov writes: "I have never encountered a writer more unliterary, more intricate, more abstruse, or unsystematic. . . ."[4] Berdiaev adds: "He was in no sense a writer, nor was he a philosopher in the usual sense of the word. . . . Theoretical philosophy and contemplative metaphysics are completely alien to him."[5] And Lord tells us: "Fedorov was certainly no writer. His disconnected, rambling style, with its frequent repetitions and even apparent contradictions, will quickly exhaust the reader's patience. . . . It is only a pity that his poverty of expression has left serious blemishes on what is otherwise highly significant and original:"[6]

While Fedorov's repetitious, contradictory, and unsystematic writing style cannot be entirely excused, it can and should be understood in the light of his theories about philosophical writing in general. For Fedorov, philosophy is a task involving more than writing. Words must be followed by deeds. In his own method of writing, Fedorov enabled Peterson and Kozhevnikov to join him in a "common task"—here, the task of getting his ideas into writing. Fedorov did not want to create a polished monument to himself or to his ideas. While we cannot be certain that he deliberately left his work unfinished in order that others might take up what he had begun, he did make it clear that his own writings were intended only as a call, a summons to a task, and not as a literary work so perfect and authoritative that successors would have no reason to readdress the questions he had raised. Fedorov was not at all interested in contributing to the discussion of traditional philosophical questions. Rather, he believed that the entire history of western philosophy, from Plato through Nietzsche, had wasted its time discussing the wrong questions, and had ignored the only questions of real importance: why do the living die? What can be done to bring the dead to life? Fedorov, then, was not seeking to join the mainstream of western philosophy, nor was he seeking to write a work that could be compared to the works of his illustrious predecessors, such as Descartes, Kant, or Hegel. He was, rather, attempting to point out that the course of western philosophy had to be changed, that understanding the world and even writing brilliant, systematic interpretations of the world would no longer suffice. He wanted to call the attention of all men to the need to integrate all knowledge and action in a task that would eventually make all philosophical literature, including Fedorov's own writings, obsolete. So, at least part of the unfinished, unsystematic character of Fedorov's writings can be understood as a reflection of his idea that the true purpose of philosophy was not to create perfect systems but to call all men to the common task. That Fedorov often treats the same question in different ways indicates, I think, not so much a tendency toward inconsistency, as a dogged attempt to demonstrate that the task of resurrecion can be presented credibly to any kind of audience (believers or unbelievers, scientists or aesthetes) and that no matter what problem is originally addressed, the conclusion will always be that we must all join the task of resurrection. Thus, in one essay, the task of resurrection seems to be chiefly a scientific task, while in another passage it seems to be primarily a religious task. While many of Fedorov's critics have viewed every question that he raises as an either/or, Fedorov himself usually intends his solutions to be "both/and." The task must be sacred and secular, religious and scientific, political and philosophical.

So if it cannot be said that Fedorov is a systematic thinker and writer, it can be said that he thinks and writes with a single goal constantly in mind. His work, externally disjointed and chaotic, derives its wholeness from the single idea that recurs throughout. No formal, external unity is apparent in Fedorov's works—his points do not follow each other in any strict, arithmetic, sequential order. In his works, A can often just as easily be followed by W as by B. But an organic unity, a coherence from within, holds all the apparently disparate parts of his writings together, for no matter what topic is ostensibly under discussion—Russian churches, Kant's imperatives, or the weather—the underlying topic, which will inevitably surface, is the project of resurrecting the ancestors.

In his use of language, Fedorov's precision is more nearly that of the poet than that of the mathematician.[7] Instead of choosing the word that will eliminate all ambiguity, the word that can be read in one and only one sense, Fedorov more often chooses the word that works on several levels of meaning. He does not seek words free of unphilosophical connotations, but, on the contrary, chooses precisely those words which are richest in connotative and allusive value. For instance, for "pedant", Fedorov uses *bukvoed*, "letter-eater", and one pictures some kind of large, heavy, bearded, bespectacled, grazing animal. For "pedantry" Fedorov uses "*bukvoedstvo*", "letter-eating" elevated by the *stvo* suffx to pseudo-philosophical activity. In writing of the significance of the autocrat, he tells us that it is the Russian autocrat who stands in the "*ottsov-mesto*"—the "fathers' place" meaning: that the autocrat represents the dead fathers, that the autocrat takes the role of father for the living children of the world, that the autocrat represents the God of the fathers, and that the autocrat now stands watch not only over Russia proper but, through a treaty, over Pamir, the place where the bones of Adam, the father of all men, are supposedly buried. By "*ottsov-mesto*" Fedorov means all of this and possibly more. So critics who have accused him of being an inept writer must assume, I should think, that the best philosophical writing is that which uses language with mathematical precision. But Fedorov's precision is that of a poet's He chooses his words carefully not to eliminate apparently extraneous connotations, but to add connotative levels of meaning that mathematical diction would not allow. He chooses the word that says the greatest number of things rather than the word that says one and only one thing best. Fedorov plays with language, using the roots and etymological meanings of words to suggest connections between ideas that might otherwise seem utterly unrelated. Superficially, Fedorov's sentences seem to be loose and rambling, but when examined closely they display stylistic qualities that cannot be attributed to literary ineptitude. An example of Fedorov's peculiar strengths and weaknesses as a writer is his argument against the idea of "progress."

> The triumph of the younger generation over the older—that is the essential feature of progress. Biologically, progress is the younger swallowing the older, the sons crowding out the fathers; psychologically it is the replacing of love for the fathers by a soulless exaltation over them, hatred for them, it is the moral, or, more truly, the immoral ousting of the fathers by the sons. Sociologically, progress expresses itself as the attain-

ment of the fullest measure of freedom accessible to man—(not in the greatest participation of each in the common task of restoring life to the fathers) since society, which is the same as the absence of brotherhood, demands that the freedom of each individual be limited; thus the demand of sociology will be a demand for the greatest freedom and the least unity and association, i.e. sociology is the science not of association but of dissociation and subjugation if society is permitted to swallow up the individual; as the science of dissociation for some and subjugation for others, sociology sins against both that which cannot be divided and that which cannot be confused, against the Triune God. Progress is precisely that form of life in which the human race is able to taste the greatest sum of suffering while striving to attain the greatest sum of delight. Progress is not satisfied with recognizing the activity of evil, but wants the activity of evil to have full representation, and revels in it in realistic art; while in ideal art progress struggles toward a firm conviction that the good is impossible and unreal, it revels in a representation of nirvana. Although stagnation is death and regression is no paradise, progress is veritable hell, and the truly divine, truly human task is to save the victims of progress, to take them out of hell. (I, 19-20).

In translation, one can get Fedorov's main idea and a feeling for his rambling prose style. What is missing in my translation is Fedorov's playfulness, his poetic depth. In translation, the passage may seem to be a string of unconnected clauses, but in the original each clause is naturally connected to the one before and after it, and the thread of meaning is never twisted or broken. A good example of Fedorov's literary skill (not brought out in my translation) is his claim that sociology is the science not of "association" but of "dissociation" and "subjugation" (*sotsiologiia est' nauka ne obshcheniia, a razobshcheniia, ili poraboshcheniia*). In this single phrase, the foreign sounding word "sociology' is contrasted to the Russian idea of society or community that is contained in the native Russian word, *obshcheniia,* and the foreign, latinate, western "sociology" is defined as the disintegration of all common ties. Then, by a leap of poetic imagination that one might expect of a Pasternak or a Mandelshtam, but not of a person who was "certainly no writer", Fedorov lets us see that "dissociation" and enslavement, or what I translated as "subjugation" are separated by only a thin, unstable layer of consonats. To translate all the connotations implicit in Fedorov's simple Russian sentence into English, one would have to say: "Sociology, a learned discipline foreign to Russia, is not the science of association, of integrity, of what is common, not the science of society, but the science of dissociation, of disintegration, of the destruction of the common, of the breakdown of society—or—of enslavement, which is the unnoticed shadow of dissociation and which, after a small slip, could replace it." More than sixty words of translation still do not capture all that Fedorov said in nine. And what the difficulty in translating Fedorov suggests is not that English is a clumsier language than Russian, but that Fedorov was a master of his own language, that he expressed so much in so few words that any translation into any language will have to either ignore or go to great lengths to express much of what Fedorov expressed by carefully choosing his words.

In language, as in other matters, Fedorov is very much a neo-Slavophile. He does his best to avoid, or to use only in negative contexts, words with a foreign, latinate flavor. A typical example is his contrast of *"otechestvennost'"* [true feeling for the fatherland] to *"patriotizm"* [*patriotism as affectation*]. In *otechestvennost'*, a person shows genuine feeling for the land of his fathers, whereas in *patriotizm*, a person merely uses patriotism as a mask for his own self-love.

Avoiding traditional philosophical terminology and bookish expressions in general, Fedorov formulates his basic concepts in words drawn from everyday speech. Even his neologisms, such as *"bratotvorenie"* ["brother-making"] and *"miropadenie"* ["*world-fall*"] are concocted from the most familiar common Slavic roots and would immediately be understood by even an illiterate speaker of Russian. One of Fedorov's central concepts is that of *rodstvo* ["kinship"].

In Russian the root, *rod-* is more or less the equivalent of Greek and Latin *gen-*. But where our English *gen-* words sound slightly bookish or artificial, the Russian *rod-* words are those most commonly used in everyday life and include the most ordinary words for: "to give birth," "to be born," "parents," "relative," "homeland," "nation-people-folk," "relationship" etc. *Rodstvo*, then, is that which joins one to life, to parents, to relatives, to homeland, and is the basis for most of the unchosen, ineradicable, enduring relationships that one carries throughout life. "*Nerodstvo*" ["unkinship"] is, to Fedorov, the present condition of man and the world, and the restoration of *rodstvo* is central to the common task.

It is *rodstvo* that should join the one to the many, the present to the past, the living to the dead, and man to the universe. *Nerodstvo* is the alienation of man from his original identity, the isolation of the part from the whole, the gulf between the present and the past, between the living and the dead, and the separation of man from the earth and from his true place in the cosmos. Fedorov sees *nerodstvo* everywhere and in everything: it is what idle intellectuals, believers in progress, arrogant youths, sooty cities, and cursive writing all have in common with a disintegrating corpse. It is *nerodstvo*, the absence of deep, enduring ties, that is responsible for capitalist exploitation as well as for the calls to socialist revlution. The only way to end war and death is to restore *rodstvo*.

The bridge between *nerodstvo* and *rodstvo* is *delo*, which, in Fedorov's works, is perhaps best translated "task." But *delo* means more. Like the *rod-* words, *delo* is one of the most common words in the language. It means: "affair," "business," "cause," "deed," "act," "work," etc. It is the word that Russians use in one of the most common expressions of greeting: "*Kak dela?*", "How are things?" Fedorov most often uses *delo* to mean practical activity, or, action toward a realizable goal. A sign of the disintegration of contemporary life, he believes, is the separation of thought from *delo*, both in the individual and in society at large. In the individual, this separation manifests itself as idle dreaming, philosophizing, solving all problems on paper and doing nothing to realize these solutions. Goncharov's Oblomov, planning grand projects without getting out of bed, is the best literary illustration of what Fedorov means by thought without *delo*. In society at large, the separation is manifest in the division of men into intellectuals and workers. In the absence of a common task, an *obshchee delo*, both the individual and society at large are doomed. Only when intellectuals and workers, advanced thought and everyday activity, are unified in a common task will solutions to long-standing problems begin to appear.

Fedorov's longest essay, "Brotherhood" [8] is subtitled: "a note from the unlearned to the learned." This is the role that Fedorov chooses for himself throughout his writings. He speaks not as a learned man seeking to enlighten the unlearned, but rather as a representative of the unlearned, attempting to remind the learned of truths they have forgotten and to indicate to the learned the necessary task which they are capable of directing but which they have preferred to ignore.

By adopting this literary stance, Fedorov seeks not only to disarm his potential opposition by writing up to his reader instead of down to him, but also seeks to give voice to what he believes is the broad-based view of life commonly held by the Russian people, by those who have for centuries suffered at the hand of nature, but who have, to paraphrase Pushkin, "remained silent." [9]

Fedorov never uses the pronoun "I" in his works except to denigrate the concept of individualism. And the "we" he uses is not the lofty, editorial "we" but the "we" of the nameless collective, the mass of the unnoticed, the victims of nature and history.

But if he begins by stating the separation that obtains between the "we" and the "they", between the unlearned and the learned, his goal is to reunite the two, not only by enlightening the masses from above, but by enlightening the intellectuals from below. Past attempts to enlighten the masses from above have resulted only in the uprooting of the masses, in the false separation of all from the earth. Enlightenment of the intellectuals from below, on the other hand, can re-establish contact between the intellectuals and their origins, and can restore to human thought the roots in earth that the intellectuals have continually attempted to deny or sever.

As his writings indicate, and as Kozhevnikov confirms,[10] Fedorov did not study philosophy as an academic subject (in the Richelieu Lyceum he studied law) but turned to philosophy as a young man in an attempt to find meaning in what he had seen and experienced. His early influences were, as various commentators have noted, probably Herzen, Fourier, and Comte.[11] It was probably later, after his own ideas were formed, that he made a thorough study of the major eastern and western systems of thought. Much of his commentary on other philosophers is to be found in his essay: "*Supramoralism*, or the universal synthesis (i.e. universal unification). The synthesis of the two kinds of reason, and of the three objects of knowledge and action (God, man, and nature; man as an instrument of Divine reason and himself as the reason of the universe); the synthesis of science and art in religion." Supramoralism is what Fedorov calls his own philosophical system, and in the essay of this title other philosophical systems are not carefully analyzed, but are contrasted in their main points to Supramoralism. But from this essay, and from other passages scattered through his works, we can put together a general outline of Fedorov's idea of the history (i.e. gradual disintegration) of eastern and western philosophy.[12]

Before Greece, ancient India, Iran, and Israel were the world's centers of philosophy. In ancient Indian thought, Fedorov saw only an elaborate expression of an essentially passive attitude toward life. Death and evil are deeply ingrained in the world. The universe is pantheistic, man is insignificant, and, ideally, all, instead of joining a common task to struggle against evil and death, should submit to the turning of the great wheel of life and death against which it is futile to struggle. The goal is not the transformation of the world, but, rather, through submission, individual enlightenment and release from the world. (I, 117, 211, 271)

Where the ancient Indians were pantheists and pessimists, the ancient Hebrews were monotheists and optimists (in the sense that they believed that they had been chosen for a glorious future). But the ancient Hebrews relied on God, rather than on their own efforts, to overcome evil in the world. Therefore, according to Fedorov, the ancient Hebrews represent the principle of passive optimism, just as the ancient Indians represented the principle of passive pessimism. (I, 47, 103-104)

It is in the ancient Iranians that Fedorov finds the principle of optimistic activism, the attitude which, he believes, has been inherited by the Slavs.[13] The *Zend-Avesta*, in which all men are urged to join the "beautiful task" [*"frasho kerete"*] against the forces of death, offers an ancient precedent for "the common task." The ancient Iranians, to whom Fedorov believes the Slavs are related, were land-tillers, and, in their close relationship to the earth, recognized that life is won only by struggle. Evil, for the Zendo-Slavic peoples, is not an inescapable condition of existence, but can be overcome by concerted human effort. In modern times, Indian pantheism is represented by the Germans, Hebrew monotheistic passivism is represented by Islam, and Zendic active optimism is represented by the Slavs. The Zendo-Slavic principle is the "reconciling link" between the Indo-Germanic and Judeo-Islamic Semitic extremes. (I, 346-347; II, 48-49.)

But since the beginnings of Greek philosophy, Western thought has more often sought to define (and therefore, according to Fedorov, to perpetuate) the differences between good and evil, matter and spirit, heaven and earth, etc. than to overcome them. With Socrates, thought became separated from action and was viewed as superior to action. And once the separation of thought from action was established, the course of Western thought could only be one of greater and greater isolation of the part and disintegration of the whole.

In the inscription at the Delphic Oracle, "Know Thyself," which became the principle of Socratic knowledge, Fedorov sees the crucial first step toward the disintegration of knowledge. "Know Thyself" was mistakenly interpreted to mean "Know Only Thyself," that is, according to Fedorov: " '*Know thyself*' (consequently do not trust in the fathers, i.e. in tradition, do not believe in the witness of others, or of the brothers, know only thyself) says the demon (Delphic or Socratic). '*I know, therefore I exist*' replies the Cartesian; that is—as Fichte explains— '*The knowing I is an existing I; all else then is merely that which I know, i.e., that which is thought, consequently that which does not exist.'* And so: *'Love thyself with all thy soul, with all thine heart'* conclude Stirner and Nietzsche,—i.e. *find thyself within thyself, be alone and recognize nothing but thyself. . . ."* (I, 407)

But Fedorov finds the fullest reflection of the disintegration of the Western mind in the thought of Kant. "The philosophy of Kant is the *legalization, the sanctification of evil—of the disintegration* in which the world rests. In the absolute separation of the three ideas—or of the objects of reason—God, man, and nature—is also included the cause of evil; out of this division also proceeds the division into two kinds of reason." (I, 442) The separation of theoretical from practical reason, Fedorov believes, has provided false justification for the division of mankind into classes of thinkers and classes of toilers, a division which runs deeper than that between rich and poor.

Essentially, then, in Kant Fedorov finds the Western mind in an advanced state of disintegration. After Kant, Western philosophy proceeds toward self-destruction. Fedorov retitles Schopenhauer's *The World as Will and Representation:* "The World as Carnal Lust." Nietzsche's *Will to Power* is, to Fedorov, "The Will to Death and Destruction."

But where Western thinkers traditionally have attempted to separate thought from action, and have attempted to separate various functions of the intellect (reason, feeling, will, faith, etc.) and have usually attempted to assign to one of these functions priority over all others, Russian thinkers have traditionally attempted to emphasize wholeness, the unity of thought and action, the need to redintegrate the various faculties. But even Russian thinkers, Fedorov argues, have not succeeded in putting back together all that Western thinkers have, for centuries, indefatigably labored to take apart.

The Slavophiles, according to Fedorov, understood the need for unity, but did not consider the problem of *unity for and toward what end.* They valued the Russian idea of *sobornost'* ["community"] but looked for it only in the past instead of projecting it into the future. In general, Fedorov considers the Slavophiles to have been new Pharisees who stood for an imaginary brotherhood and an unreal kinship, and opposes them to the new Sadducees (Westernists) who stood for the elimination of brotherhood and the severing of close ties to the fatherland (*"defraternizatsiia"* and *"depatriatsiia"* II, 192). "The Slavophiles saw *sobornost'* both in the structure of the *mir* in Slavic lands (in the commune and the *artel*), and in the church community, (in the *sobor*). Of course, they viewed this structure not as something actual and complete, but only as the harbinger of a great, though utterly indefinite future. But the Slavophiles did not even consider or trouble themselves to think: in the first place, *for what*, or *for what task* such a united force was needed; what *duty* it was necessary to fulfil; what *goal* it was necessary to attain; in the second place, they did not consider *how*, or *by what means* it would be possible to achieve the most intimate unification of the whole and part; and in the third place, the Slavophiles did not raise the question, *in the name of what* or *according to what form or model* collective activity must arise. In a word, the Slavophiles' attitude toward the future was not active, but passive, and they talked vainly of love and truth-justice [*pravda*], all the while misusing these words, especially the latter." (II, 193)

In Solov'ev and Dostoevskii, who, Fedorov believes, have most clearly recognized the need for redintegration, he finds, as we have already seen, only an unrealistic, transcendent, mystical resolution of the problem. "Mysticism also proposes a uniting for the purpose of resurrection, but this unification is to be achieved mystically, i.e. by incomprehensible means, by unverifiable research, which can be presented only by adepts to each other. Resurrection itself in this instance is achieved not through knowledge of the natural or through the regulation of blind force, not by means of experiment, or by empirical knowledge, not by scientific illumination, but by secret, occult means, by some sorcery, such as, for instance, the materialization of spirits." (I, 439)

Through his friend, the philosophyer Kozhevnikov, Fedorov became interested in the philosophy of F. H. Jacobi (1743-1819). But Fedorov believed that one must go beyond

Jacobi's defense of faith and feeling to create a philosophy that would unite all forms of thought and action.

Supramoralism, the name that Fedorov gives to his new philosophy, postulates, as its epistemological base, that knowledge is neither subjective nor objective—but "projective" [*proektivnoe*]. The universe, not only of human interactions, but of physical and chemical interactions as well, is not an "object" whose existence is dependent on or independent of our existence as "subjects", but is a "project" which we shall either direct or fail to direct, but for which we must bear ultimate responsibility.

"Projectivism" is Fedorov's bridge between idealism and materialism. Where the pure idealist would hold that ideas exist independent of the material world, and where the pure materialist would hold that nothing is real or can be said to exist that is not, ultimately, matter, and where Kant would say that ideas do at least exist in our minds, Fedorov would argue, further, that ideas exist in our minds as projects to be realized in the material world. "That which Kant considered inaccessible to knowledge is precisely the object of action [*delo*]." (I, 16) Projectivism, then, is neither idealism nor materialism, but the task of realizing ideas in the material world. Projectivism is an epistemology for artists rather than for critics, for engineers rather than for theoretical scientists. The present universe, "the world as fact," or "the world as it is" [*mipb*] is what it is because we have so far failed to turn it into "the perfect world" or "the world as it ought to be" [*mupb*—literal meaning: "peace"]. (I, 447) By failing to realize that the world is our project, we have allowed nature to shape the universe. Our task is to assume control over everything that nature now controls, including the courses of celestial bodies, and the composition of matter. Until we make the universe our project, i.e. until we have reshaped matter to conform with our idea of the universe "as it should be", the universe will not be a "cosmos", that is, will not have meaning and order, but will remain a "chaos" of large and small particles of a disintegrating whole.

Kinship, brotherhood, immortality, paradise, universal order, and even God, are real neither as facts nor as ideas, but

THE COMMON TASK 91

as projects. For them to become real facts we must make them real. At present, we have some evidence that God, paradise, etc. exist, but for the evidence to be conclusive we must make God's world our project. When we have realized the project, there will be no more doubt, for we shall see God "face to face"[14] (II, 262)

Fedorov accepts the traditional Orthodox Christian picture of the world—but as a project rather than as either a worldly fact or an other-wordly idea. That God created the universe and it was good can be proved not by rational arguments but by human effort to turn the world we know into the world as we believe God intended it to be. On this point, it is clear that Fedorov does not imply that God created an imperfect world, but, rather, that God created the world so that it contained the project of its own perfection. If God created man in His own image, then He made man active and creative, not a passive spectator. By being active, i.e. by controling nature, man could have kept the world perfect, i.e. he could have stayed in paradise. But, abusing his freedom, man failed to hold nature in check, and instead of remaining nature's master allowed himself to become nature's slave. This would seem to be Fedorov's interpretation of the Fall.

As Golovanenko points out in his discussion of Fedorov's ontology,[15] life, not death, is the first principle in Fedorov's universe. Life is primordial and primary—death came after and is secondary. Man's principle is life, nature's is death. Man gave up life to nature and must win it back from nature. As Golovanenko formulates Fedorov's idea: "Life is good: a unity unfused and undivided [*edinstvo neslitnoe i nerazdel'noe*]. Life is kinship (*rodstvo*). Death is evil: a multiplicity mixed and divided [*mnozhestvo smeshannoe i razdel'noe*]. Death is discord [*rozn'*]. The victory of life over death lies in the annihilation of world discord and of cosmic dissociation, throughout the universe. (I, 79; II, 62, 407)[16]

The model for life, i.e. for unity that can neither be divided nor fused, is the Icon of the Holy Trinity, the perfect three in one. Our project is to remake the world in the image of the Holy Trinity. Men must model themselves after Christ, the Icon of perfect sonship, women after the Holy Spirit, the

disembodied

Icon of perfect daughterhood, and together, as sons and daughters, we must remake our fathers (the dead) into living images of the Eternal Father.". (I, 13, 33-36, 67-72)

Fedorov's "projectivism" may be considered a form of pragmatism.[18] But there are important differences between Fedorov's idea that a truth must be known by its results, and the ideas later advanced by James, Peirce, Dewey, and others. The American pragmatists, especially James, held to a pluralistic idea of truth. At least in religion, if not in science, what "worked" for one person might not "work" for another. Truth is not necessarily universal. Moreover, a given truth need not be eternal: truth based on our knowledge today need not remain true if our knowledge changes tomorrow. In American pragmatism, truth is constantly being made and remade. But built into Fedorov's projectivism is the idea that to be true a project must be universal, i.e. that it must be made true by all and for all. Moreover, while in Fedorov truth is not static and fixed at present but is constantly in the process of being realized (not made or remade, but realized), it is being realized absolutely and forever. Truth, for Fedorov, is temporarily relative and in flux, but is potentially absolute and eternal. The temporary, relative, fluxuating truths of our present world of facts are, potentially, absolutely and permanently untrue. Thus, permanent truth and untruth are immanent and exist in potential even in the present, mixed, changing world.

But here we come to a point that Fedorov leaves unclear: namely, whether the ideal world actually *exists* only in potential, or whether we from our perspective in the present can only *conceive* of its existence in potential. In other words, Fedorov does not clearly state his idea of time. In some places, he contrasts eternity to temporality, e.g.: "nature is our temporary enemy, but eternal friend" (I, 447). If there is such a thing as "eternity" (and Fedorov does claim that when the dead are resurrected they will live for eternity), then it cannot exist only in what we call "the future" but must exist even now and must have existed for all time. Thus our temporality ("past", "present", and "future") must be contained within "eternity". If we *shall live* in eternity, we must *already be living* in eternity, hence we must be living in not simply one, but in at least two dimensions of time. Fedorov seems to recognize this when he writes: "Our view is as follows: at the present time there exist God and the *world* [*мiръ*], and "the *world*" means the world in its present condition, i.e. the world in which we have not fulfilled our duty. When our duty is fulfilled, then the *world* will become the *perfect world* [*мupъ*]. When we say: '*God is not in nature, but God is with us*', we are acknowledging the sovereignty of reason over blind force, i.e. we are talking about the *perfect world*, and not about the *world*, where the opposite relationship prevails. The *world* is a fact, but the *perfect world* is our project." (I, 447) He seems here to be talking about two kinds of existence: absolute existence in eternity, and present existence in temporality. In absolute existence, in eternity, we exist with God, the world is perfect, and nature is our eternal friend. In temporal existence, we are not with God and He is not with us, we are subject to nature, and we die. Fedorov seems to recognize that we live simultaneously in two kinds, or dimensions, of time. He confuses the matter, however, by sometimes implying that "eternity" will exist only in "the future." What he must mean is that we shall realize eternal life in our future, i.e. that we shall someday be as fully aware of our eternal existence as we are now aware of our temporal existence. At present we have only fragmentary evidence of the existence of the perfect, eternal world: icons, liturgies, and other "child-guidance" materials that we may use to help us pass from immaturity to maturity, and from ignorance to knowledge.

But if the "perfect world" is to be our project, we must first begin the only task that can unite all people living on earth, namely, the task of restoring life to all our dead ancestors. And it is to this "task" that we must now direct our attention.

Resurrecting the Dead

The idea that we must resurrect the dead is clearly the central and most important idea in Fedorov's philosophy. As Dostoevskii indicated in his letter to Peterson,[19] the idea of resurrection must be made clear, otherwise the rest will remain incomprehensible.

The first question we must address however is: why is the resurrection of the dead necessary? Fedorov's answers, if not entirely persuasive, are at least clear. He writes: "So long as there is death, there will also be hunger and there will be disease; and conversely, so long as there are disease and hunger, there will also be death." (II, 271). Death, in Fedorov, is not a force of radical evil and is not an ineradicable condition. Death is a consequence of our passive relationship to nature. Death, in man, is a manifestation of the blind force of nature that disintegrates whole entities throughout the universe. Death is the disintegration of the body and the person by blind natural force. In our present passivity, we allow nature to kill us. But, created in God's image, we are intended to take an active rather than a passive role in relation to nature. We are blind nature's eyes: her will, her feeling, her rationality. We are nature's consciousness. Since nature has neither will nor feeling or consiousness, we must be more than natural creatures. But we have hardly even begun to exercise those qualities which make us more than natural. Since death is in nature, and since man is more than a creature of nature, man should, by extending and developing the qualities that set him apart from and over nature, be able (at least theoretically) to exercise control over nature, and, hence, over death.

But it would be selfish and immoral of us to control death, i.e. to obtain immortality, only for ourselves. We should live neither for ourselves alone (egoism) nor for others alone (altruism), but for all and with all (kinship.) (II, 201) And "all" includes not only the living.

The mistake previously made by all who have called for the unity of mankind is that they have considered only the living. But we cannot all be brothers and sisters unless we are, first of all, sons and daughters, a point so obvious that it might seem trivial were it not so often overlooked. If we do not add to the idea of brotherhood the idea of sonship, then brotherhood will inevitably turn into a conflict between generations, i.e. the "brothers" of one generation will band together, setting themselves apart from and against the "fathers" of earlier generations, and will eventually be banded against by a future generation of "brothers", etc. In history, e.g. the French Revolution, the call to brotherhood is inevitably accompanied by a call to regicide or some other form of parricide. So any call to brotherhood alone must lead eventually to further discord and division. Only the idea of sonship-daughterhood will lead to the unity of all. As small children, we think only of what we can get from our parents, but as we mature we must begin to think of what we can give back to them. In history as fact, the human race is still at a stage of immaturity, but in history as project we must assume the responsibilities and tasks of mature sons and daughters. Hence we must look for a way to return to our parents the life we took from them. Not to do so is to prolong our immaturity. To create immortality for ourselves, and to withold it from our parents and ancestors, would be to consign ourselves to eternal adolescence.

All of this is based on two assumptions, which Fedorov seems to accept as given, but which in fact are open to question: that death is undesirable, and that the unity of all, indivisible and at the same time infusible, is to be desired. We shall return to these questions in due course, but for now let us follow Fedorov's idea further.

Taras Zakydalsky has attempted to demonstrate that Fedorov's theory of the natural world is best understood as a form of reductive materialism.[20] He cites Fedorov's clear statement of preference for the position of the materialists to that of Western Christians. Fedorov writes:

> The most extreme materialists-naturalists can take precedence over the disciples of Papism and Protestantism in the Kingdom of God. In rejecting immortality, i.e., in arguing that thought is the product of matter, of dust, they do not realize that as soon as this were proved, i.e., as soon as we were able to bring this dust to a condition in which it would produce thought, we would be immortal. Furthermore, in arguing that the world is a blind mechanism and that man is the only rational being, that the world was not created by any

gods and is not something miraculous but something very simple, a mechanism which could have come into being without the intervention of God's supernatural, mysterious power, do they not imply that this mechanism can be controlled by reason? Finally, in rejecting purposiveness do they not suggest this absence of purpose contains a higher plan, to make man the agent that introduces purposiveness? They can of course stop short of accepting the natural consequences of their premises...." (I, 206, Zakydalsky's translation.)

Zakydalsky is careful to point out that in this passage Fedorov is not adopting the position of the materialists as his own, but is simply indicating that the initial assumptions of the materialists offer a good starting point for the common task. Moreover, Zakydalsky points to many passages in which Fedorov objects to the views of materialists. But, citing, in addition to the passage quoted above, many other statements by Fedorov that can be intereprated as being of a generally materialist tendency, Zakydalsky concludes that the system implicit in Fedorov's thought is best understood as a materialist system. Fedorov's project essentially involves only man and nature. Both man and nature are composed of atoms, and since the only causes at work in the universe are efficient and not final causes, the system is basically mechanistic, and man is ultimately a physical mechanism like any other body in the system, unique only in that his organism is more complex than others. God is present in Fedorov's system, but is not necessary to it. Had Fedorov altogether omitted the idea of God, his system would have lost nothing and would have gained in clarity, consistency, and efficiency. Zakydalsky is not, of course, attacking here the idea of God itself, but is simply arguing that Fedorov's idea of God is presented so vaguely and inconsistently, and seems so much at variance with the rest of his thought that Fedorov either should have clarified God's role or not tried to incorporate God into his system.

Zakydalsky makes I think as good a case as can be made for Fedorov as a materialist, and neither ignores nor oversimplifies possible counterarguments in arguing that Fedorov's system would be more consistent without the idea of God. But the problem is that while one can cite chapter and verse to demonstrate that Fedorov was a materialist, one can also cite chapter and verse to indicate that he was an idealist, or, perhaps better, a "psychist." His basic idea, after all, is that *reason* must control matter. Here is one of his clearest statements on the relationship between the spiritual and the material:

> Just as the cooperative activity of a unified human race extends beyond the limits of the laboratory and factory, and is not confined to cultivated fields, but embraces meteorological processes as well, so also the unification for such activity is not a juridical and not an economic task, but a *psychological* and a *moral* one; it is a question of creating a society in which there is no need for surveillance or penalties or punishment or compulsion, or, to be more precise, it is a question of the transition of society from compulsory activity to activity that is voluntary and cooperative, and worldwide as well. When such activity is begun, the rational force will control the material. Even if the ideas have been created or given birth by a carnal human being, they will all the same not have arisen in order that flesh might control thought, but in order that thought and spirit might control matter. Thus, even proceeding from the materialist understanding of life and the world, one must, from the marxist materiocracy, arrive at a psychocracy. Here one will find a materialism without swinishness [*svinizm*] and a psychism without mysticism. (II, 272)

One could interpret this and any number of other passages to mean that in the project all that is now matter must become spirit. Indeed, the word he uses when he speaks of populating other planets is *odushevlenie* ["*animation*"]—matter will be provided with a soul. (II, 205).

But it is wrong, I think, to try to classify Fedorov's project of resurrection as either materialist or idealist (or spiritualist or "psychist.") He stands for neither one *ism* nor the other, but attempts to offer a new synthesis of the material and the spiritual. His "psychocracy", as he explains, "is not a kingdom of bodiless, fleshless spirits, but an instilling of spirit [*vlozhenie dushi*] into all material functions." (I, 303) All that now lacks soul or spirit will be inspirited. Similarly, ideas, projects, and dreams that now exist unembodied will be realized in material form: "the wings of the soul will become bodily wings." (I, 318) "The illusion of poets, which has personified or patrified [celestial] worlds will have become the truth. But that personification or—more precisely—patrification will be done no longer by thought, no longer by imagination, but in fact, by action." (II, 205) And in describing the man who will have mastered his own nature, who will no longer be driven to cause new births but will direct himself by his own will to restore life to those from whom he received it, Fedorov writes: "Such a creature, being *material*, will in no way be distinguished from a spirit [*dukh*]." (I, 315)

So clearly, then, Fedorov is talking about the unification of matter and spirit. We cannot say that in Fedorov's thought spirit is subsumed under matter or that matter is subsumed under spirit. He believes in both matter and spirit, and insists that if they exist separately now they must be unified in the project. And like his other unities, the unity of matter and spirit will admit of neither division nor fusion.

Now this raises a problem. If Fedorov were a mystic, like Solov'ev, we could call the unification of matter and spirit a mystic union to be accomplished by means unknowable to man. But Fedorov insists that he is not a mystic, and that this union, like all others, must be achieved by human knowledge and effort. So how is this to be achieved? Moreover, if Fedorov were a dualist, we could classify his matter-spirit problem as a dichotomy traditional to dualistic thought and leave it at that. But Fedorov was attempting to overcome Cartesian (and all other) dualism. Dualism, after all, in Fedorov, is a sign of intellectual discord [*rozn'*] and, as such, manifests the principle of death. Only monistic thought can point the way toward life. So, if matter and spirit are not to be separate, but at the same time are not to be fused, or one swallowed by the other, how is this unity to be understood?

It is here, I think, that we must consider whether the idea of God is actually inessential to Fedorov's project. Without the idea of a God who exists now and eternally, we are left in Fedorov with only man, nature, the world "as it is", and the project of a perfect world. And without God and eternity, the project of the perfect world exists only in temporality and only in our minds. But Fedorov constantly refers to God not only as an idea, but as a real being, as the God of the Fathers, and as the Creator. Moreover, he says that by fulfilling the task we shall fulfil God's will. He begins his prayer for universal salvation: "Our Father! God of the fathers, not dead, but living! Enable us to become instruments of Thine holy will" (II, 12). Note that he does not say "Who art in heaven", but that he does explicitly say that the fathers, who are dead to us and dead to our world, are not dead but living.

If the fathers are alive, but are not alive in our world, where are they alive? Fedorov does not try to say. But he has faith, even if he has no scientific verification, that somehow and somewhere they are even now alive. But for Fedorov, faith is a way of knowing, and, as a way of knowing is more advanced than present science. Only in their passive states are faith and science at odds, When faith and science both become fully active, rather than passive, ways of knowing, the differences between the two will disappear, and science will discover the truth that faith has already told us. Faith alone is not enough, just as science alone is not enough. Faith tells us of the existence of God and of the life of the dead fathers, i.e. faith tells us what we cannot yet see with our body's eyes and touch with our body's hands in this world. Faith in the Trinity tells us what unity will be when we have developed to our full human potential and when we have completed the project. Faith tells us that God is with us and not with nature. Our task is to make the passive knowledge that we have through faith active. That is, we must not merely believe, but must act to realize our beliefs. And as action in this world based on knowledge of things not of this world, faith cannot help but draw closer to science. Just as science, which is now knowledge of only this world, cannot help drawing closer to faith as it becomes action, for to become action science must have a goal, and the goal cannot be from within the world as it is but must come from some notion of the world as it ought to be, i.e. from that which is now the special province of faith.

It is clear, then, that Fedorov fully accepted not just one, but at least two kinds of truth and two ways of knowing. Moreover, he did not confuse the two: he did not try to advance scientific proofs for the existence of God, nor did he try to claim that scientific discoveries can only be taken on faith. He had too great a respect for both science and faith to confuse the two before they were ready to be united. Since in eternity, with God, truth is one, he knew that the separation could only be temporary, but living in the temporal world, he did not try to claim that the two are one here and now.

It is also clear that Fedorov not only accepted the legitimacy of faith as a way of knowing in the present world, but also accepted the real and true existence of the objects of traditional Orthodox Christian faith. God and eternity both exist, and not only in our minds. But how or where they exist, Fedorov, not a mystic, did not attempt to say. He accepts the existence of transcendent reality on faith, but he does not attempt to offer a mystical claim that somehow transcendent reality and everyday reality are already one and the same. Fedorov's thought develops out of, but does not depart from, traditional Christian belief. He does not reject belief in transcendent reality, (as we shall see he does not even altogether reject a transcendent resurrection), but simply insists that what we now consider transcendent reality can and must be a project for our world. This is not to reduce transcendent reality to mundane reality, but, rather, to elevate, gradually and by human effort, our mundane reality to the reality that we can now only call transcendent.

As science, working with faith, matures, develops, and advances, we will not need to be mystics to know more and more about God and eternity. For at the end of the project, we shall see God "face to face." By this, Fedorov must mean that we will have grown to God's level, that just as a crawling child cannot look straight out and see his standing father's face, so we are not yet on a level to see God's face. And when we do reach that level, we may have an entirely different idea of what a "face" (or "person"—the word Fedorov uses is *litso*) is than we now have.

It is essential to any understanding of Fedorov to realize that he considered us, as human beings, to be still in the early stages of our eventual development. We accept ideas now that may seem ridiculous later, and we may well later accept ideas that seem ridiculous now. We have not yet begun to learn what reason can accomplish, and our initial, mostly ineffective or even disastrous attempts at the regulation of nature are like the first wobbly steps of a child who must for the moment assume that no one is watching or helping him walk.

Fedorov believed both that the task of the perfection of ourselves and the world was ours, and that God is essential to the task. For Fedorov accepts Divine Creation. Fedorov does not dismiss or disregard scientific claims of a natural origin, but merely points out that even by proceeding from materialist premises one still arrives at the idea of a purpose to be fulfilled by men. Fedorov's faith is that no matter where we start, from scientific or religious bases, we will eventually reach the same conclusions, and that then we will have full proof of what we now assume by faith, in this case, of Divine Creation. What else God has done in eternity, we do not know. We know Him only as the Creater of our world, our Father, and the God of our fathers. God, Fedorov believes, created us with the responsibility and the capability to regulate nature. So the Creation was perfect: not static, but dynamic, consisting of that which was to regulate (man) and that which was to be regulated (nature.) We are responsible for the present state of the world, and our failure to carry out our our task, i.e. to fulfil God's will, has resulted in all the miseries we now know. Our task, then, assigned by God, and defined as the fulfilment of His will (to which our wills must conform) is rooted and concluded in eternity, i.e. in transcendent reality. Our task is finite, but issues from and concludes itself in the infinite. Without the real existence of God and eternity, we have only ideas of the infinite within the finite. But with a real God and a real eternity, i.e. with the reality of the infinite, the idea of the infinite within our finite world is "realizable". It would be logically impossible to "realize" the idea of infinity within a finite world. Hence, without an already real and existing God, and an already real and existing eternity outside the framework of our finite, material world, the resurrection of the dead to eternal life and the perfection of the world (including "eternal" friendship with nature) would be logically impossible, and could be understood only mystically, i.e. as a mystical union of the finite and the infinite, God and man, paradise and the world, etc. Thus, to interpret Fedorov's thought as a form of materialism is inadequate. The contradictions and inconsistencies that inevitably arise in Fedorov's project if it is considered to be a project in which the existence of God is irrelevant and inessential, and if it is considered to be a project for science alone, a project both acting upon and grounded within the material world alone, can only be resolved, I think, when we realize that Fedorov was both an idealist and a materialist, and when we realize that his project is set both within and beyond the existing world.

Fedorov writes: "All matter is the dust of ancestors. . . ." (I, 329.) I think that this statement must be interpreted in both the materialist sense, that the particles of our disintegrated ancestors have dispersed throughout the material universe and have entered into the composition of all substances, but also in the spiritual sense, that in every piece of matter in the universe there is a trace of something that was alive and that can be made to live again. Fedorov does not abandon religion for science, but attempts to show that what is held to be true by religion can be discovered to be true also by science. The task is both a holy one and a scientific one. As a holy, sacred task, it has been set and will be concluded in eternity. As a scientific task, it is set in and for our world. Faith, knowledge of the sacred, must point the way, i.e. must tell us that the dust of our ancestors is waiting to be discovered in matter; but science must accomplish the discoveries and must work to realize the objects of faith in the material world.

Just as Fedorov accepts the existence of God the Father-Creator on faith, so he also accepts both the divinity and humanity of Christ, the Son of God and Man. Our actions as sons of our fathers will be the proof of our faith in Christ as Son of God and Man. By intellect alone, we may never acknowledge the reality of Christ. But by participating in the task of resurrecting, we will become in fact followers of Christ, and, sooner or later, our intellects will catch up with our actions.

Christ is Fedorov's icon of the complete resurrection. He is both the one who resurrects and the one who is eternally resurrected. Christ's act of resurrecting Lazarus, and His own Resurrection were miracles, divine acts to show us what can be done. Because the Jews then were and we now remain immature and undeveloped creatures, miracles were the only way Christ had to convince men of the possibility of resurrection. (II, 271) But we are not divinities, and we cannot resurrect the dead by miracles. Christ showed us what was to be done, but not how. He began the universal resurrection which it is our task to complete. (I, 66) He is the icon or model of the complete resurrection which we must make real in and for our world.

By gradually developing our own power over nature, through science and art and directed by faith, we shall eventually be able to accomplish for ourselves and for all men what Christ, through miracle, once accomplished for his beloved friend Lazarus. When our powers of love are as highly developed as Christ's love, we too shall be able to resurrect our loved ones.

The resurrection of all did not immediately follow Christ's Resurrection because Christianity wrongly viewed itself as a religion of commemoration alone, and not as an active task of resurrecting. Correctly understood, the "Good News" of the Resurrection is our summons to the task of resurrecting all our ancestors. (I, 139) In history as fact, Christianity has not assumed its proper role in the world. Properly understood, as a project, "Christianity is the unification of the living for the resurrecting of the dead" (I, 133).

As theology, the project of resurrection shifts the emphasis from the Western, Catholic and Protestant idea of Christ as Atonement, to the Eastern, Orthodox idea of Christ as Resurrection. And, within Orthodoxy, Fedorov's project would require a shift from passive commemoration of the Resurrection to active participation in the process of resurrecting. The

Eucharist, instead of being a holy mystery, an invisible transubstantiation of bread and wine into Christ's body and blood, would become a factual, literal rearrangement of bread, i.e. of matter that we now prepare and ingest for our own nourishment, into the living bodies of our ancestors.

It should now be clear that in Fedorov no theological question can be considered a question for theology alone. Inevitably, in the project, theological problems will also be scientific problems, and sacred acts will of necessity be also scientific and technological acts. The question of the Eucharist, or of how bread and wine can he turned into flesh and blood, receives its fullest answer in an article that Fedorov called "The Question of Sanitation" [*Sanitarnii vopros*] (I, 276-289; II, 316-318). The problem essentially is that since all matter, including what we eat to stay alive, is dust of our ancestors, we literally and figuratively feed ourselves by swallowing our fathers. Both morally and as a matter of fact we cannot continue to do this if we accept the task of resurrection. Instead of taking life from them, we must return life to them. But the decomposition of organic matter is essential for germination and the growth of crops. On the other hand, it is the decomposition of matter that causes the worst epidemics and plagues. So, to protect ourselves from disease, and to restore life to the fathers, we shall eventually have to resynthesize our own bodies so that they no longer require nourishment from organic matter, i.e. so that they no longer require the dust of our ancestors. The knowledge that will be required to resynthesize our bodies will probably turn out to be the same knowledge that will be required to restore life to the fathers, i.e. a biology that has not only attained a full understanding of life but that has also attained full control over it. Moreover, to collect every last particle of every last ancestor, we shall have to send expeditions beyond earth to the most remote ends of the universe, for even there, according to the Copernican principle of unity, matter is the same as matter here, namely, ancestral dust. The problem raised by Malthus of overpopulation of earth, even by the living, can be solved by synthesizing the bodies of resurrectees so that they will find it possible to live under conditions that could not support life as we now know it on earth. The peasant saying, "it is not earth the feeds us, but heaven", (I, 280) will become literally true. In the short term, we shall insure adequate harvests by regulating the weather, and in the long run we shall no longer need organic nourishment.

In another place, Fedorov describes how gradual a process the universal resurrection will be:

> The difficulty for each generation of restoring the generation that immediately preceded it will be absolutely equal; for the attitude of the present generation toward its fathers, and of that generation which will first acquire the art of restoration toward its fathers is exactly the same as the attitude of our great grandfathers toward their fathers. Although the first resurrectee will be, in all likelihood, resurrected almost immediately after death, hardly even having died, and after him will follow those in whom very little decomposition is evident, nevertheless each new experience in this task will make subsequent steps easier. With each new person resurrected knowledge will be growing; it will reach the height of the task just when the human race arrives at the first person who died. Moroever, for our great-great-greatgrandfathers resurrection should be even easier, incomparably easier, i.e. for our great-great-greatgrandchildren it will be incomparably more difficult to resurrect their fathers than for us and for our great-great-greatgrandfathers; for in the resurrection of our fathers we shall make use not only of all previous experiences in the task, but shall even have the collaboration of our resurrectors; in this way it will be easiest of all for the first son of man to resurrect his father, the father of all people. (I, 330)

It is, then, through resurrection that we shall obtain "knowledge of all." For now we do not really know the past. We guess at it and generalize about it. But through people, resurrected, we shall know the entire past, and since we shall have attained immortality for ourselves and for all, we shall know both the entire past and the entire future. This is what Fedorov means, then, by his often repeated formula that knowledge must be "of all, by all, and for all." By these words he does not simply mean widespread literacy or general education, but personal knowledge of all time and of all space. When we know all that is to be known of man and of the physical universe, then we will be ready to know God, our Father. The day when our kinship is established as a fact, the day when every person who has lived on earth sees the resurrected first father, Adam, is the day on which we will, for the first time, no longer be orphans. Fedorov writes:

> The awaited day, the day longed for through the ages, the jubilation of the immense heavens, will arrive only when the earth, having swallowed generations in darkness, moved and directed by heavenly filial love and knowledge, will begin to return those swallowed by her and with them begin to populate the heavenly, starry worlds that are now without souls and that are now coldly and as if with sadness gazing down at us;— when, gathering and giving life to the dust of those who gave—or more truly—gave up life to us, we will no longer be turning that dust into nourishment for ourselves and our descendents, which we have been forced to do because of the isolation of worlds and the necessity to live by the means that can be accumulated on our small planet. By their knowledge of matter and of the powers of restoring it, succeeding generations will already have found it possible to create their own bodies from the basic elements, and will populate the worlds and eliminate their tendencies toward discord. Then indeed the sun will begin to palpitate, as even now simple people believe they see ti do on the Easter morning of Holy Sunday; then indeed even the multitudinous choirs of stars will begin to rejoice. The illusion of poets, which has personified or "patrified" these worlds, will have become the truth. But personification, or, more precisely, patrification will be done no longer by thought, no longer by imagination, but in fact,

by action (*delo*). Premature pacification, alive in folk poetry and other poetry, clearly testifies that the awaited day is the hope of all ages and peoples, awaited from time immemorial. That day, *the one which the Lord shall accomplish through us*, will be brought about not by the the apparent movement of the sun, and not by the actual movement of the earth, but by the joint activity of sons who have loved the God of the fathers and who have been filled with great compassion for all those departed. The earth will be the first star in heaven to be moved not by the blind force of gravity, but by reason, which will have turned against and prevented gravity and death. Nothing will be remote when in the integrated totality of worlds we shall see the integrated totality of all past generations. (*Note*. The universal meeting. This, then, is the great future which awaits the past, if the present will comprehend its function, its task, its goal. N.F.F.) *All will be kindred, nothing alien;* nevertheless, for all an immense breadth, depth, and height will be opened, but this will not be overhelming, or terrifying, but will have the capacity to satisfy the boundless desire, life without limits, which so frightens the present, emaciated, sickly, Buddhist-tending generation. This will be life ever new, regardless of its antiquity, spring without fall, morning without evening, youth without old age, resurrection without death. However at that time there will also be not only autumn and evening, there will also be dark night, as the hell of sufferings remains, in the present and past life of the human race, but it will remain only as a representation, like grief that has been lived through, and will raise higher the value of the bright day of resurrection. This day will be divine, awesome, but not miraculous, for *resurrection will be a task not of miracle but of knowledge and common labor*.

The awaited day, the day longed for through the ages, *will be God's command and man's fulfilment*. ("The end of orphanhood; limitless kinship", translated in full, II, 205-206)

This is as close to a full description of the resurrection as Fedorov gives in any single passage of his writings. Just as immortality and perfection (paradise) exist not as facts but only as representations or projects in our miserable present, so in our glorious future mortality and imperfection (hell) will no longer exist as facts but only as representations or memories. Nevertheless, between here and "spring without fall, morning without evening, youth without old age" etc. lie many obstacles, some of which Fedorov considers, but many of which he does not.

One problem first raised by Solov'ev, and later echoed by Losskii and others, is how we can be certain that we will not resurrect death. Solov'ev's example is the cannibal—what do we do when it is time to resurrect the cannibals? Or mass murderers? Or suicides?

Fedorov wrote in the margin of Solov'ev's letter that the idea of resurrecting death was "an absurdity",[21] but he does not give a direct answer to the question. Nevertheless, if we cannot quote a direct answer from Fedorov, we can from all his writings put together an answer that would be consistent with his ideas.

Man is not, in Fedorov, radically evil. Even a murderer is not fundamentally evil, but is simply not in control of his nature. Presumably by the time the resurrection begins, all living people will be in a state of "psychocracy", i.e. in a state of universal inner consensus in which all will participate in the task freely and without external compulsion. People will be far advanced, psychologically, over us as we are now. Resurrected into such an environment, a murderer could not help but be affected. All cause for crime (hunger, disease, sexual passion, greed, etc.) would have been eliminated. With nature completely under control, crime would be unthinkable. Health, both physical and mental, would be assured. In Fedorov's view, mental and physical defects are not part of a person's essential makeup, but are disfigurements caused by nature. In reassembling the dust particles of our ancestors into whole persons, we shall not be eliminating anything essential to the whole person if we leave out the defects which did not really belong to a person in life but which were, so to speak, foisted upon that person by nature. People who were weak in life will be made strong in the resurrection. They will not be changed essentially from what they were, but will be "fully themselves"—which they were not strong enough or active enough or sufficiently developed to be while subject to nature.

Berdiaev's chief criticism of Fedorov is that he did not have an adequate understanding of the power of evil. It is true that Fedorov understands evil chiefly as weakness. By being passive toward nature, we allow nature to drive us to actions that we would not take if we were wholly guided by love and reason. In Fedorov's system there is no transcendent force of evil, no malicious divinity, and no active force of evil with a potential strength greater than man's. Even nature is not inherently evil, for, when controlled, nature will be our "eternal friend." On this point Berdiaev is right to criticize Fedorov. As Losskii points out, Fedorov does not consider the possibility that "the body composed of impenetrable particles (atoms)—i.e. of particles performing the processes of repulsion in relation to the environment—is of necessity bound up with the struggle for existence and, therefore, with evil." [22] If evil is inseparable from bodily existence, i.e. from our "atoms", then any attempt to rearrange these atoms into new bodies will necessarily perpetuate evil. Moreover, Fedorov does not consider the possibility that a will for evil may be as basic in man as a will for good, or that good and evil might be inextricably tangled, and that to eliminate man's capacity for evil might also be to eliminate his capacity for good. Fedorov does not consider that spite, malice, and outright perversity (as in Dostoevskii's Underground Man) might be something more than lack of control or a remediable defect cause by a failure to resist the onslaught of nature. And that there may be good, as well as evil, in irrationality and in the unconscious seems not to have crossed Fedorov's mind.

Another theoretical problem which Fedorov does not address directly has to do with the difficulty of establishing the ownership of individual particles. Our bodies, like all matter, in Fedorov's view, are composed of the dust of ancestors. In the resurrection, what happens to those particles that have belonged to more than one person? If, for instance, a given particle belonged at one time to the monk Nestor and at another time to the poet Pushkin, who will get it?

The underlying problem here is that Fedorov made no attempt to suggest criteria of personal identity. Just what makes a person that person? This is one of the more difficult theoretical questions that must be solved before Fedorov's project can be considered even theoretically feasible, and is a problem to which one Fedorov specialist has devoted considerable attention.[23] Another problem which Fedorov did not consider, but which might become important if the project were undertaken, has to do with the limits of the task. At some points, Fedorov entertains the thesis of evolution. He implies that whether man was created as man by God or evolved from lower animals, the task of resurrection will be the same. But this is not necessarily so. If man was created as man, then the backward limit is clear: after the resurrection of Adam, the task would be complete. But if man evolved from, say, the apes, how can a clear line be drawn between the first man and the last ape? Would not the apes also be our "ancestors"? Where is the line? The definition of man that Fedorov is fondest of is: "Man is the creature who buries his dead." (II, 33, and elsewhere). But as Boranetskii has pointed out, ants, and possibly other creatures also bury their dead.[24] The idea of sons resurrecting fathers and of those fathers resurrecting their fathers loses some of its grandeur when we begin to consider the resurrection of apes and ants. What is clear here is that Fedorov thought his idea through to a certain point, but did not think it through to the end.

Another point, again purely theoretical, which Fedorov perhaps should have but did not consider, is: after the dust of ancestors is extracted from all matter, what will remain of the universe? If all matter is the dust of ancestors, and if all the dust of ancestors will be reassembled into living ancestors with physical bodies, what will be left?

> All matter is the dust of ancestors, and in those infinitesimal particles, which might be accessible to microscopic animals invisible to our eyes, and even then only if these animals were armed with such powerful micro-

scopes that their field of vision would be increased as much as ours is by our microscopes, and there, in the square and cube of those microscopic particles, we can find the traces of our ancestors. (I, 329)

This may be a beautiful idea, an imaginative prose-poem that contains a certain moral truth, i.e. that all the universe is somehow organically related—but if we are to take it as anything other than that we immediately run into serious problems. First, assuming that we could extract these traces, what what happen to the rest of the particle? Trying to imagine this is like trying to imagine what would happen if all the protons were extracted from every atom. Fedorov has directed us here up a blind alley. All matter, including the bodies of the resurrectors, contains the dust of ancestors; if that dust is not removed the ancestors cannot be resurrected; but if it is removed, then what happens to the resurrectors and to the rest of the matter in the universe? The only way out is to say, as Fedorov sometimes does, that anything considered from a purely theoretical standpoint is bound to end in apparent contradictions and absurdities, for theory alone can never solve a problem. In practice, the confusion raised by theoretical consideration alone should, if the task is a true one, disappear.

But even putting all theoretical questions aside, and even ignoring many of the apparent logical contradictions that arise when Fedorov's project is given serious consideration, we still must encounter at least one very basic problem that, for me at least, makes Fedorov's project impossible to accept. This problem is that neither Fedorov, nor presumably anyone living, actually knows what death is. It may be utterly undesirable, as Fedorov assumes, and it may even be eliminable, as he argues. But we do not know even what death is, or what happens to a person when he dies, much less whether what happens is or is not bad for him and for the world. Our beliefs about death are matters of faith, and while faith tells Fedorov that death is bad and must be eliminated, faith tells others (e.g. the Buddhists and most Christian mystics) that death is not to be lamented or feared. If the claims of Buddhists and mystics are false and we accept them then we are deluded, but others need not join us or suffer the consequences of our error. But Fedorov, who does not know what death is, would nevertheless have us rearrange ourselves and the entire universe on the slender hope that we might defeat what we do not know. The price that we might pay for tinkering with the organic structure of the universe might well be higher than the value of possibly eliminating something which may or may not be to our benefit to eliminate. Thus, Fedorov's ideas about resurrection are fascinating, and valuable as visionary literature on a mytho-poetic plane, but the likelihood that he is wrong about a few very important things makes his work unacceptable as a program for universal action.

Solov'ev's ideas on the resurrection are, in the end, better grounded than Fedorov's. By holding that resurrection is a spiritual, rather than a sacred-scientific task, Solov'ev assumes that we must work on our souls much more before we will be ready to work on the organic structure of the universe. Fedorov's project, though more comprehensive and ambitious than Solov'ev's, seems, ironically, much less practical and realizable than the great mystic's project which calls upon all men to make their souls immortal and then to allow the immortal souls to create appropriate new bodies for themselves. Theoretically, at least, man's potential for spiritual development is unlimited, for spiritual development leads ultimately toward a merging with God and union of the finite with the infinite. Within Solov'ev's framework, resurrection is possible. But within Fedorov's framework, in which the resurrection must first and foremost be physical and must be within the limits of the material universe, many modifications, alterations, and extensions must be made before the resurrection is even theoretically possible.

That Fedorov himself had some doubts about the feasibility of his project is indicated by his insistence that even if we do not resurrect ourselves, then God will, in His own time and way, resurrect us. But this resurrection, which Fedorov calls a "resurrection of anger" (I, 418, 471, II, 294) will result in the eternal separation of the wicked from the righteous. Upon this resurrection, the wicked will be condemned to eternal agony which the righteous will be eternally condemned to witness. It is to prevent eternal separation and eternal torment, then, that Fedorov proposes his project of the common task. Although Fedorov leaves many details of the resurrection project unclear, and although he does not consider a number of problems that would have to be considered if the project were to be undertaken, he does clearly indicate that the task must be gradual, that it must be universal, and that almost any activity people are now engaged in could serve as a starting point. What is also clear is that the project of resurrection is not a project for science, or politics, or philosophy, or religion alone. All forms of knowledge and action must be redintegrated into one task. The activities that must be brought into this one task are as many as the activities now engaged in by men. But among those to which Fedorov devotes most attention, and to which we shall now turn, are: the regulation of nature, the integration of thought and knowledge, the role of the autocrat, and the Christian task of becoming sons of man.

Regulating Nature

"Nature is our temporary enemy, but our eternal friend." (II, 247) Nature, in Fedorov, is not essentially evil, but is blind. Left unregulated, the blind force of nature drives the universe toward disintegration, drives men and women to abandon their parents in order to turn themselves from children into parents, and divides even the individual against himself. In nature "as it is", Fedorov does not see a balanced organic wholeness, or a grand unity of perfectly inter-related parts, or a total ecological system whose equilibrium is too magnificent to improve upon and too delicate to tamper with. Man's place, in Fedorov, is not within but over nature. Man's duty is to check the destructive force of nature, and to govern with consciousness and love a universe that is now dominated by blind force. The icon for the perfect universe is the Holy Trinity: wholeness, unfusible, yet indivisible. Man's sacred-scientific task is to reshape the entire, disintegrating universe into an icon of the Holy Trinity.

Like the task of resurrecting the dead, with which it is interdependent, the task of regulating nature is to be long, gradual, and, ultimately, universal. The idea of turning the universe into an icon of the Trinity is now imaginable only as a distant goal. But it is the goal which must constantly be kept in mind and toward which all regulative activities must be directed. Without such a goal, attempts to regulate nature would remain uncoordinated, would lead toward conflicting ends, and would only further contribute to the forces of disintegration now operative throughout the universe. But if the task of regulation must have only one goal, it may have any number of starting points. One of Fedorov's favorite examples for how the task might begin has to do with the aiming of cannons.

In the early 1890's, which happened to be years of terrible drought and famine in Russia, Russian newspapers were full of articles about the discovery by American scientists that cannons fired into the air could sometimes bring rain. For Fedorov, this discovery served as a model for the radical shift in direction needed to transform all death-bearing force into life-bearing force. At present, men turn their weapons against each other while nature is allowed to send drought and storm to the misery of all. By redirecting all our weapons, and our general orientation, from a horizontal aim to a vertical one, we may turn all our blind, instinctive death-bound activities toward the conscious task of restoring life to all. Present weapons need not be discarded, but must be redirected. These first, clumsy attempts to bring rain to dry regions by firing cannons into the air would eventually be developed into a more sophisticated science of climate regulation. Meteorology would gradually change from a passive science of observation and prediction to an active science of regulation. In a similar manner, biology would become a science of the restoration, rather than merely the observation of life; linguistics would gradually turn from the study of existing languages to the task of restoring and permitting all men to reacquire the original language of Adam. As sciences changed from passive to active, they would gradually merge together into one science whose scope of activity would be universal. An intermediate step toward this merging would be the incorporation of all present sciences into an active version of astronomy. (II, 251-253)

Implicit in most of Fedorov's writings on the task of regulation, and explicit in his article, "Falling worlds and the being that counteracts the fall" (II, 253-279) is the idea that we can and must find a way to counteract the force of gravity throughout the universe. He writes: "Under 'falling stars' we mean to include all worlds, from cosmic dust particles and bolides to the largest planets and suns, which seem unmoving, but in actuality are also falling, differing only in the time and manner of their fall. Nature is an aggregate of falling stars (or worlds), whose slow falling is taken for stability. The falling of the world is thus taken for the state of the world, world destruction for world order! But falling is connected with death and dying; falling is an expression of the difference between an income and expenditure of force, a deficit. . . . The falling of stars, or the end of the world, is in accordance with its beginning; and the end of the world will accomplish itself if the force of reason remains inactive." (II, 253)

Using the little information that was then available about the nature of the earth's electro-magnetic field, Fedorov attemped to speculate on just how men might begin to regulate the force of gravity. He imagined that it might be possible to erect huge cones or "conductors" at strategic points on the earth's surface in such a way that the earth might be freed from the sun's field of gravity. We might then be able to steer our planet out of its natural orbit into some flight pattern of our choosing. Eventually, we should be able to free the entire universe from its enslavement to the forces of gravity, and thus rearrange all particles of matter into a consciously and rationally, rather than blindly and naturally, determined order.

This fantasy of Fedorov's is a logical extension of his hypothesis that man first demonstrated his potential to counteract gravity when he raised himself from a four-legged, horizontal orientation to a two-legged, vertical posture. "Man's vertical position itself is already a counteraction to falling. All construction erected by man, all architecture and sculpture are expressions of that same act of arising, of an intellectual or a material (aerostat) lifting up." (II, 254) The natural animal in man tends toward the horizontal, which is the position of the corpse in the grave, the position in which man is utterly subject to the force of gravity. The gravestone, all funeral sculpture, and, indeed, all art represents a protest against and an imaginary victory over the force of gravity. By the first, and by every subsequent act of arising, man has broadened his horizon. Ultimately, when man escapes the earth's field of gravity, the entire universe will be his horizon. If in the present we may overcome gravity only by imagination, by thought, and by art, in the future we should be able to overcome gravity by our science. Then the differences that we now observe between our science and our art will have disappeared.

The theologian, Fr. G. Florovskii, one of Fedorov's harshest critics, finds Fedorov's ideas for regulating nature to be essentially an exaltation of technologism. "Man for Fedorov is, first of all, a technician, and comes close to being nature's mechanic, her foreman and overseer." [25] Moreover: "One gets the impression that he intends to prepare new homunculi *in vitro*... Fedorov would actually like to rebuild or transform the cosmic *organism* into a *mechanism*.... Fedorov always prefers that which is made to that which is born, and the artificial to the natural..." [26]

There is some truth in Florovskii's contention. In explaining why Russia is the country best suited to direct the world to its common task, Fedorov includes among the country's virtues its flatness "which does not draw the gaze earthward by its beauty" (I, 212). And similarly, the dull gray sky has the virtue of not permitting us to idolize it or make it the abode of imagined deities. The Russian landscape's lack of beauty is precisely what makes Fedorov prefer it to all others. In part, Fedorov's philosophy of regulation can be understood as the philosophy of a man who had looked all around him and seen only Russia. The insistence that we must all labor ceaselessly to control the savagery of nature might not have been expressed with such urgency had Fedorov grown up in, say, Tahiti. But Fedorov looks at nature not only from the viewpoint of a Russian, but from the viewpoint of the powerless "unlearned" rural masses for whom life is indeed a struggle against nature. Fedorov speaks for those who cannot possibly view nature as a temple, but who would, like Turgenev's Bazarov, given the knowledge, view nature as a laboratory.

Florovskii misrepresents Fedorov by implying that he glorifies technology above all else. Clearly Fedorov did not value technology as an end in itself. Throughout his works, Fedorov insists that technology must be united with art and with religion, and must be directed toward the single goal of restoring life to all men and harmony to the entire universe.

In his essay, "Supramoralism," Fedorov projects, in addition to his utopian future of redintegration and resurrection, an alternative, anti-utopian future in which present divergent tendencies have reached their grim, inevitable conclusions. Scientific technology will have outdistanced morality, and progress will have continued without the common task and without God. Fedorov calls this bleak, alternative future by several names, among them: "Pornocracy," "Anti-Easter," and "Counter-Easter."

In this "pornocratic" future, many features of which seem uncomfortably familiar, men will have abandoned the theological world-views of their grandfathers, will have abandoned also the anthropological world-views of their fathers, and will regard themselves and their fellow creatures from the zoological standpoint alone. Then, "having acknowledged themselves animals, people will then turn themselves into animals." (I, 428) Religious faith will be considered to have been "an unneeded appendage," "something that belonged to the youth or infancy of the human race." (I, 428) Both theoretical and practical reason will have atrophied. Living wholly in the present, people will have lost the sense of history, and memories of the ancestors will have faded forever. Technology, not the product of true applied reason, and not the application of reason toward a task, but "unconscious technology—an atrophied form of practical reason—will be master." (I, 429) Instead of bringing life to the dead, unconscious technology will bring death to the living. "Sexual feeling, or lust, having created *childless marriage*, will then drive out love both for fathers and for children." (I, 429) The goal of life for these human animals will not be to restore old life or to create new, but to obtain the maximum degree of satisfaction and comfort and luxury for themselves. All technology will be directed toward making life easier and more comfortable, and people will gradually eliminate everything that poses even the most minor threat to their comfort. All human effort and energy will be directed toward the elimination of minor annoyances and petty inconveniences, and everyone will try to ignore the fact of death. In the Anti-Easter, men will attempt in every way to pretend that their vices are virtues, but, locked in the present, neither resurrecting the past nor giving birth to the future, arrested in a state of "permanent adolescence," people will finally turn upon themselves and upon each other with loathing, and will destroy themselves and each other until what has traditionally been prophesied as "The Day of Wrath" will have been fully accomplished. (I, 429)

Like his paradise, Fedorov's hell is one of man's own making. If we do not by our own efforts bring about the general Resurrection, we shall surely, by our own efforts, accomplish the terrible Last Judgment. This is the either/or with which Fedorov confronts us. Total regulation of nature, or total submission to her, paradise or hell—Fedorov, like many Russian thinkers before and after him, abhors the idea of a middle course. That nature contains within herself equal powers of destruction and generation, or that the limits of human reason may fall within rather than extend beyond the limits of nature are ideas not to be found in Fedorov. The basic problem with Fedorov's view of nature is that he asks us not only to consider nature our chief enemy but to treat her as such, to wage war against her, to bring her under our will—all on the basis of assumptions that may or may not be true. If nature is not now our real enemy, but only seems so because we do not properly understand her, then we may well turn her into a real enemy by trying to shape her to our specifications. Fedorov, who had seen much evidence of nature's power to destroy the works of man and little evidence of man's power to destroy the works of nature could look hopefully toward the day when man would at last be able to redesign the universe. Today, the most common reaction to the idea that men might someday be able to free our planet from its solar orbit and set it spinning in some other direction might well be: "Thank God it's not yet possible!" In Fedorov's day, the most radical and novel side of his project was that spiritual development must be accompanied by advances in technology. In the future, the most important idea in Fedorov may be that advances in technology can only lead to disaster unless accompanied by comparable spiritual development.

Integrating Knowledge and Action

One of the most important of the many interconnected and interdependent projects of the common task is that of integrating knowledge and action. Fedorov writes: "Of all divisions the split between thought [*mysl'*] and action [*delo*] (which have become the properties of separate classes) is our single greatest misfortune, incomparably greater than the split between rich and poor. Socialism, and our age in general attributes the greatest significance to the division into rich and poor, supposing, of course, that with the elimination of this division the former will also disappear, i.e. all will become educated. But we have in mind not popular education, which with the elimination of poverty would indeed become more widely and evenly distributed; rather we have in mind the activity itself of sharing knowledge, and in fact the universal participation of all; participation and sharing in the knowledge of all, without which the division into learned and unlearned will not disappear, and which cannot result from the mere elimination of poverty." (I, 7)

Some commentators have interpreted this and other similar statements to mean that Fedorov was simply arguing that the elimination of illiteracy must precede the elimination of poverty, and that universal education must be understood as a condition for rather than a result of an equal distribution of wealth.[27] In this view, Fedorov shares the socialist's goal of equality of wealth and education but simply reverses the order of priority. Fedorov's insistence that knowledge, like life itself, must be "by all, of all" (I, 7), "through all" (I, 320) and "for the sake of all" (I, 36, 118) is, however, much more than an appeal for mass education. By "universal" knowledge, Fedorov meant, literally, that all people must work together until all that is now outside human knowledge becomes the knowledge of all. We shall, for instance, know the past by resurrecting those who lived in it, i.e. our ancestors. We shall know the entire universe by inhabiting it. We shall know God by seeing Him "face to face." Our knowledge of everything will not be theoretical but practical, not impersonal but personal, not passive but active. Essentially, then, Fedorov believed that we, not individually but together, as the human race, could, not only in theory but in practice, attain omniscience. Living forever and throughout the universe, our knowledge would no longer be bounded by traditionally accepted limits of space and time. But like the project of resurrection, with which it is interrelated, the project of universal knowledge will result from the gradual expansion of collaborative efforts that could begin almost anywhere and at any time. The existing institution, however, which is now best suited to begin the task of reintegrating knowledge and action is not the university, but the museum.

Disparaging remarks about the university—retreat for "the learned" (I, 5), tabernacle for the "New Pharisees" (II, 206), etc.—are scattered throughout Fedorov's works. Essentially, Fedorov's argument is not against specialized or advanced learning, but against the isolation of each branch of learning from all others. In the project, advanced specialists would cease to view themselves as a separate, established class, and would instead assume the duties of a temporary taskforce whose assignment would be to point the way toward a solution to the problem of death. Working toward the single goal of eliminating death and restoring life, specialists in all present divergent fields of knowledge would eventually begin to cordinate their efforts, collaborate on research, and, ultimately, share all knowledge. So Fedorov does not suggest that scientists should abandon their specialities for, say, Bible study, but that each should turn his special knowledge toward the solution of the one problem common to all men, namely death, and thus lead the way for all to share the knowledge that is now held only by isolated specialists. In Fedorov's project, then, one branch of knowledge, e.g. cosmonautics, is not to be developed at the expense of another, e.g. paleography—rather all sciences and arts are to be developed toward a common end: biology toward the restoration of Adam's body, and linguistics toward the restoration of Adam's language, so that ultimately all aspects of learning will be united. All that can be known is relevant, and all is needed to complete the task.

Fedorov discusses the integrative function of the museum in many of his works, but the most detailed discussion of the role the museum must play is found in an article entitled "The Museum, its Meaning and Importance" (II, 398-473).

He begins by arguing that the museum, scorned by "progressive" intellectuals, offers, paradoxically, the very opportunities for the betterment of mankind that the institutions promoted by "progressive" thinkers lack. To the standard argument that whereas museums are only repositories for dead objects, progress benefits living people, Fedorov replies: "But progress is precisely the production of dead things, accompanied by the displacement of living people.... For the museum a person is infinitely higher than a thing; while for the industrial part of the city, for factory civilization and culture, the thing is higher than the man. The museum is the last remaining trace of the cult of ancestors...." (II, 339)

The museum is, then, not a repository of dead objects, but "a gathering of departed souls, an assembly of the dead, in the guise of old things (rummage). But these souls reveal themselves only to those who have a soul." (II, 399) Thus, the first step in the task is one of perception: we must realize that the museum is not a house for mere objects but for what has been left by departed souls. We must start looking for the people behind the objects. By viewing the museum in this way, Fedorov suggests, we shall gradually turn the museum into an "observatory" for the discovery of our ancestors. (II, 403) Just as stronger telescopes reveal the existence of previously unobserved heavenly bodies, so shall new developments in museum technology eventually reveal much more information than is presently available about the lives of our ancestors.

In the project, every village and settlement would establish its own museum, in which every available scrap of information about the locality's past and present would be gathered Not only scientists, but everyone in the locality would participate in the collection of essential data. "A museum is *not a collection of things, but a community of persons (sobor lits)*; its activity consists not in the accumulation of dead things, but in the returning of life to the remains of what no longer lives, in the restoration of the dead, through their products, by living agents." (II, 407) It is by collecting and reassembling data about the ancestors that the learned and unlearned shall begin to work together and to realize their interdependence. For both the intellectual and the peasant, learning will at last become directly relevant to life.

As the religious, scientific, and educational functions of museum work become more apparent, museums will gradually expand their activities until new institutions, which Fedorov calls "museum-temple-laboratory schools" eventually replace the separate institutions we now know. Study, worship, experimentation, and preservation will gradually and naturally turn into one sacred, scientific, educative, restorative task whose one goal will be the resurrecting of all the dead. Since villages, and even abandoned villages, will become resurrection centers, the migration from country to city will no longer be a problem. Urban life represents to Fedorov a clear example of all that is wrong with the world. Separated from his parents and country ancestors, avoiding the confrontation with nature, slaving to produce and acquire lifeless objects, his mind no longer in touch with the earth, urban man is Russia's Prodigal Son. The search for more and more luxury, the exploitation of the country, the contamination of the soul, the need to wage war—all this, Fedorov's Slavophile instincts tell him, can end only if Russians return to the countryside and fathers they have abandoned. The need to establish resurrection centers in every village and former village will offer the natural incentive, no longer provided by agriculture, to draw intellectuals and skilled workers back into the depleted country. Thus Fedorov goes beyond those Slavophiles and Populists who merely contrast the virtues of rural life to the miserable conditions of modern urban society. For Fedorov, reversing the flow from country to city is not an end in itself, but only a means to fulfil the necessary task of resurrecting the ancestors. In the project, the resettling of the countryside is not only desirable, but absolutely necessary—the resettlement, however, would be accomplished not by directive or coercion, but freely, by sons and daughters whose one thought is to resurrect their parents and ancestors. In working for the new museum, people would use whatever skills they had acquired in previous occupations. Diplomats would negotiate the exchange of relics between localities and countries, merchants would scour the countryside in search of discarded materials now recognized to be of great value, soldiers would use their military skills in the battle against nature. (II, 429) At first, most present activities and occupations would simply be redirected toward the new goal of resurrection. Gradually, over several generations, narrow specialities would broaden and overlap each other until eventually all people would have not one but many skills and would have thorough knowledge of most of the present fields of specialized study. Ultimately everyone would be engaged in the same all-sided activity of resurrecting ancestors.

The only place more important than the museum in Fedorov's project is the cemetery. (II, 399) Properly understood, the entire earth is a cemetery. (I, 9) For now, we must continue to till the earth for our food, but eventually, as we find ways to live without organic nourishment, i.e. without swallowing our ancestors, we shall stop taking life from our fathers and start returning life to them. The museum-temple-school is the institution which must lead us through the transition from expoiting to resurrecting the dust of our ancestors.

The museum-temple-school, then, has many functions in the project: to redintegrate knowledge and action, to transform cities back into villages, to turn strangers into brothers, and to direct us from exploitation toward resurrection.

Fedorov's ideal society would thus be made up of a network of more or less self-sufficient communities in which all activities would be coordinated, through a local museum-laboratory-temple-school, toward the task of resurrecting the ancestors. There would be no need for heavy industry, for all products necessary for the task would be manufactured locally. Energy would be from the sun—earth and men would not have to be expolited in the mining of fossil fuels. (I, 5) Regulation of the climate would insure adequate harvests, and since there would be neither shortage nor excess, commercial interactions would not be needed. People would live as families of brothers and sisters working for the sake of their parents. Everyone would devote all his energy to the task, not as an act of self-denial but as self-fulfillment. The task, which would combine learning and labor, and which would focus the mind, the heart, and the hand toward a single goal, would be infinitely more rewarding and joyful than any work now known.

Pretty as this picture is, it raises many questions which Fedorov does not even attempt to answer. One very mundane question would be: how can technology advance without centralized heavy industry? The only manufacturing that Fedorov includes in his utopia is of the sparetime, cottage variety. And yet each community of regulators and resurrectors is expected to undertake advanced scientific research and even, eventually, to send its own explorers on extraterrestrial expeditions. How the benefits of rural life and advanced technology are to be combined is a matter which Fedorov did not try to think through. In his future, a picture of a space capsule beside a log cabin would illustrate the opposite of the gaps, paradoxes, and incongruities that such pictures are taken to illustrate today.

But a deeper and more basic problem has to do with Fedorov's assumption that the human mind has an unlimited capacity to learn. Those systems of thought or belief, such as the Hindu, which posit the infinite range of the mind, usually suggest that to expand to infinity the human mind must somehow mysteriously merge itself into the limitless mind of God. To become infinite the human mind must find release from its human limitations, must free itself from a specific body, and lose itself as a river loses itself when it flows into the sea. But Fedorov is not an Indian mystic, and yet he insists that as finite, specific human beings we can somehow possess minds whose range is infinite. We can interpret this, as we did earlier in discussing Fedorov's apparently contradictory concepts of eternity and temporality, to mean that Fedorov believed that we posses at one and the same time both finite and infinite capacities of mind. But Fedorov himself seems not even to have been aware of, much less to have attempted a solution to, the apparent contradiction inherent in the idea of a finite person with an infinite mind.

Fedorov does not want to suggest anything vague or mystical, but when he speaks of "knowledge by all of all' he does not clearly state just what he means by these words. All he seems to be saying here is that when all of us who have ever lived are resurrected, we shall all then "know" one other and shall be able to obtain from each other direct, personal knowledge of all that happened during each other's lives. If we want to know just how the pyramids were built we can ask the people who built them. But even if, by some stupendous feat of public communications, everything that everyone could say about himself and his life were made known to everyone else, we still might not know all that could be known. What of the world beyond human experience—the state of the world the day before the first man arrived? What can we ever know of the inner world of even another human being, much less of some animal that may have flourished and become extinct before the advent of man? And will anyone ever be able to recall at will everything that has ever happened to him? And even if he could, would he want to—and even if he wanted to, should he? That forgetfulness, like unconsciousness, might sometimes be more nearly a blessing than a curse seems not to have occurred to Fedorov.

Just what Fedorov means by saying that we must all know all, then, remains unclear. If he means that we should literally become omniscient, then he does not offer an adequate case for either the possibility or the desirability of human omniscience. If he does not mean omniscience, then he does not give any clear indication of what else he might mean by "knowledge by all of all."

But, theoretical problems aside, probably no one has considered the question of omniscience or of the unification of all knowledge as fully, from the practical standpoint, as Fedorov. Despite oversights, inconsistencies, and a few apparent contradictions, Fedorov does leave the reader with at least some sense of what "omniscience" might be if possessed by humans on earth. Omniscience would be not some vague idea, not something unimaginably abstract, but *people* milling around and sharing with other *people* all that they can share of what they know. It is this deliberate simple-mindedness, his dogged, *muzhik* insistence on the literal, his concreteness, his ability to give body to words like "omniscience" that, in the beginning, so attracts and, in the end, so repels the serious student of Fedorov's thought.

The Role of the Autocrat

Marxist commentators neatly divide Fedorov's thought into two categories: his "progressive" ideas about the need to unify thought and action, about the importance of technology, and about not only the possibility but the necessity of creating paradise on earth; and his "reactionary" ideas about the importance of Christianity and the need for a Christian autocrat. To the Marxist, and perhaps to many who are not Marxists, Fedorov's scientific and political ideals can only be understood as mutually contradictory. What Fedorov attempts to demonthrate, however, is not only that there is no contradicion between the ideas of a Christian autocracy and of a technological paradise on earth, but that the one without the other is unthinkable.

Fedorov recognized that uncontrolled technological advance could only lead to disaster. A single goal must be established, and a single taskmaster must direct and supervise the universal task. The only task in which all humanity, living and dead, can be united is the task of overcoming the enemy of all humanity, namely, death. Moreover, Fedorov concludes, the only person on earth who can unite and direct all people in the task is one who will stand in the "father-place", namely, some future Orthodox Christian Russian autocrat.

Several questions immediately come to mind. Why an autocrat, why an heir to an existing throne, rather than the head of some international organization, or the leader of some hypothetical "Universal Resurrection Party", or someone elected by popular majority? And why a Russian, rather than, for instance, a European, an Asian, an African, or an American? And why an Orthodox Christian, instead of a Protestant, a Roman Catholic, a representative of some other major religion, or a leader who represents no religion at all? Fedorov's reasons for insisting that Orthodox Christians must initiate and direct the task will be discussed in the concluding section of this chapter. We shall turn to the other two questions now.

In defending the idea of autocracy, Fedorov takes his stand within a tradition of Russian political thought that goes at least as far back as Ivan the Terrible's epistles to Kurbskii.[28] The Tsar is not only a ruler of men, but an instrument of God's will on earth. Although the idea that the autocrat is God's representative on earth did not originate with Ivan the Terrible, and, indeed, did not even originate in Russia, the immediacy with which the atheistic Bolsheviks proclaimed themselves instruments of an invisible higher will (the mysterious "laws" of history) indicates the enduring appeal that the idea has had for Russians. Fedorov's idea, then, that without an autocrat we would all follow our individual inclinations and would never undertake our common task, expresses a conviction that has dominated Russian political thought for centuries.[29]

Thus, to organize the task of resurrection, and to direct all people, divergent in their interests, toward a single goal, both individual and social life need what Fedorov calls *samoderzhavie*, "autocracy," or, in the broader sense, "self control." Politically, autocracy is Fedorov's synthesis of despotism and constitutionalism. In the individual, self-control is the synthesis of self-repression and self-will. We may talk and dream all we wish of unity and of resurrecting the dead, but without *samoderzhavie* we will never turn our ideas into activity. As Fedorov writes: "but it is true now that if all of us do not unite in the task of resurrection, in what is surely the brother's task, then we will not be brothers; and if man is a moral creature, then in order to remain moral it is necessary for him either to return life to the dead or to die himself, but to survive the death of his father, having assumed that to resurrect is impossible, means not to be a son, not to be a brother, and not to be, in the end, a moral creature. What is required, then, for the restoration of brotherly unity, for the gradual extension and preservation of this unity in the human race, and what is necessary in order to lead a brotherly union of sons of dead fathers in the common paternal task, in the task that has arisen because of the sense of loss—what is required is a deputy [*namestnik*—"one who stands in place of"], a steward of the soul [*dusheprikazchik*], *who stands in the father-place*, and this is the autocrat." (I, 367)

By "standing in the father-place" Fedorov means "standing at Pamir" as well as representing the ancestors. (I, 378) Pamir, for Fedorov, is the father-place, the site of the Biblical Eden, the site of Adam's grave (according to Turkic legends), and, according to theories of Fedorov's time, the original homeland of the Aryans. (I, 218, 233, 247, 348, 350-351). Fedorov wrote his article on "Autocracy" not long after England and Russia had signed an agreement permitting British scientific expeditions to explore the Pamirs. This meant, to Fedorov, that the Russian Tsar was autocrat not only of Russia, but of the Pamirs, the father-place, as well. For this reason, the Russian Tsar stands in the father place not only for Russians, but for all the human race as well. Russian history is mankind's history. "The autocrat as the one standing in the father-place, in being crowned Tsar receives from God of the fathers, from the Triune God, a higher sanctification, and becomes an instrument of God's will in order to lead the task of all sons of men, that is, sons of all the dead fathers, sons who have survived their fathers and who are even guilty for displacing their fathers and for having contributed to their deaths—in order to lead them in the father task, uniting these very sons in that task in the image of the Triune God." (I, 367-368)

And just as society must be united by the one who stands in the father-place, so the individual must redintegrate his conflicting mental faculties and must regulate his errant nature by that part of him that is of the fathers. The ego must seek not self-fulfillment but self-direction in fulfillment of the duty to the fathers. Reason must control the sex drive. Part of oneself must stand firmly in the father-place. (I, 386-391; II, 97-98.)

"*Autocracy is in its original meaning dictatorship*, provoked by danger not from other people like oneself but from a blind force which brings the threat of death to all without exception. . . . Autocracy, that is, power to the one in the father-place, appeared immediately after the death of the first father had united all in a single will, in a single desire, caused by loss and death. . . ." (I, 375) For Fedorov, dictatorship is not the same as tyranny or despotism. Despots and tyrants are men who attempt to dictate without "standing in the father-place," that is, without directing the living sons to the task of resurrecting the dead fathers. In the world as it is, one-man rule has always been despotism. But constitutional government is, for Fedorov, an unacceptable alternative to despotism. Constitutional government was the first work of the first sons who had forgotten their fathers. Constitutions are the legal handiwork of prodigal sons. If despotism is the abuse of father-power, constitutionalism is the decimation of that power. (I, 375)

In advocating autocracy, then, Fedorov is not attempting to defend the abuse of power by Russian Tsars. He recognizes, even insists, that in the world as it is, even in Russia, there have been no true autocrats, no true exercise of autocracy as he defines it. The task of politics is not to abandon the idea of autocracy for some lesser idea, such as constitutionalism, but to change autocracy as it is to autocracy as it ought to be.

Fedorov's articles on "Autocracy" (I, 353-398), in which he formulates his political ideas, are in part a response to an 1897 article by Solov'ev entitled "What Russia Is."[30] But his fullest discussion of Russia's role in world history appears in the section of the long "Brotherhood" essay entitled "What History Is." (I, 128-247.) And it is to this work that we must turn for Fedorov's answer to the question of why the Tsar of Russia, rather than the leader of some other country, must direct the project of resurrection.

Although Fedorov is no more systematic in his discussion of world history than he is in his discussion of any other topic, he focuses most of his attention on three centers: the Pamirs, Constantinople, and Moscow, representing respectively the centers of pre-history, history as fact, and history as project.

We have already mentioned, in other contexts, the special significance that Fedorov attributes to the Pamirs. For evidence that the Pamirs are *the* center of mankind's pre-history, Fedorov points to the legends that have gathered, like cloud banks, around the peaks that dominate the region. These unchanging legends, unquestioned by the simple people (who represent, to Fedorov, the "forefathers" of modern history) tell us as much, if not more, truth about our common unwritten past as do the changing, conflicting accounts of literate historians about the most recent past. Thus the legend that Pamir is the grave of the first father is in itself, for Fedorov, sufficient testimony to its central position in the distant past. That other, modern historians have overlooked the importance of the Pamirs testifies more to the narrow, Western orientation of written history than to the insignificance of the place.

If, as legend holds, these rocky wastes were once the lush, verdant Eden of the Bible, then the very desolation of the place must now serve to remind us of all that we have lost. Every pagan people had, in its world picture, a mountain that was looked upon as the center and axis of the world, the meeting point of earth and heaven, where the ancestors' spirits were supposed to reside. For the Chinese, Fedorov tells us, this sacred summit was Kuen-Lun; for the Mongols, T'ian San'; for the Finns, Altai; for the Semites, Ararat, Nazir. By poetic logic, Fedorov deduces that the center of all these various centers is Pamir, "the original first grave, to which all other graves point." (I, 247).

Pamir, then, is the focal point for all remorse for the loss of kinship and life. Once paradise, the barren, uninhabitable crags which now separate peoples of the most diverse linguistic and racial stocks, make the Pamirs the emblem of all that our failure to regulate nature has cost us.

According to Fedorov, the geographical position of the Pamirs has made control of the region essential for anyone who would unite East and West. Alexander the Great was the first European conqueror to understand the significance of the Pamirs. The underlying purpose of his march to India was, in Fedorov's view, to find and control the father-place. In more recent history, it was from the barren heights of the Pamirs that the Mongol invaders swept across Russia and into Europe. Control of the Pamirs is necessary for the defense of Constantinople from the east, and, Fedorov believes, failure to control this desolate region was one of the most important (and still unrecognized) reasons for the fall of the holy city. And in Fedorov's own time the threat of invasion by a new wave of Scythians, new Golden Hordes, the new "yellow peril" that captured the imagination of *fin de siècle* Russia made control of the Pamirs doubly important. But by "control" Fedorov meant more than military occupation. The task of a future Tsar, in history as a project, must be to restore life to this kingdom of roaring winds, deep snow, and silent stones: to regulate the meteorological forces so that the ruined, abandoned garden of our collective memory will again be made green. Thus the Pamirs, now a center of repulsion, from which Adam, the Aryans, and the Mongols have all fled, the place from which men have turned as prodigal wanderers to assault their more peaceful brothers, must become a center of attraction, where people will come to till the earth and to restore life to the remains of our common ancestors. The centrifugal center must become a centripetal center—and as the sovereign responsible for the future of the Pamirs, the Russian autocrat alone can redirect our attention back toward our forgotten common center.

But if Pamir is the center of the world's unrecorded history, Constantinople (which Fedorov usually calls Tsargrad) is the center around which the recorded history of our world (history as fact) has turned. Written history begins, Fedorov finds, with the account by Herodotus (the "father" of the historiography to which the people are "forefather") of the first encounters between Europe and Asia. The first remembered collision between the two continents had been recorded earlier in the *Iliad*, and for Herodotus, and consequently for all subsequent historiography, the collision between Asia and Europe as narrated by Homer became the paradigm for all military struggle, the archetype for all subsequent war. All human conflicts recorded in history, then, can be understood as the issue and likeness of the collision between East and West. World history, according to Fedorov, is essentially the story of our repeated attemps, on a thousand battlegrounds, to resolve the conflict between East and West, to gain control over the center that represents the world's dividing point.

The founding of the city that became Constantinople represents, to Fedorov, the first attempt to unite the world at its dividing point. The son of the East, father of the West, Constantinople, not Rome, Fedorov argues, has the greatest right to the name eternal, for Rome was only a prelude to Constantinople and was not universal but only Western. Rome rose and fell, but Constantinople has always marked the point of the world's division.

The attempt at Christian unity represented by Byzantine Orthodoxy failed, Fedorov believes, chiefly because the Byzantine Christians thought that the resurrection would occur in the very near future and without their effort. The Byzantine Christians did not seriously attempt to make their church the world's church. Thus Christianity did not become a universal religion, but remained only the faith held by the people who happened then to be living at the world's center. In neglecting the task of Christianizing the world and restoring life to all, Constantinople affirmed the erroneous view that salvation could be partial, that is, that part of the world could be saved and part not, and ignored that salvation and restoration must be total. Thus instead of joining all men in the activity of resurrecting, Constantinople allowed herself, and Christianity's best opportunity in history as fact, to be mired down in disputes over dogma, that is, in disputes over thought without action. Thus, in the very city that could have been the center from which the activity of universal resurrection spread, the door was opened to discord, to philosophy, and to the Turks.

Fedorov argues that the rise of Islam was a direct consequence of Constantinople's failure to Christianize the world. Because Constantinople did not restore life to the desert that surrounded her, the desert was allowed to rise in whirlwind. Islam, to Fedorov, is the religious manifestation of the principle of blind, destructive force. "Holy war" is its creed, and the will of the individual is swept into the principle of death. Because Constantinople did not live by the Christian idea she professed in dogma and represented in art, the center of the Christian world was lost.

To Fedorov, Constantinople at her peak represents the unstable combination of Christian doctrine and Anti-Christian practice. In her fall, she passed her Christian spirituality to the Russians (Moscow—the Third Rome), and passed her Anti-Christian pagan practices (in the form of Greek philosophy and art) to the West. But Russia, having received the White Cowl [31] and the icons of redemption, was not yet able or ready to lead the universal task that Constantinople had failed to begin. With the fall of Constantinople the focus of history as fact passed not to Russia, but to Western Europe, where the influence of Byzantine art and learning brought on the "rebirth of paganism" (I, 167) which Western historians call the Renaissance.

The part of Fedorov's essay on history that deals with Western Europe anticipates most of the conclusions that Spengler announced in his celebrated 1918 work, *Der Untergang des Abendlandes*. But in the Russian tradition, Fedorov's ideas seem little more than individual variations on the basic Slavophile positions best articulated by Khomiakov and Kireevskii and later supplemented by Fedorov's contemporaries Dostoevskii and Danilevskii. But in addition to offering a general synthesis of the major criticisms, prejudices, animadversions, and valid objections to westernism that had accumulated in nine or more centuries of Russian thought, Fedorov adds a number of fresh negative observations of his own.

He finds, for instance, that even the geography of Western Europe can be understood as an emblem of her disintegration. In history, as well as in prehistory, mountains represent, for Fedorov, the quality and intensity of a people's spirituality. Mountains are what people look up to, and what they see or don't see in their mountains reflects their spiritual development. Where the Pamirs stood in the center of the East, and where Parnassus stood in the center of Greece, the Alps stand in the center of Europe. In the prehistoric world, the Pamirs stood for what we had all lost. In the pagan world, Parnassus stood for art and cultural unity. But in Europe, the Alps stand for craft and division. At the top of the mountains of Europe stands not the first father's grave, or the oracle, but Switzerland: scenic, but with no greatness; skillful, but in the way of the craftsman, not the artist. Where the Greeks had the appearance of unity, but lived in fact by the principle of discord, the Europeans have had the appearance of diversity and discord but in fact have lived under an artificial and externally imposed unity, Catholicism. Moreover, within Europe, every country has its own Alp, its peak that divides peoples into discordant tribes united under the "Papal Oracle". (I, 168)

Catholicism, for Fedorov as for the Slavophiles, represents a false unity without freedom. Protestantism represents freedom without unity. Orthodoxy is the synthesis of freedom and unity.

The crucial difference between Russian and Western religious life, Fedorov suggests, results from the comparatively late date of Russia's acceptance of Christianity. He divides the history of Byzantine religious debate into two parts: arguments over dogma and arguments over ritual. The Slavs entered Christendom and adopted Orthodoxy, fortunately, during the second phase, and thus participated in and carried back to their own lands the debates over ritual, i.e. over the embodiment and practice of dogma, rather than disputes over dogma itself. The fathers of the Eastern Church, then, were more concerned with creating artistic and didactic guides to the practice of Christianity than with developing a scholastic theology and attempting to convince the intellect of what intellect alone could never comprehend. (I, 177-178)

Thus, in Fedorov's account, while the Eastern Church attended to the spiritual life of the community, Christianity in the West became more and more an intellectual exercise of the rational and imaginative faculties of clever individuals on the one hand, and unthinking mass obedience to the dictates of the papal hierarchy on the other. In the mind of the Western Church, the imaginary was more and more regularly mistaken for the real, until in Dante, fantasy utterly replaces reality, and the inner life of the individual is substituted for the whole life of the community. (I, 179)

Fedorov, then, sees Dante not as the glorious summit of Western spirituality, but as the most obvious landmark of its descent. He sees in Dante the capitulation of spiritual community to fantastic individualism, the ultimate expression of the pagan cloaked as the Christian. What Fedorov does not tell us is that Dante was careful to define the point at which Virgil, his pagan guide, could no longer accompany him on his journey. Dante understood more clearly than Fedorov the extent, but also the limits, of his debt to pagan thought.

Fedorov views the history of Europe as a series of futile attempts to regain control of the lost center. The Crusades failed because the goal was not to restore life to all through the center, but merely to slay or drive out the heathens. The Crusades, like Dante's work, illustrate to Fedorov the degree to which Latin Christianity had become an acting out of fantasies. The victories the Crusaders sought were utterly imaginary, and only the losses they suffered and inflicted were real.

Fedorov even suggests that it was in many ways better for the world that Latin Christianity failed to recover its lost center. The discovery of America would not have occurred so soon had Latin Europe controlled the Bosphorus, and, with it, the overland route to the East. Constantinople was the impassable center around which the navigators sailed, enlarging the known world. The discovery and exploration of the earth as a globe, the mental shift from a Ptolemaic to a Copernican view of the world, can thus, Fedorov suggests, be understood as a consequence of the battle between East and West for control of their common center.

Fedorov also traces the seeds of the dispute between Catholics and Protestants, as well as the seeds of resolution in Orthodoxy, back to Constantinople. Byzantine dogma (future Catholicism) had provoked criticism (future Protestantism), and criticism had led to the conception, though not to the actualization, of the project of the common task (future Orthodoxy). In this way, according to Fedorov, the history of Constantinople can again be seen as an emblem of the history of the world: an age of dogma is followed by an age of criticism; the age of criticism must lead to an age of projectivism, first in idea, then in reality.[32] (I, 188-189)

In Western Europe, the age of criticism began with Protestantism. So long as criticism remains a mere idea it remains religious Protestantism or secular protestantism (liberalism). When criticism becomes action, it becomes revolution. In either case, the spirit of collective consensus of the whole is replaced by the spirit of subjective individual or partial group rejection of the common. To Fedorov, this smacks of parricide.

The secularization of Western Europe, according to Fedorov's view, in no way changed the basic mindset of the continent. Slavery to the Pope was replaced by slavery to commerce and industry, while its protestant antithesis, subjective individualism, merely lowered its goals from spiritual salvation to worldly power. The French Revolution, then, in Fedorov's history, is not the beginning of the age of revolution, but only the end of the revolution of the mind and the beginning of the repeated revolutions of the body politic. Western science may have circumnavigated the globe many times, but it has still not recovered its lost spiritual center.

But the extreme East offers no better alternative. Fedorov sees the principle of Islam to be that of destructive activism, that of Buddhism to be pessimistic inaction, and that of Confucianism to be stagnant legalism. Islam has as its goal the annihilation of the world, Buddhism the rejection of the world, and Confucianism seeks not to resurrect but to embalm the world. The Moslems recognize neither brothers nor fathers, but only enemies. The Buddhists see other human beings as only roadblocks to their escape from the world. The Confucianists worship the memory of ancestors, but do not try to restore life to them, venerate death and dying instead of attempting to overcome death. While Fedorov finds more to praise in Confucianism than in other systems of Oriental thought, he concludes that their worship of the dead is at best a passive, cerebral veneration unaccompanied by action.[33]

Our hope, Fedorov concludes, lies neither in the West nor in the East, but in the vast land mass between the two extremes. The centrality of Russia, no matter what problem is under discussion, is one of Fedorov's major themes. In religion, Russian Orthodoxy holds to the center of Christianity and offers a middle way between the unity without freedom of Catholicism and the freedom without unity of Protestantism. The traditional Russian idea of *sobornost'*, a community of individuals freely united in spiritual consensus, bridges the gap between the extreme individualism of the secularized West and the sense of the worthlessness of the individual that dominates the East. In geopolitics, Russia offers a continental center to the insular and oceanic extremes. Autocracy is the middle way between the "prodigal" constitutional democracies of the West and the despotic governments and colonial slavery of the East.

That Russia has failed to lead the world in history as fact qualifies her all the more for leadership in history as a project. For with the Slavophiles, Fedorov is convinced that Russia has been marked for a very special destiny. While in history as fact, Russia slept through the centuries in which most other countries awakened, during this long sleep Russia was storing up vast reserves of spiritual energy while her neighbors were wasting theirs. Through long centuries, the feet of conquerors, moving from north to south, east to west, and west to east, have etched the sign of the cross deeply into the Russian land. Since Boris and Gleb, passive, kenotic suffering has been the mark of Russian spirituality. In history as fact, Russia has remained passive while her neighbors and enemies have exhausted themselves by misdirected action. Now, as the history of facts draws toward its inevitable conclusion and modern civilization hastens its own disintegration, Russia must transform her passive qualities into active tasks of universal salvation, and Moscow must become the world center from which the project of resurrection radiates.

Fedorov lists ten instinctive Russian qualities [*zadatki*] that make her uniquely qualified to assume the leadership of the universal project. Fedorov recognizes that: "These instinctive qualities, which we consider to be conditions of advanced development, could be viewed by others as merely lower forms of life...." (I, 211) Like many (notably Khomiakov) before him, and like many (notably Trotskii) after him, Fedorov believes that it is precisely Russia's "backwardness" that will enable her to play a leading role in the world's future. Because she has not even entered the long stage of development out of which the supposedly "advanced" countries are now trying to struggle, Russia can leap from last place to first without passing through the intermediate stages. The "backward" qualities that destine Russia for future command are:

1. A way of life based on kinship. [*Rodovoi byt*]. That Russian life is, or at least was at one time based on deep feelings of kinship is indicated by the continued use of the patronymic, and by the common reference to strangers and acquaintances alike as "father" and "mother" and "brother" [*batushka, matjushka, brat*]. All Russians must begin to look upon themselves as orphans, just as, Fedorov tells us, the Russian peasants consider themselves orphans. And as the peasants beseech their masters and landlords to be their "fathers", so all Russians must look to the father-autocrat for protection and direction. In this way, all human relationships would be considered relations of kinship. Brotherhood, sisterhood, daughterhood, and sonship would replace citizenship. (I, 211-212; 318-319)

2. The commune [*obshchina*]. In communal life, no enmity can arise between father and son, one works for the welfare of all instead of for one's own profit, and the goal of agriculture is to provide adequate nourishment for all rather than to obtain the maximum (and hence most profitable) yield. In communal life, people must regulate rather than exploit the land. On this point, Fedorov's ideas coincide with those of the Russian Marxists. Although Fedorov's utopia is far more ambitious, lofty, and comprehensive than the materialist "paradise" of the Russian Marxists, his antipathy toward capitalism, and indeed toward exploitation of any kind, is, if anything, even keener than theirs.

3. Tilling the earth. In Fedorov's ideal society, we would all return to the simpler, rural life. Cities, he argues in "The Sanitation Question", are the centers of isolation, decomposition, sick fantasy, and prodigal living. Although compared to her own past, Russia was rapidly becoming an urbanized country, compared to most countries in Europe she was still a rural nation. Fedorov believed that in his time it might still be possible to avert the catastrophe of urbanization on a European scale. It is especially here that Russia's backwardness could make her the "most advanced" major country in the world.

4. The classless society. Fedorov maintains that the class

system in Russia is not as deeply entrenched as the class system in Europe. In Russia, the greatest division is between learned and unlearned. By eliminating this difference, Russia could establish a classless society more easily than could countries in which divisions are more numerous and run deeper. On this point, Fedorov's analysis of Russian society is probably unique. Fedorov does not deny the traditional division between rich and poor, but argues that this division is more nearly a consequence than a cause of the division into learned and unlearned.

5. State service, based on the principle of self-sacrifice, having as its goal not the well-being of bureaucrats, but selfless service to all. Everyone without exception would serve the universal task. All should seek not exemption from duty but extension of duties. Only in the task of overcoming death, now master of all, will men find true freedom. We should seek freedom through duty instead of freedom from duty. The Russian tradition of obligatory service to the state has for centuries trained people to seek fulfillment in duty to a higher cause. "Freedom to live only for oneself is a great evil" (I, 195) would seem to reflect not only Fedorov's attitude, but also that of many of his countrymen. While Westerners may look upon the Russians as a weak, slavish people who allow themselves to be herded like cattle by dictators who for some reason are best loved when most oppressive, Fedorov interprets the Russian lack of self-assertion as a subtler and more advanced understanding of freedom. Where in the West, the Christian idea that we must give up our freedom (and our life) in order to find it has often been treated as a paradox, in Russia that freedom comes through duty has seemed less like a contradiction.[34]

6. A state governed not by those who proclaim their rights, but by those who proclaim their guilt. Presumably, Fedorov is referring here to the many Tsars in history who have confessed their failures (and sometimes even their crimes) to their subjects. In Fedorov's thought, we are all guilty for the death of our fathers. The project should be directed by a leader who acknowledges that he is willing to assume responsibility for our collective guilt. And just as leaders should cease pro-

claiming their innocence and begin acknowledging their most grievous faults, so every member of society should cease to demand his rights and should direct all effort toward atonement for his responsibility for the death of his fathers. The state must forever renounce its right to take life and forever assume its duty to restore life. In attributing a deep sense of natural guilt to the Russians, Fedorov has uncovered a trait that underlies some of the most perplexing events in Russian history, from the gratitude of the Novgorodians who were punished by Ivan the Terrible to the willingness of Stalin's purge victims to pass the harshest of sentences upon themselves for crimes they may not even have committed. The confessional tone of so much of Russian literature, the guilt that someone like Tolstoi could feel for having been born a wealthy nobleman, the Dostoevskian insistence that all must share the blame for everything—all this indicates the depth of the sense of guilt that Fedorov considered to be a basic trait of Russians. The ability to accept, even to seek the blame makes the Russians the natural candidates for leadership in the task of removing the cause of universal guilt. People who insist on protesting their innocence, or who instinctively refuse to blame themselves for whatever goes wrong have not reached the Russian level of maturity. The sense of guilt that has led to passivity and even paralysis in the past must, in the future, become the basis for the active task that will free the world from the universal guilt that Russians feel keenly but that many other peoples have not yet even become aware of.

7. *Extending the sentry lines.* According to Fedorov, Russia is unique in having expanded her territory over vast areas by swallowing her invaders instead of attacking her neighbors. While not all military historians would concur with Fedorov's assertion that Russia has never been a belligerent power, Fedorov is probably correct in emphasizing that traditionally Russia has proved more successful at defense than at offense. In viewing Russia's military past, Fedorov tends to write not "history as it was" but "history as it should have been." He argues that Russia finally overcome the Mongols not by open offensive, but by extending her natural radius of activity until the enemy was peacefully surrounded and absorbed. So in the

future, in the project of history, Russia must expand her beneficent influence not by open conflict but by gradual extension of her sentry lines until the powers of the world are surrounded and absorbed into the Russian principle. The Mongols came as fierce, nomadic horseman, but by gradually being absorbed into Russia, slowly turned into peaceful farmers. By gradually taming and russifying neighboring savages, Russia increased her territory and population and turned diverse pagan tribes into a united people. Only a struggle of this character, then, a struggle whose purpose is to turn the nomads who live by theft, assault, and war into peaceful tillers of the soil—only a struggle of this kind can, Fedorov argues, genuinely be called disarmament and be waged by a Christian people. (I, 198, 212)

8. Russia's geographical position. Russia's mountain heights and her great breadth demand a life of hardship and self-sacrifice. Her plains, Fedorov argues with some justification, do not permit the gaze to be riveted and the mind to be paralyzed by excessive beauty. For the Russians, nature is not a beautiful picture. Of her flat gray skies men will not be able to create false idols. Her expanse and flat space does not permit internal feuding but necessitates close ties between neighboring familier for mutual protection against the incursions of foreign marauders and the devastating force of the natural elements. Her inland, continental position, her country backwardness, prevents her from becoming aggressive in the way of insular and peninsular peoples. At present the world might be seen, Fedorov suggests, as Russia surrounded on all sides by England. But by absorbing the insular and peninsular, Russia can passify these naturally assertive and aggressive races. She can turn land-seekers into earth-tillers, as she did with the peninsular Varangians. That Russia offers the best overland route to Asia makes her the natural link between East and West, both in the physical and spiritual sense. Her climate, which tempers people by exposing them at one moment to desert heat and the next to arctic cold, has created a hardy race capable of naturally enduring conditions which others might not be able to withstand. This adaptability of the Russian should make him the natural leader, Fedorov suggests, in

the future tasks of space exploration and genetic engineering.

9. Gathering the lands. Just as Russia's past has been one of gradual expansion and gathering so her future will be. But in the project, her experience in gathering living peoples will enable her to lead the task of gathering in the particles of the dead, and her experience in expanding her control over a large portion of the earth will enable her to direct the project of expanding human control over the remainder of the universe.

10. The absence of any deals or compromising transactions between the spiritual and the secular, and between the clergy and the laity. The clergy, which has been denied power in the world as it is, will in the project be able to devote full power to the task. Though he does not elaborate, Fedorov seems here to be contrasting the Russian Church, which has not traded its purity for political power, to the Catholic and Protestant churches, which have compromised themselves in bargaining for wordly power. Because it has not attempted to accommodate itself to the political realities of the world, the Russian Church has presumably retained its pure energy and should now be free to devote to the creation of eternal life all the spiritual power that Western churches have wasted on maintaining influence over the disintegrating world.

Fedorov's list of Russian "instincts", national character traits that have kept her a "backward" nation in history as fact, but that should make her the most "advanced" nation in history as a project, owes much to the Slavophiles.[35] And in rough outline, Fedorov's writings on universal history can be understood as an elaboration of the fifteenth century "Tale of the While Cowl" in which the White Cowl, the radiant symbol of resurrection and Orthodox Christianity, was moved from Rome to Constantinople when the Popes began to distort the original teachings of Christ. And when later the Greeks also began to corrupt Christianity, and God sent the Turks as punishment to them, the White Cowl was passed on to Russia, which, a century before the fall of Constantinople, had been designated by God to become the seat of Orthodox Christianity. Another related medieval doctrine which Fedorov follows in his historiosophy is that of "Moscow, the Third Rome," as formulated by Philotheus: "All Christian realms will come to an end and will unite into the one single realm of our sovereign, that is, into the Russian realm, according to the prophetic books. Both Romes fell, the third endures, and a fourth there will never be." [36]

Fedorov's version of universal history, then, is a strange edifice, constructed from many materials never before hammered into a single building: medieval Russian legends, folklore from the Pamirs, a dozen ideas from the Slavophiles, half a dozen others from the Westernists, futuristic speculations that still read like science fiction, all propped up by encyclopedic erudition and structured around a modified Hegelian dialectic. It is a unique and fascinating edifice—but can it stand? And gigantic as it is, will it hold everybody?

Probably not.

Fedorov is asking us to step out of the history in which we live and to which we contribute, and to step into a new kind of history, in which the past and the future will gradually be incorporated live and whole into a present which will expand until it is eternal. This is like asking fish to turn their river first into a pond, then into a lake, and finally into a universal ocean. Fedorov insists that outside help is unnecessary. People, even as they are presently constituted, can initiate and complete the transformation. As with river fish, so with men, we may be dimly aware that an alternative to life within our familiar current is possible, but how we ourselves are to engineer the passage from what we know to what we can conceive only dimly remains a problem to which Fedorov offers no adequate solution.

Russian nationalism pervades Fedorov's essay on world history. Fedorov's assumption that any international enterprise must begin as a national enterprise seems based on common sense. But thinkers representing other constituencies could draw up lists of "national qualities" every bit as persuasive as Fedorov's list of "Russian instincts" and argue that France, China, Israel, or America alone is capable of initiating and directing the universal project.

Built into Fedorov's project in history is the insistence that we all must become one. What, then, happens to the nationality, group, or individual that ignores the call to unity and insists on going a different way? Presumably, in the project, recalcitrance would be considered a family matter and would be treated as such. Dissidents would be viewed not as criminals but as immature children who must be dealt with firmly but with love. But the Finns, the Czechs, the Hungarians, and others who have experienced Russian acts of "brotherly love" in the world as it is might not be eager to second the nomination of Russia for the position of head brother in the world "as it ought to be."

Fedorov does not consider the question of what differences between individuals and between peoples will remain after worldwide unification. He does say that we will all speak the same language and understand our universal kinship. There will be no discord [*rozn'*]. But does this mean that there will also be no individual or cultural differences? Since Fedorov talks constantly about realizing what we have in common and about the need to eliminate all that separates and differentiates us, we probably should assume that by the end of the project almost everything that now makes one person or group different from all others will have disappeared. In this respect Fedorov's idea of all-unity would differ little from the nightmarish "One State" depicted in Zamiatin's novel, *We*. The impediments to the creation of the one "perfect state in *We* are the same as most of the obstacles the lie between Fedorov's world "as it is" and his world "as it ought to be": individualism, irrationality, the rule of "nature", competition, discord, and individual differences. The most important part of Fedorov's project—the resurrection of ancestors—is not part of Zamiatin's One State. But after the ancestors are resurrected, the "one family" in which Fedorov would have both resurrectors and resurrectees living would seem to differ in few significant respects from the sterile "One State" projected in Zamiatin's novel. Like the moon, Fedorov's utopia of a totally unified humanity might appear lovely—or even inhabitable—when it is half hidden, viewed through mist from a great distance. But the closer we approach it, the less appealing it may turn out to be.

Christ as the Icon of Sonship

In the second part of his essay, "Brotherhood," Fedorov repeats, after a thousand years, Vladimir's "test of the faiths". (I, 54-117). But where Vladimir's task was simply to choose the right faith for the people of Russia, Fedorov attempts to determine which of the world's major faiths could best guide all people in the world. After a consideration of Judaism, Islam, Hinduism, Buddhism, Catholicism, and Protestantism, both in their original form and in their more recent secular variations (Fedorov considers Tolstoyism, for instance, as a secular variant of Buddhism) Fedorov concludes that Orthodox Christianity, Vladimir's choice, remains the best religion not only for Russians but for all mankind.

"There is one true religion, and this is the cult of ancestors. . . ." (I, 46) All religions began as a cult of ancestors, but Orthodox Christianity remains the only religion that gives us proper direction in the exercise of the one true religion. Christianity teaches us not merely to be good men, but to become sons of men, and Christianity guides us not by a code of laws or by a set of procedures to follow through this life, but by the eternal model or icon of Christ, the Son of Man. By following Him, we enter into a perfect relationship with the rest of creation: we turn ourselves into living members of the Icon of the Holy Trinity, the model for the perfect universe.

Viewing ourselves as sons and daughters, rather than as independent entities, we realize that we have a duty to our parents. If our parents are no longer living, then the only way that we can truly be sons and daughters is to restore life to them—to bring them back into the empty spot their departure has left in the Icon.

Christianity, as the religion of sonship and daughterhood, tells us that we are incomplete without our parents. Our world is incomplete without the resurrection of all our ancestors, i.e. without the resurrection not only of our parents but of the parents of our parents, and so all the way back to the original parents of all mankind. "Christianity, inseparable from universal resurrecting, is the full expression of the cult of ancestors." (I, 46)

Faith, for Fedorov, is more than a set of beliefs: "we take the word '*faith*' not in the modern, current, learned-class sense, i.e. not in the sense of certain nations about God, the world and man, according to which the acceptance of a new faith would signify merely a reshuffling of ideas, or the mere adoption of a new idea. The word '*faith*' is taken here in its old sense, in the popular sense, for the Russin people, probably like any other people, and like Vladimir himself, sought and still seek not knowledge or dogma, but a task, which, unless it carried with it an obligation or a promise to carry it out, could not be accepted." (I, 55) The obligation which Christianity imposes on the faithful is the obligation of restoring life to the dead ancestors.

As the perfect Son of Man, Christ is also our model for both the act of resurrecting and for the promise that we too shall be resurrected. In first restoring life to Lazarus, and then returning from the dead Himself, Christ stands for the complete resurrection.

The fault with Christianity as it now exists is that it has not seriously attempted to carry on the task of resurrecting outside the walls of the church. The Orthodox Church has preserved the ritual but has not expanded the ritual to embrace all human activity. Hence, the institution that must lead the project of resurrecting is not the Church, but the temple-school-laboratory-museum, which will turn Christianity into a sacred, scientific, political task that embraces all knowledge and action.

Individually, by becoming Christians, i.e. sons of men, we restore to ourselves the balance and harmony that as individuals in the modern world we have lost. At present, we are torn between the demands of what Fedorov calls the ego [*Ia*] and the non-ego [*Ne Ia*]. Ego is that self-consciousness and self-knowledge that would separate each man from his fellows. Ego is that which makes one wish to be original and unique. But acting against the ego is the non-ego, which is foreign, and which would annihilate the self. Nature, which is behind both, work's through the ego to drive us to death by isolation, and through the non-ego to drive us to death by fusion. Egoism and altruism are the behavior patterns that reflect the divided self. (II, 97-98; 200-201)

The morality which Fedorov advocates is "Neither egoism, nor altruism, but kinship!" (II, 97) And the resolution to the conflict between ego and non-ego is what he calls the generic or kinship ego [*rodnoe ia*]. The generic ego is that in us which recognizes our relationship to others. The generic ego recognizes ourselves in others and others in ourselves. The generic ego refuses to see the world as "I" versus "Not I" and instead sees the world as "We." And it is the generic ego that begins to guide us when we become Christians, or sons of men.

It is only after we recognize ourselves as sons that we may begin to engage in what Fedorov calls "brother-making" [*bratotvorenie*]. At present the most powerful force in us is that which drives us to become fathers and mothers. In the project we must redirect our sexual energy from the creation of new children toward the creation of brothers and sisters. By viewing ourselves as sons, grandsons, and so all the way back to Adam, we realize that we are, ultimately, brothers of all men now alive. But we shall remain brothers only in our minds until we accomplish the actual resurrection of our common ancestors. All talk of the "brotherhood of man" today is empty rhetoric and will remain so until we resurrect our ancestors. Therefore, Christianity is the only way to true brotherhood, and "universal brotherhood" will arrive only after we have undertaken the task of universal sonship.

Orthodox theologians differ on the question of how much Fedorov's project contributes to or deviates from Orthodox tradition.[37] The real question for theologians is whether Fedorov merely spells out ideas that have always been implicit in Christian doctrine, or whether he distorts the entire idea of Christianity by treating spiritual truths as projects for the material world. The problem of Fedorov's general relationship to Orthodox tradition comes clearly into focus when we consider Fedorov's interpretation of Christ's mission. All Christians believe that Christ came to save us. The question is: has Christ already saved us, or, has He merely demonstrated what we ourselves must do to save ourselves? According to one view, supported perhaps by most theologians, we as men could not save ourselves, but God "so loved the world that he gave his only Son, that whoever believes in him should not perish but have eternal life" (John, 3:16) Through Christ, God accomplished for us what we could not accomplish for ourselves. Christ's death saves us from death: in the words of the Orthodox Easter hymn, Christ has "trampled death by death." Fedorov, on the other hand, insists that death has not been overcome, that Christ was sent only to show us that we could and must conquer death ourselves. According to Fedorov, we are not saved, but have only been given a model to follow in the task of our salvation.

Fedorov criticizes the traditional Christian understanding that while we know that we will be resurrected we do not know how this will be accomplished. Belief that God will raise us in ways unknown to us seems to Fedorov nothing more than a passive resignation to an uncertain fate. The idea that God's ways must remain a mystery to man represents to Fedorov our supreme self-delusion. Mysticism then becomes the refuge of those who consider themselves believers but who lack the fortitude to act on their beliefs.

But what Fedorov considers to be passivism and mysticism takes as its base a more realistic view of man and his capabilities than Fedorov based his project on. Fedorov scoffs at the mystic for assigning infinite powers to God, and at the same time Fedorov himself assigns infinite powers to man. The Christian who accepts the Resurrection of Christ as a real and unique event in the past and who anticipates his own resurrection, and the resurrection of all Christian believers, in the future does not claim for himself powers and abilities that he has never encountered among men. He realizes that he is a limited, deathbound creature who can attain eternal life only through a mystery that he has had intimations of but cannot fully comprehend. Fedorov calls such faith "unreal" and rejects it for a faith in man's ability to take actions that even Fedorov admits no man is known to have taken before. The traditional Christian believer knows that people have been imperfect since the Fall, and that, barring miracle, they will remain imperfect until the Second Coming. The traditional Christian believer does not deceive himself about man's capacity for self-perfection. But it is precisely on imperfect man's necessarily imperfect efforts to perfect himself that Fedorov places all his hope. The traditional believer knows that on at least one occasion in the past God acted upon human history—it could happen again. Fedorov does not claim to know of even one instance in the past when a person combined all knowledge and all action in the manner and to the degree that he insists we must all combine knowledge and action in the future. The traditional believer can at least claim a precedent for the event he believes will happen. Fedorov cannot.

Fedorov does not make the mistake of completely humanizing Christ. For Fedorov, as for most traditional Christian believers, Christ is both perfect God and perfect man: the Son of God and the Son of Man. By resurrecting Lazarus and by Himself rising from the dead, Christ did what no man in history has done. The difficult theological question that Fedorov raises—and for which he offers no adequate solution—is just how, without divine intervention, man "as he is" can ever become man "as he ought to be." All Christians believe that Christ "came into the world to save sinners" (1 Tim. 1:15) Fedorov is perhaps distorting the very heart of Christian doctrine by insisting that "to save sinners" means "to show sinners that they can and must save themselves from sin." The idea that Christ's kingdom "is not of this world" (John, 18:36) seems clearly to mean just that, and not, as it would have to be interpreted to fit Fedorov's project: "is not of this world as it is, but is of this world as we shall remake it". Fedorov himself was obviously not trying to depart from Christian doctrine, but was trying rather to discover and universally apply the very heart of Christian teaching. But in his efforts to make Christianity totally relevant to this world, Fedorov may well have misrepresented both Christianity and the nature of this world.

CHAPTER III

FEDOROV IN CONTEXT

Fedorov And His Time

What was Fedorov's "time"? His writings are full of religious and political ideas that could only have seemed archaic to progressive nineteenth century thinkers. Fedorov's reaffirmation of "Orthodoxy, Autocracy, and Nationality"—at a time when "advanced" thinkers were infatuated with Marx, Darwin, or, later, Nietzsche—would surely have placed him in the camp of the "reactionaries", had his thoughts been published at the time they were written. The idea that Moscow was the "Third Rome", or that the Holy Trinity ("indivisible and infusible") remained the icon for the perfect world, belonged to the medieval picture of the world and not to the Russia of aerostats and railroads.

On the other hand, Fedorov's writings were full of ideas that still seem futuristic almost a hundred years after they were written. Space travel, genetic engineering, and the resuscitation of the dead could only have seemed fantasies to most of Fedorov's contemporaries. So it is no wonder that Fedorov was reluctant to try to publish his writings during his lifetime. Editors and readers alike might well have considered Fedorov's vision of the world a strange one indeed: with one eye rolled back toward the middle ages, and with the other focused on an unimaginably distant future, Fedorov would seem to have been looking at everything except what was immediate and present.

But in fact Fedorov was, among other things, very much

a thinker of his own time. No matter how "untimely" his solutions, the problems he addressed were those which troubled all thinking Russians of that day. He carried on a spirited, if one-sided, polemic not only with the "timeless" figures of the past and present, not only with the likes of Plato, Kant, Tolstoi, and Marx, but also with any number of minor figures, with buried writers, obscure academics, and forgotten journalists, with people whose names are now mentioned only in footnotes to Russian intellectual history, but whose writings on the large and small questions of the day filled the newspapers and journals that Fedorov and his contemporaries regularly followed. Those whose ideas won Fedorov's respect or provoked him to attack included, in addition to those whose names are familiar to all students of Russian literature and thought, such lesser figures as: the journalist A. I. Voeikov (II, 259), the naturalist Veresaev (II, 267), the science reporter (not the famous artist) N. Vereshchagin II, 282), the Tolstoian T. M. Bondarev and the populist writer Gleb Uspenskii (II, 362). In discussing the ideas of foreigners, Fedorov names only those of universal stature — the rest he refers to simply as "Englishmen", "socialists", or whatever. But from Kozhevnikov, we learn that that among those to whom Fedorov referred by species rather than by individual name were: G. Barlow (author of *A Lost Mother*, London, 1862), the German chronicler of culture Biese (*Die Entwickelung des Naturgefüls im Mittelalter und in der Neuzeit*, Leipzig, 1888), the Fabian pamphleteer Headlam (*Christian Socialism*, London, 1896), the industrialist Andrew Carnegie (whose *The Gospel of Wealth* appeared in French in 1891), and E. Belfort Bax (*The Religion of Socialism,* London, 1891.)[1]

Fedorov begins many of his essays by reminding the reader of some news item or opinion piece that appeared in a newspaper or journal. Current events, then, served Fedorov sometimes as an inspiration, sometimes as a provocation, and sometimes merely as a pretext for developing a new side of his idea. Fedorov kept abreast not only of the political and social daily news, but of the current state of research in many specialized fields. But in his readings, whether of the evening news or of the classics of literature and philosophy, he moved his eyes up and down the page with a single goal in mind: to discover new evidence, new reasons, or new approaches for the common task. Thus, while Fedorov read the same pages, witnessed the same events, and considered the same questions that his contemporaries did, he saw much that others missed. Others readers, for instance, might have overlooked the connection between a front page story on the threat of famine and a back page story on rainmaking experiments. But to Fedorov, everything fit in. In a later section, we shall consider some of the intellectual and social concerns that link Fedorov to, and distinguish him from, the entire tradition of Russian thought. Now, however, let us take a closer look at the uncommon solutions that Fedorov proposed to a number of the questions most commonly debated in late nineteenth century Russia.

Perhaps no event in Fedorov's time that was intended to unite all Russians split them into more factions and caused more protracted enmity than the 1861 Emancipation of the serfs. In principle, the idea of eventual Emancipation had few opponents. Since Catherine's time, it had appeared inevitable. Those who by the late fifties still did oppose Emancipation were generally either wealthy landowners, whose defenses of the *status quo* could easily be dismissed as based on self-interest, and perhaps some contented serfs whose misgivings could easily be attributed to ignorance. So by the middle of the nineteenth century the question that divided most Russians was not whether the serfs should be freed, but rather when, how, and with how much land. The consensus of historians is that Alexander II chose the best of the many options open to him. By acting from above, he accomplished what could have been accomplished only violently from below. By announcing the act in 1861, and, at the same time, by allowing up to forty-nine years for full implementation, he seemed to satisfy the demands for both precipitate and gradual change. And by establishing that the liberated self would receive approximately half of the land he had been working, and by setting what appeared to be a reasonable plan under which the state would compensate the landlord for his loss and the peasant would gradually pay the state for his gain, Alexander appeared to have arrived at a policy fair to everyone. And the initial reaction, not only on the part of liberals like Turgenev, but also on the part of conservatives like Samarin and radicals like Chernyshevskii, was one of wholehearted approval.

But unanimity dissolved as implementation of the decree proceeded. Some landlords cooperated, others resisted by every device possible. Some clever and enterprising peasants, now able to hire out their labor, took good advantage of the new policy and quickly began to improve their lot. Others found themselves not free but simply uprooted, or bound to the peasant who ran the community instead of to the nobleman who had formerly owned them. For some the new situation was worse than the old. Conservatives, now relieved of whatever guilt they might have felt for being "slaveholders", regarded the Emancipation as a satisfactory conclusion to long-standing problems. Liberals and radicals, however, had greeted the Emancipation as only the grand opening of a long overdue period of fundamental reforms, the start of Russia's long needed transformation. And as the process of land redemption dragged on into the seventies, and even into the eighties, the main split deepened, new splits appeared, and the rhetoric did not grow softer.

Fedorov's position might, at first glance, seem to have been with the "reactionaries." But in fact he aligned himself with neither side. The solution he offered was far more extreme and radical than anything either of the opposing sides could imagine.

Fedorov believed that "freedom to live for oneself alone is a great evil." (I, 195) And on the question of the Emancipation itself, he writes: "The people always stood firmly for autocracy and demanded for themselves not *liberation*, but *service*, but service *immediately* to the tsar and fatherland, the kind of service that the nobility bore before its liberation under Catherine II. And the people held to their amazing and high-principled demand not for liberation but for service, not for freedom but for slavery [*rabstvo*] to God... until the Tsar-Liberator stepped to the throne." (I, 379) Instead of freeing the serfs, then, Fedorov believes that the tsar should have reinstated obligatory service for nobles and peasants alike. Even the intelligentsia should be enlisted in the "slavery" to God and the task. According to Fedorov, before the Emancipation "not only the people were demanding service at that time, but even the intelligentsia; all the best and especially the young members of the intelligentsia, while irrationally demanding freedom, were actually wishing for a task, for service, and one might even say, for a *yoke*." (I, 382) From his experience with Peterson and other young revolutionaries of the sixties, Fedorov clearly understood that the "freedom" the young, self-sacrificing members of the intelligentsia wanted was freedom to serve a great cause. In Fedorov's view, Alexander II had wanted to act in the peasant's interest, but in emancipating him Alexander followed bad advice. Not knowing the Russian peasant, Alexander assumed that the Western course, toward more and more individual liberty, was the one the Russian peasant wanted to take. Alexander's greatest mistake, according to Fedorov, was that he failed to realize that the Russian peasants (and noblemen and intellectuals) lived on a higher spiritual plane than their counterparts in the West. By rescinding Catherine's act freeing the nobility, Alexander II would have truly been the Tsar-Liberator, for he would forever have freed Russia from the fatal Western pursuit of the wrong kind of freedom. (I, 379-384)

Although "Autocracy", the essay containing Fedorov's thoughts on the Emancipation, was probably not written until the late nineties, the ideas expressed are simply a logical extension of the the position he stated to Peterson at their first meeting in 1864.[2] From the start, then, Fedorov believed that Emancipation was not a step in the right direction but merely another necessary step in a direction that had been wrong from the beginning. Since he owned no property and was probably himself the son of a serfwoman, Fedorov cannot be accused of tailoring his principles to fit his own personal or class interests. Thus while it is clear that he did not belong to the camp of the radicals, it should also be clear that he did not belong to the camp of the reactionaries, where some Marxists would like to put him.[3] During a time in which every thinker felt increasing pressure to declare himself "either-or", Fedorov stated his position as "neither-nor." His own solution to the problem was far more radical than that advanced by either of the polarized camps. Fedorov understood that even when the serfs were liberated, men would still be divided into masters and slaves. True freedom and equality could only come not by liberating those regarded as slaves, but by offering voluntary enslavement to all who regarded themselves as free. Where a Westernist thinker might argue that we must all have complete individual liberty before we can begin to think of voluntary universal service, Fedorov would argue precisely the opposite. This is a profoundly Christian and profoundly Russian position, but in Christian Russia of the late nineteenth century, Fedorov appears to have been the only one who tried rationally and consistently to apply this principle to social and political questions. Considered by itself, Fedorov's idea that Alexander II should have enserfed the free instead of freeing the serfs could only have seemed at the time a call for a giant leap backward. But within the context of the resurrection task, Fedorov's idea can be understood as merely a small preliminary step toward not a wild leap but a carefully regulated acceleration forward.

Closely related to—and compounding—the problems that arose from Emancipation was the problem of the emergence of that special new class, which Fedorov called "the learned" but which is usually referred to as the intelligentsia. Some of these people were from the nobility, but most were *raznochinsy*, "people of different ranks," young men and women descended from the peasantry, the clergy, or from the civil servant or merchant class. Some members of this class, like Chernyshevskii, had taken university degrees. Others had been excluded under Nicholas I, and still others attended or dropped out of universities, depending in part on their own inclinations and in part on the state's constantly changing policies toward student activism. When they studied, they usually specialized in economics or the natural sciences. Anatomy was a particularly popular subject. When they wrote, they did so as "literary critics", using literary texts as launching pads for attacks on social conditions in Russia. Their leading spokesmen, young men like Pisarev and Dobroliubov, were gifted polemicists. But, with highly developed critical faculties and utterly undeveloped creative faculties, they were terribly one-sided people. Even those who were formulating the intelligentsia's positions had only the vaguest notions of what kind of new society should replace the old one. And if men like Chernyshevskii, Dobroliubov, and Pisarev, as soft-headed in affirmation as they were rigid in negation, represented the head of the movement, what about the trunk and tail? From testimony recorded during the Karakozov trial, and from memoirs and descriptive accounts of the period,[4] a picture emerges of an entire generation of disappointed idealists, dreamers who believed that in the life of social activism they could find whatever they had not found in ordinary life. They wanted to commit their lives to fight for their idea of the peasant and against their idea of the landlord, but they had almost no knowledge of either peasants or landlords in real life. Disengaged, disaffected, long on conviction, short on experience, these eager but often ill educated young men and women, began first to demand, and then to try to precipitate, in the name of the peasants, an end to the only society they knew, but a society which they had found—and which they demanded that all others find—unjust, oppressive, unresponsive, and outdated. And while Alexander II and his advisors continued to try to mediate between conservatives and liberals, the intelligentsia shifted the battle lines so that in the war for public opinion the real fight was between liberals and radicals. Thus liberals of the older generation, such as Herzen [Gertsen], and Turgenev, now found themselves under attack from both sides and simultaneously losing to the conservatives whatever influence they had had on Alexander and losing to the radicals much of their former influence on public opinion. So as the conservatives increasingly gained Alexander's ear, and as the radicals increasingly gained the public's ear, the gap between what was actually being done and the public's radically informed notions of what should be done grew ever wider.

At the intelligentsia's influence on public opinion became more apparent, the question of just how these young people related to the rest of Russian society became a matter of heated controversy. The conservatives, who loathed them from the start, considered the intelligentsia a threat to all that was sacred in Russia. When Pisarev, in his now famous article of 1865, "Pushkin and Belinskii"[5] set out to demolish the greatest Russian poet, conservative readers were probably not won over by the young author's boldness and wit. The liberals, at first sympathetic, eventually found the young people to be conceited, arrogant, and reckless, but generally objected more strongly to the manner than to the direction of their efforts. The intelligentsia's own opinion of themselves, subsequently accepted by Marxist historians, was that they gave voice to the people's aspirations and were the only bearers of light in this dark period of Russian history. Pisarev wrote: "the moving force of history is intelligentsia, the path of history is marked out by the level of theoretical development of intelligentsia."[6]

In 1862, the appearance of some broadsides addressed "To Young Russia" which advocated a number of terrorist acts including the assassination of Alexander, and, soon after, the outbreak of a series of Petersburg fires believed to have been set by revolutionaries, provided a good excuse for the crackdown on radicalism long advocated by such conservative government officials as Valuiev, the Minister of the Interior. Chernyshevskii's journal, *The Contemporary*, and Pisarev's *The Russian Word* were both shut down; Chernyshevskii himself was sentenced, on very loose evidence, to a twenty-four year prison term in Siberia; and Pisarev was given a two year sentence. During the remainder of Alexander's reign, attempts to suppress the radicals alternated with attempts to suspend further suppression. As a result the intelligentsia was neither totally muzzled nor allowed a free and open voice. Discussion circles treated as conspiracies, became such. Dreamy idealists became fanatical terrorists. The conviction that it was "our side" against "their side", and that all good rested with "us" and all evil with "them" forced people into terrible and impossible choices. Even as early as the mid-sixties, which "side" one was on seemed more important to many people than the reasons for one's choice.

But Fedorov again rejected both sides. He criticized the intelligentsia for looking upon itself as a separate class and for considering itself the highest step on the evolutionary ladder. Nevertheless, he also believed that, having emerged, the intelligentsia now had and important role to play in the universal task. The autocrat, according to Fedorov, should not try to suppress the intelligentsia, but should turn it into a temporary task force to solve scientific problems that stand between us and the resurrection. The intelligentsia, as a class, is not capable of directing even itself, much less the fate of Russia. Left by itself, the intelligentsia will only continue to do what it does best: question whatever is decided, and criticize whatever actions are taken. The intelligentsia as a class has gained power and influence only by criticizing, i.e. by demonstrating its superiority over, whatever falls into its view. By directing the energy of this class of eternal critics toward the one object of knowledge that has never been criticized, i.e. the fact of death, the autocrat can put otherwise destructive energy to productive use. Fedorov, then, would assign the intelligentsia to attack death instead of wasting all their brilliant fury upon the ideas and actions of their fellow men. Instead of asking *why what exists exists*, the intelligentsia should turn all its intelligence to the question "*why does what is living die?*" (I, 12.)

Fedorov's description of the present "learned class" is similar to Pisarev's description of "aestheticians" and "men of letters." [7] In contradistinction to those who have separated themselves from the people, to those who have separated thought from feeling, Pisarev describes the "new man", whom he calls "the thinking proletariat."

> The basic features of the new type of man I have thus far spoken of may be formulated in three main propositions which are very closely interrelated.
> I. New people have acquired a passion for work for the benefit of society.
> II. The private benefit of new people coincides with the benefit for society and their selfishness contains the broadest love of humanity.
> III. New people's reason is in perfect harmony with their feelings because neither reason nor feeling are distorted by chronic enmity for the rest of people.

This may be summed up briefly as follows: new people is the name given to workers who think, who love their work. So there is no reason to be angry with them.[8]

But one difference between Fedorov's "task force" and Pisarev's "thinking proletariat" is that Pisarev believes that his new men already exist, that Chernyshevskii depicted them in *What is to be Done?*, and that they are already working for what he vaguely calls "the good of mankind." Fedorov believes that even Pisarev's "new people" remain separated from the people, that the intelligentsia has not truly begun to view itself as a temporary task force because it has not yet accepted the common task of resurrection. Moreover, where Pisarev speaks vaguely about work for the common good, Fedorov insists that one and only one task can ultimately improve our lives. Here, then, as elsewhere, Fedorov treats problems of contemporary interest not by aligning himself with one of the opposing sides, but by incorporating ideas from each side into a solution considered by neither.

On the question of whether Russia should have more railroads or no railroads, Fedorov argued that each village should develop and operate its own fleet of dirigibles (I, 283). On the question of whether during the war of Balkan liberation, Russia should have seized Constantinople, Fedorov took the position that if Russia had demonstrated that she was prepared to lead the world in the common task, then the allies might have permitted her to annex the city peacefully. But since Russia entered the war for the wrong reasons, she succeeded only in alienating the Christian nations that she should have been able to unite. By failing to fight for the right cause, Russia allowed the world's dividing point, Constantinople, to be once again a point over which potential friends acted as bitter enemies. Russia's designs on Constantinople turned all Christian nations of the world against her instead of uniting them behind her. (I, 200-201)

On the question of how the government could best aid the victims of the famines of the early nineties, Fedorov took the position that in the long run only regulation of meteorological and all other natural forces could prevent the recurrence of famine. And when, toward the end of the century, drug addiction and hypnotism began to be looked upon as problems about which something should be done, Fedorov pointed out that if everyone joined the task of resurrection the apparent need for such escapes from the world as opium and mesmerism would quickly disappear. (I, 13)

Throughout Fedorov's work we find assumptions that have lost or are beginning to lose the wide base of acceptance that they enjoyed in the late nineteenth century. Fedorov's theories on race, for instance, follow the general line established by such now discredited thinkers as Johann Blumenbach and Arthur de Gobineau.[9] All races have certain, definite attributes. In history, one race, one people has evolved whose duty is to lead all others. In Fedorov's plan, of course, we are not to be led by Germanic masters, but by Slavic servants. As heirs to the ancient Zendo-Aryan principle of struggle against evil, the Slavs are our natural leaders in our universal struggle against nature. (I, 252-257; 346-348)

Similarly rooted in the nineteenth century are Fedorov's assumptions about language. The studies of Grimm, Rask, and other linguists had recently demonstrated that many apparently unrelated languages were, in fact, of one family. "Grimm's Law"[10] established the regularity with which consonants from the Indo-European parent language changed during the development of the various Germanic languages. Leaping far ahead, Fedorov assumed that if Grimm had discovered the laws that linked one Germanic language to another, then it would only be a matter of time before some new linguist would discover the laws that bound all languages together. If no one had yet discovered that Chinese and Dutch were both descended from the same parent language, then the task of future linguists would be to make that discovery. (I, 254-256) Although no one would claim that enough is known about all the languages in the world to dash Fedorov's hope absolutely and forever, the likelihood that we will soon discover a Grimm's law applicable to all languages on earth seems smaller now than it seemed in the first decades after Grimm's discoveries.

Another assumption that Fedorov shared with many thinkers of the last century is that mass education is the solution to most social problems. The radical generation of the sixties, as one member later wrote in her memoirs, "believed passionately in the all-powerful significance of the natural sciences, in the great power of education... and with many of them this faith extended to childish naivete."[11] Chernyshevskii and Pisarev, despite their reputations as "nihilists" both propagandized for the education of the peasants, believing that education, especially scientific education, would cure Russian society, bring an end to evil, and result in monumental changes for the better. Pisarev wrote:

> There exists only one evil among mankind—ignorance; for this evil there is only one remedy—science; however, this remedy must be taken, not in homeopathic doses, but by the bucketful, by the cask. This remedy taken timidly increases the sufferings of the sick organism. The remedy taken boldly leads to a radical recovery. But human cowardice is so great that a saving remedy is considered poisonous.[12]

As we have seen, Fedorov insists that the gap between "learned" and "unlearned" is greater than that between rich and poor. And like Chernyshevskii and Pisarev, Fedorov believes that science should have a major place in the curriculum. But there the similarities end. For Fedorov, science must not replace religion and art, but must be wholly integrated with all other forms of knowledge and action. And Fedorov's idea of "universal education" is not simply that everyone must go to school. "Knowledge of all by all" will not be possible until we resurrect the dead. Science must be studied not simply to "transform society", but to transform the entire universe into a living icon of the Holy Trinity.

And as in his view toward education, so in his view toward art, Fedorov shares a number of assumptions with the radicals, but develops his idea toward different ends. With Chernyshevskii, whose 1855 master's thesis "The Aesthetic Relations of Art to Reality" is the definitive statement of the radicals' position, Fedorov agrees that art should be didactic, that art is inferior to reality, and that a work of art should be judged by its potential for improving socity. But, again, where Chernyshevskii's idea of the good is general and vague, Fedorov's is specific. Art must first give us images of the task of resurrecting, and finally, merged with science, religion, and all other forms of knowledge and action, must become the very act of resurrecting. All our art will be used to remake ourselves and the universe.

One of the great debates of Fedorov's time had to do with the relative importance of science and art. In *Fathers and Sons,* Turgenev illustrated this conflict in the confrontation between Bazarov, the spokesman for the new "scientism" of the 1860's, and Pavel Petrovich Kirsanov, the spokesman for the "aestheticism" of the 1840's. Kirsanov quotes Pushkin and views nature as a "temple"; Bazarov quotes from Ludwig Büchner's *Kraft und Stoff* (1855) and views nature as a "laboratory." For many radicals in life, as for Bazarov in fiction, the affirmation of science required a rejection of art. To respect the works of Darwin, Jacob Moleschott, and Karl Vogt meant to have contempt for the works of Pushkin, Shakespeare, and Schiller. Fedorov, of course, not only rejects this dichotomy, but also the dichotomy between science and religion. All three have the same task and the same goal, and as all three advance toward the goal the differences between them will disappear.

Fedorov was no doubt influenced by the "nihilist" worship of science. But he was probably also inspired by the great advances that Russian science made during his lifetime. D. I. Mendeleev (1843-1907), I. I. Mechnikov (1845-1916), I. P. Pavlov (1849-1936), V. V. Dokuchaev (1846-1903), I. M. Sechenov (1829-1905) and others made Russia in the second half of the nineteenth century one of the world's great centers of scientific achievement. Fedorov's heady speculations about the future of science, then, were based in part on the extraordinary breakthroughs that Russian scientists in widely different fields had made during his day. If such discoveries could be made when only a small portion of the population had received an education, then the potential for scientific achievement when everyone received training in science seemed to Fedorov all but limitless.

Fedorov himself did not claim to have a specialist's knowledge in any of the natural sciences, and the more detailed his attempts to describe just how scientists might solve certain problems—for example, in his suggestion that great cone-shaped devices mounted at strategic points on the earth might enable us to liberate our planet from its solar orbit and thus allow us to steer the earth on a course of our own choosing—the more ridiculous his ideas might seem to people who know something about the field. Nevertheless, Fedorov did propose a number of tasks for scientists that scientists themselves no longer regard as foolish: solar energy should replace the burning of fossil fuels (I, 54), new artificial organs should replace our old ones (I, 283), we must find substitutes for the food we now eat (I, 317), and we must cease to view nature as a field for us to exploit and must start to view her as an ecological system which we have a responsibility to maintain and regulate (I, 278). In general, then, Fedorov looked upon the scientific achievements of his day as a token of even greater achievements that awaited scientists in the future. By the time Fedorov was seventy, discoveries had been made that had not even been imaginable when he was twenty. Fedorov reasoned that if scientists knew what they should be looking for, major breakthrough might be more frequent. As a projector of goals, Fedorov was a man of great foresight. That even now many of the goals that he projected in the last century have not begun to be approached may well indicate just how far ahead he was looking rather than how little about science he actually knew.

As Professor Chizhevskii has shown in his valuable study, *Hegel in Russia*,[13] no major Russian thinker of the second half of the nineteenth century escaped the enormous influence of Hegel. Fedorov was no exception. Although the calls Hegel "the philosopher bureaucrat" (II, 86) and criticizes him for having tried to organize all that exists into an idea instead of into an active task, Fedorov nevertheless pays Hegel the compliment of imitation, and whether consciously or unconsciously, organizes his own discussion of history as a project to correspond roughly to Hegel's discussion of history as a self-realizing idea. To Fedorov, Hegel was "the last philosopher-thinker" (II, 88)—after him we must become "philosopher-activists". And although Hegel himself did not always use the terms "thesis, antithesis, and synthesis" to describe the path of *Geist* through history, Hegel's Russian followers did, and Fedorov, like many Russians of his time and since, saw dialectical process at work everywhere. Projectivism is for Fedorov the synthesis of idealism and materialism, kinship is the synthesis of egoism and altruism, Russian *sobornost'* the synthesis of oriental fatalism and occidental individualism, etc. Fedorov's entire system, "Supramoralism", is termed "the universal synthesis" [*vseobshchii sintez*]. To a point, then, Fedorov's entire philosophy can be viewed as an attempt to oppose an active, Russian task to Hegel's German idea. Fedorov believed that with Hegel, thought by itself had reached its limits, and that to go further thought would now have to unite with action. Future philosophy should not simply attempt to give us new ideas about the present and past, but should attempt to provide us with blueprints for a rational future.

Marx, of course, had already reached the same conclusions. And by the 1880's, when Plekhanov and others began to introduce Marx's ideas to Russia, Russians seemed ready for a philosophy of activism. But, strange as it might at first seem, Fedorov saw in Marxism not a philosophy of action, but a doctrine of unacceptable "moral quietism." He writes: "The philosophical doctrine of Marxism is a moral quietism, an advocacy of inaction and will-lessness.... The Marxists demand not cooperation; they demand instead only mutual opposition through the dispossession of all and the destruction of village handicraft and light industry." (II, 323) By "quietism" Fedorov did not mean that Marxism was a call to no action, but rather that the action Marxism called men to was not in opposition to, but in conformity with, the forces of division and destruction inherent in nature. So, in Fedorov's view, Marxism calls only for opposition within mankind, and not for the opposition of all mankind to nature. Marx's "activism", then, is, ultimately, "quietism"—men struggle actively against each other but remain passive against the real enemy, nature. Another major point of divergence between Fedorov's thought and Marxist philosophy is in the Marxist insistence that we are basically economic creatures. Fedorov attacks the capitalist system with the same arguments that a Marxist might use, but he always insists that economic conditions are a reflection of spiritual and religious conditions, where the Marxist would argue the opposite. Like Weber after him, Fedorov understood capitalism to be a secular form of Protestantism. Socialism, for Fedorov, is a secular form of western Catholicism. The same conflicts are continually present in Fedorov's vision of history. The combatants fight under new names on new fields of battle for constantly diminishing stakes. Battles between faiths diminish to battles between states, which in turn diminish to battles between economic systems. More lives are lost each time, and more of the earth is destroyed, but for smaller causes. Capitalism (understood as economic individualism) is neo-Protestantism, which in turn is neo-paganism. Socialism (economic collectivism) is neo-Catholicism, which in turn is neo-Judaism. Fedorov's answer to Marxism, then, is not some other economic system, but Russian Orthodoxy, which has retained the spiritual center lost by the faiths that have degenerated into economic systems. Where Marxists held that economic differences could only be resolved through class struggle, Fedorov held that they could only be resolved through the unification of all classes of men in the task of resurrecting all our ancestors.

In Nietzsche, who seemed to many Russians at the turn of the century the only real alternative to Marx, Fedorov found a thinker who attacked but could not himself escape the fundamentally erroneous course of Western thought. "Nietzsche's great contribution is in his call to pass beyond the borders of good and evil. His mistake is that instead of planting a tree of life beyond these borders, he plants a tree of death." (II, 117)

Fedorov was sympathetic to Nietzsche's admiration of will and power, but he believed that Nietzsche failed to consider the goal of that will and power. Nietzsche stands for the glorification of adolescence. The great man, for Fedorov, is not the one who seeks to be the Overman, but the one who seeks to become a son of man and who seeks to enlist the support of his brothers in the task of restoring life to the fathers.

As the end of the nineteenth century approached, Fedorov shared with most of his compatriots a sense that more than just another century was coming to a close. He believed that European civilization as a whole was about to destroy itself, and that a new age, which he hoped would be led by Russians, was about to begin. With Solov'ev, he recognized the threat of a new violent force from Asia. But where Solov'ev prophesied new Golden Hordes, and "Panmongolism", Fedorov emphasized the threat from nature. The desert was the real enemy, and the task of stopping the growth of the desert would be the task that united Russia and China. By working together against their common enemy, the wasteland that separated them, Russians and Chinese could begin to recognize their natural brotherhood. Fedorov placed great importance on the discovery, by archeologists, of an ancient inscription on a Christian monument in central China. According to the inscription, the Christianity brought by Syrian missionaries in the seventh or eighth century had made a very favorable impression on the Chinese. The statement to the effect that not even among the Buddhist priests could such holy men as these Christians be found served as proof to Fedorov that Orthodox Christianity, spread with love, could still succeed, even with the people who at the moment Fedorov was writing were cursing and trying to drive from their land the Christians who preached with guns. The link between the Chinese and Orthodox Christians was love for the ancestors. Presented as the task of resurrecting the ancestors, Orthodox Christianity could not fail in China.[14]

Fedorov's approach to the "eastern problem" then, like his approach to other problems, shows that he shared the major concerns of his contemporaries, and was, at least in that respect, very much a thinker of his own time. But the solutions that he proposed to contemporary problems evince a power of hindsight and foresight uncommon even in that past-scanning and future-seeking day. His stature long underrated, Fedorov deserves to be recognized, with Dostoevskii, Tolstoi, and Solov'ev, as one of the giants of his age. His flaws, like theirs, seem large when compared to the flaws of lesser figures, but small when we consider what he undertook. Like his great contemporaries, Fedorov sank his roots deep into his own time, grew high above it, and spread far beyond it. At the same time, utterly unlike anyone else, Fedorov surrounded himself with a cloud that has broken only intermittently and that may not disperse entirely for centuries.

Fedorov And Russian Thought

Berdiaev wrote of Fedorov: "I do not know a more characteristically Russian thinker." [15] No matter what conclusions one may finally reach concerning the feasibility, or even the desirability of Fedorov's project, one must, I think, agree with Berdiaev that probably no thinker who ever lived between the Bug and the Pacific was more thoroughly or characteristically "Russian" than Fedorov. His project is, among other things, a grand synthesis of any number of the previously divergent intellectual tendencies discussed in the standard histories of Russian thought. He combines the religious and anti-Western views of the Slavophiles with the scientism of the Nihilists, the broad humanistic concerns of the Westernizers, and the faith in simple people that characterized the Populists. Berdiaev has found much in Fedorov that prefigures Russian Communism.[16] Zenkovskii has found traces of the occultism popular among Russian freemasons of the eighteenth century.[17] Both Odoevskii's utopianism and Chaadaev's dismay that Russia has not taken her role in world history find their way into Fedorov's synthesis. And in Fedorov alone, among Russian thinkers, do we find a single idea sufficiently comprehensive to encompass both the Christian messianism of the sixteenth century Monk Philotheus, who formulated the "Third Rome" doctrine, and the cosmic messianism of Konstantin Tsiolkovskii, the rocket pioneer who believed it was our destiny to populate the stars. And looking even farther back than the middle ages, we may also find in Fedorov something of the ancient cult of ancestors that Fedotov calls the Pre-Christian Slavic "religion of the gens," [18] the veneration of the *rod*, the eternal kinship community. The idea that the father's identity is an essential part of the son's, an idea which Fedorov places at the center of his thought (e.g. I, 319), is at least as old as the Russian patronymic. The roots of Fedorov's thought, then, extend back through the centuries to the very sources of Russian mental life. But before bogging down in the dark, humid fertility of the Earth Mother cults, it might be best to turn to individual thinkers whose works lie closer to Fedorov's time, if not to his mind.

Despite Fedorov's attempt to establish the seventeenth century thinker Krizanich, or Crisanius [19] as the first father of both the Slavophiles and Westernizers (II, 191-192), it is only in the nineteenth century, with Chaadaev, that the tradition of Russian philosophy to which Fedorov belongs can truly be said to begin. Chaadaev, most historians agree, formulated the major questions that subsequent thinkers struggled with throughout the rest of the nineteenth century: what is Russia's role in world history? how is freedom to be reconciled with duty, and the individual with the whole? what is the meaning of *unity*? what is special about Orthodox Christianity?

In Chaadaev, we find the seeds of both the Westernizer and the Slavophile movements: on the one hand, the idea that Russia must look to Europe for the ideas she should live by, and on the other, that what culture Russia has she owes to the ideals embodied in the Orthodox Church. In Chaadaev also, we find many of the special features that characterize the entire tradition of Russian thought. Some of the adjectives that various commentators have chosen to describe these qualities are: "man-centered", "non-academic", "ontological", "historiosophical", "eschatological", and "totalitarian." And from Chaadaev, through Fedorov, and even into this century, Russian philosophy continually evinces these qualities.

The anthropocentric orientation of Russian thought, especially apparent in Fedorov, insists that man himself—and not, say, the question of God's existence, or the question of what knowledge is—be the focus. In Russian thought, the question of God's existence or non-existence more often than not turns into the question of the human consequences of belief or disbelief.

That no major Russian philosopher was an academician

(at least not for long) can be explained in part by the fact that for most of the nineteenth century philosophy was excluded from the curriculum of all Russian universities. During the periods when instruction in philosophy was permitted, the course topics allowed ranged from Plato to Aristotle. Hence, from the 1830's on, people seriously interested in philosophy either studied by themselves, exchanged philosophical letters, or met in small, informal discussion groups. And since philosophy could not be a profession, it had to be an irrepressible passion. So well into this century, the major contributions to Russian thought continued to be made not by trained academicians but by gifted amateurs: imaginative writers, literary and social critics, at least one ex-horseguardsman, expelled teachers, spiritual pilgrims, and unfrocked priests. That Chaadaev was officially certified a madman, and that Fedorov worked most of his life as a librarian in no way disqualified them from the mainstream of traditional Russian philosophy.

Moreover, not only in the nineteenth century but throughout the history of Russian thought, even to the present day, the line between literature and philosophy has never been as clearly drawn as in other countries. Philosophical *belles-lettres* and belletristic philosophy have, in Russia, been more nearly the rule than the exception. From Baratynskii, Gogol', Tiutchev, Dostoevskii, and Tolstoi, on through Blok, Viacheslav Ivanov, Solzhenitsyn and Brodskii, writers whose talents are primarily literary have made and continue to make important contributions to Russian philosophy. And from Chaadaev, Kireevskii, and Khomiakov, through Solov'ev, Leont'ev, Shestov and Rozanov, thinkers whose chief gift is for speculation have also demonstrated considerable literary talent. And even those who have lacked genuine literary talent, such as Chernyshevskii, have nevertheless often struggled manfully toward the ideal of thought in art. Until the end of the century, no major philosopher except Solov'ev wrote books of philosophy. Besides the novel, the poem, and the book review, the favorite *genre* was the philosophical letter: Ivan the Terrible to Kurbskii, Chaadaev to "Madam", Khomiakov to Samarin, Gogol' to "Friends", Belinskii to Gogol', Gershenzon to Ivanov and Ivanov to Gershenzon.[20] Solzhenitsyn's 'Letter to the

Rulers of Russia" is the most notable recent contribution to this long tradition. One reason, then, for much of the immediacy, the accessibility, and the existential, "man-centered" quality of the Russian tradition of speculation may be that in Russia philosophy remained the work of men of letters and did not become the work of professionals, or of men of numbers, until well after the October Revolution. In Russia, philosophy remained an art until the dialectical materialists ruled it a science. And Chaadaev is the main source of this tradition.

Zenkovskii writes: "With the exception of a small group of orthodox Kantians, Russian philosophers have tended in the solution of epistemological problems to *ontologism*, i.e. the recognition that cognition is not the primary and defining principle in man. In other words, knowing is recognized as only a part and function of our activity in the world; it is a certain event in the life-process, and thus its meaning, its tasks, and its possibilities are determined by our general relation to the world." [21]

Equally important as the questions that Chaadaev does ask are the questions that he does not ask. And one of the major questions that he is *not* interested in is: how do we know? Much more important to Chaadaev, and to all the major Russian thinkers through Fedorov, are the questions of *what* we know, and *what we do* with what we know. Especially from the middle of the century on, the unprinted subtitle, if not indeed the printed title itself, of nearly every piece of speculative writing was not some variant of "How do we know this table is real?", but, rather, some variant of *Chto Delat'?*—what is to be done? Even when not explicitly stated, it was at least understood that knowledge must be accompanied by action. Fedorov's project to unify thought and action offers probably the most comprehensive solution ever proposed by a Russian to this traditional Russian question.

The meaning of history, and Russia's role in world history, is another of the "accursed questions" that Chaadaev included on his agenda for debate. His position was that *unity* was the principle of universal history, and that Russia, by remaining isolated from the rest of the world, had contributed nothing to history. Connected to Russia's role in world history is the significance of her geographical position. Situated between East and West, or, in Chaadaev's memorable phrase, "with one elbow leaning on China and the other on Germany" [22] Russia is in a position to comprehend and unify the opposite spiritual principles of Orient and Occident. Russia should be the bridge, the reconciliation between Europe and Asia—instead, according to Chaadaev, she has remained a gap, an empty space, a land that divides rather than joins. Not only has Russia contributed nothing—she is actually standing in the way of universal history, whose principle is unity.

The Slavophiles accepted Chaadaev's thesis that Russia has remained outside world history, but viewed this isolation as a virtue rather than as a defect. By her isolation, Russia had been spared from the hell of European individualism. While the West was now crumbling, Russia remained intact. For the Slavophiles, as for Chaadaev, total unity is desirable, and division, isolation, and individualism are undesirable. But where Chaadaev argued that Russia stood against the principle of unity, the Slavophiles insisted that she stood for it, and that the West stood for every kind of disunity. The Slavophile position was that Europe should turn to Russia for guidance, not the reverse.[23]

But the Slavophiles did not specify just how Russia was to unite the world. They emphasized the differences between Europe and Russia and opposed the positive Slavic principle to the negative Eastern and Western principles that surround it. Fedorov began where the Slavophiles ended. He specified not only what "lesson" Russia must teach the world (Chaadaev's question), but also just how this lesson was to be taught. In Fedorov, the task is to universalize, to activate, the Russian qualities that the Slavophiles merely attempted to define. Fedorov wants a Russia whose elbows will not only rest on Germany and China, but whose hands will reach around the globe and whose fingers will stretch out into the expanses of sidereal space.

The Russian emphasis on eschatology, discussed at length by Berdiaev,[24] can be seen in the constant preoccupation of Russian thinkers with the Kingdom at the end of history. Whether it is the Kingdom of God or perfect Communism, most Russian thinkers have insisted that something awaits us at the end of history—and awaits not just individuals, but the entire human race. For Chaadaev, "On the day of the final achievement of the work of redemption, all hearts and minds will constitute but one sentiment and one thought, and all the walls which separate peoples and communions will fall to the ground." [25] History moves from diversity toward unity, and at the end of history we will all be of one mind. This interpretation of the Kingdom of God was adopted by most of the Westernizers. The unity of all mankind was the ultimate end toward which we should all direct all our efforts. The Westernists de-emphasized the Divine and emphasized the human part in the movement of history toward its goal. The first major Slavophiles, Kireevskii, Khomiakov, Samarin, and Aksakov wrote not so much about the Kingdom of God at the end of history as about the earthly prefigurations of that Kingdom: the Orthodox Church and the Russian sense of *sobornost'*. Only later, in such thinkers as Berdiaev and Bulgakov, did the eschatological implications of the idea of *sobornost'* receive full treatment. But through the interpretations of these twentieth century religious thinkers, we may see that the position implicit, but not fully developed, in the writings of the early Slavophiles is that what awaits us at the end of history will depend more nearly on God's grace than on our own efforts. The way to the unity of all mankind has already been given to us: it is in the Orthodox Church and in the Russian *sobor*. The essential Slavophile position is that the door to the Kingdom has always been open in Russia. People need only enter the Church. The Slavophiles did not preach a holy Slavic crusade against the West, but merely wished to establish that the door has been and still was open. The difference between the implicit eschatology of, say, a Herzen and a Khomiakov was not very great. Both believed that mankind would be unified at the end of history. For Herzen, the path to ultimate unity was through Western, humanistic progress; for Khomiakov, through the already existing Russian Church.

The real differences came later, as the Westernist line moved through materialism and the Slavophile line through mysticism, and when the spokesmen for the opposed positions were no longer personal acquaintances, like Herzen and Khomiakov, but men like Plekhanov and Solov'ev who may not even have been aware of each other's existence, so different were their spheres of interest and activity. Both mystics and materialists believed in paradise on earth. For a mystic this could mean, as it did for the boy Markel in *The Brothers Karamazov*, that the Kingdom of God was already with us, that paradise was all around us, if only we would see it so. The Kingdom at the end of history is even now visible to the "seer"—the life of pure bliss, life in eternity, which we shall all know at the end of all time, can already be discovered within each of us. The problem is not one of material progress, but of vision. We are looking the wrong way—look the right way, and we will be filled with the mysterious bliss of Sophia, Holy Wisdom. For the materialists, paradise on earth was not to be discovered by spiritual insight but rather was to be attained through socio-economic development. God is out of the picture: paradise is simply the last, permanent stage of human evolution, the perfect society.

Fedorov's paradise combines all of these ideas. It will be through the Church (redefined as the temple-school-observatory-museum) of Orthodox Russians (resurrectors), but it will also be accomplished by human effort. Mankind (including the dead) will be unified. Paradise already exists in our minds as a vision (a project), but must be realized for all of us, and be realized within the material world. The project will be both sacred and secular, both spiritual and material, both by God's will and through human effort. Fedorov's idea, then, of the Kingdom at the end of history is, probably without question, the fullest and most comprehensive expression of Russian eschatologism to be found in the entire tradition of Russian thought.

But if eschatologism is only one of several leading characteristics of Russian philosophy, it is the very heart of Russian Orthodoxy. For no idea is more important to Orthodox theologians and Orthodox believers than the idea of the Resurrection. Easter, not Christmas, is the great holiday for the Orthodox. Christ's Resurrection is viewed by the Orthodox as an occasion for even more joyful celebration than His birth. For the Orthodox, the central fact about the time we live in is that it is the time between Christ's Resurrection and ours. As Father Alexander Schmemann explains, in a brief guide to the meaning of each day of Holy Week: "Every year, on Great Saturday, after this morning service, we wait for the Easter night and the fulness of Paschal joy. We know that they are approaching—and yet how slow is this approach, how long is this day! But is not the wonderful quiet of Great Saturday the symbol of our very life in this world? Are we not always in this "middle day," waiting for the Pascha of Christ, preparing ourselves for the day without evening of His Kingdom?" [26]

Resurrection is also an important theme in Russian literature. The unfinished second part of Gogol's *Dead Souls* was intended to illustrate, metaphorically, how through faith in Christ the dead souls of all Russians could be resurrected. And Dostoevskii's narrator, on leaving the "House of the Dead" ends the novel by proclaiming that he has been resurrected. Raskol'nikov, at the end of *Crime and Punishment*, ready now to pay for his sin, is left on the verge not yet of full resurrection, but of gradual "renewal", of gradual "regeneration", and "of his passing from one world into another, of his initiation into a new unknown life." [27] But Nekhliudov, the hero of Tolstoi's *Resurrection*, is left not only on the verge, but over the line and actually in the state that at least Tolstoi is willing to consider "resurrection." Having spent the night reading the Bible, Tolstoi's hero undergoes a change of mind and heart: "A perfectly new life dawned that night for Nekhliudov, not because he had entered into new conditions of life, but because everything he did from that night on had a completely new and different significance from before. The future alone will show how this new era of his life will end." [28] Apparently Tolstoi was ready to let this pass as his understanding of resurrection. But vague and indefinite as their notions of resurrection were, Gogol' Dostoevskii, and Tolstoi nevertheless understood that some form of resurrection must follow whatever ordeals their heroes experience. By the appearance of Christ at the end of "The Twelve" (1918), and by the juxtaposition of words from the Easter service and revolutionary slogans in "Christ Has Risen" (also 1918), Blok hints and Belyi does more than hint that the Symbolists identified the October Revolution with the Resurrection and Christ's Second Coming. So in placing the Resurrection at the center of his task Fedorov gave focus and direction to an idea that has always had a deep, if not always clear, meaning for Russians.

And in a fascinating article on the tenacity of the idea of immortality in Russia,[29] Peter Wiles tells us that the theme of resurrection in Russian religion and literature is paralleled by a secular, even materialist conviction that something in us is still immortal. As he points out, Marxism in itself accepts that we shall all die. But: "When communist atheism is superimposed upon Russian Orthodoxy, a quite remarkable mysticism results."[30] Lenin's body is preserved and put on view as if he were an Orthodox saint, and posters proclaiming that "Lenin lived, Lenin lives, Lenin will live" and that "Lenin is more alive than all who are alive"[31] line the streets of atheist Moscow. Moreover, Wiles reports instances in which perfectly atheistic Soviet citizens toast their dead comrades as if they were still present, in the manner of the old Slavic Radunitsa festival, in which the dead ancestors were supposed to reappear for the feast celebrated in their memory. In conversations with communist officials Wiles finds that the most difficult idea for them to accept in the materialist system was the idea of non-existence after death. Wiles then goes on to describe the many attempts by Russian scientists—some of them qualified and respected specialists, others quacks—to discover the secret to prolonged, and perhaps even endless, life. Whether these scientists did or did not know Fedorov's ideas— most of them worked in Paris in the twenties and thirties— is not here important. What is important is that in his insistence that we must learn to extend our own lives forever and to restore life to all our dead ancestors, Fedorov again gave definitive expression to an idea that has at times seemed an obsession of Russians.

Another characteristic of Russian philosophy barely mentioned by Berdiaev, but of great importance, is the "totalitarian" cast of much Russian thought. Partial solutions, partial unity, a balance between opposing forces simply will not do. All must be united, one principle must hold. The individual must take his place in the whole, whether by "submission" as in Chaadaev, "consent" as in Khomiakov, or "freely" as in Fedorov. The choice, to be sure, remains with the individual, but not to join is clearly the wrong choice.

Chaadaev believes that the essential truth of Christianity is that its doctrine is founded upon "the supreme principle of unity" and that the true spirit of religion is contained "in the idea of the fusion of all the moral forces in the world into a single thought, a single feeling, and in the progressive establishment of a social system or *Church* which will make truth reign among men. Any other doctrine, by the mere fact of its separation from the original doctrine, rejects the sublime invocation of the Saviour. . . and does not want that God should rule on earth."[32] Moreover, the virtue of Christianity is that it can "captivate" men whether they wish it or not. "Nothing more clearly indicates the divine origin of this religion than this aspect of absolute universality which allows it to penetrate people's souls in all possible ways, to possess souls without their being aware of it, to dominate them, to subjugate them, even when they resist it the most."[33] In another place, Chaadaev suggests that our goal as creatures endowed with reason should be to rid ourselves of freedom: "There is no reason which is not obedient reason. But that is not all. Does man do anything his life long but seek to submit to something? First, he finds in himself a power which he recognizes as different from that which determines motion external to him: he feels himself alive. As the same time he recognizes that his power is limited: he feels his own nothingness. Next he perceives that the power external to him dominates him and that he must submit to it. This is his whole life. From the moment that he begins to reason, these two notions—one of an internal and imperfect power, the other of an external and perfect power—come on their own to fill his mind."[34] And he asks: "What would happen if man could make himself so submissive that he wholly rid himself of freedom? Clearly, according to what we have said, this would be the highest degree of human perfection. Every movement of his soul would then be produced by the principle which produced all other movements of the world. Thus, instead of being separated from nature, as he now is, man would fuse with it. Instead of the feeling of his own will, which separates him from the general order of things, which makes him a being apart, he would find the feeling of universal will, or, what is the same thing, the intimate feeling, the profound awareness of his real relation to the whole of creation." [35]

For Chaadaev, then, individual freedom leads to isolation, to separation from nature. Only by "abdicating his fatal actual *self*" can man recover "the idea, the vast personality, all the power of his pure intelligence in his innate bond with the rest of things." [36]

Chaadaev, then, establishes the position on the relationship between the individual and the whole that will dominate traditional Russian thought. It is not only against Chernyshevskii or against the "anthill" of contemporary socialists that Dostoevskii's Underground Man insists on retaining the right to say that twice-two is five—he is railing against the entire tradition of "totalitarian" Russian thought, which contains not only vulgar materialists but lofty idealists like Chaadaev and the dogged "projectivist" Fedorov as well.

Chadaev called his ideal "unity," Khomiakov called his "*sobornost'*," Solov'ev calls his "total unity," and Fedorov his "multi-unity" or, sometimes, "all-unity" (*mnogoedinstvo* and *vseedinstvo*, but not, Fedorov insists, *vsëedinstvo*—"unity of everything") Just what is to be unified, and by what, varies from thinker to thinker. Chaadaev emphasized unity of mind, unity of idea, and his unifying agent is the Western Christian Church. Kireevskii emphasizes the "wholeness' of the individual person, which can be attained only through "consent" or, as Khomiakov posits by participation in the spiritual concensus of *sobornost'*. For Solov'ev "total-unity" generally means the unity of God and the world, and the unifying agent is human consciousness. Man inwardly unites the "world-soul" and the divine Logos by his consciousness. Moreover, mankind as a whole forms an organic unit, a "pan-human organism" — and here love is the binding principle. For Fedorov, as we have seen, the Holy Trinity is the model for the project of universal unification, and the unity of mankind will be the unity of father, son, and daughter — not husband and wife — and our task is to make ourselves sons and daughters by restoring life to our fathers. For both Solov'ev and Fedorov, the Trinity is the perfect model and man is the agent of unification, but where Solov'ev emphasizes the role of consciousness Fedorov emphasizes the role of action. But in all these models, the individual is incomplete in and of itself. The individual completes himself, becomes whole, only by becoming part of a greater whole. Russian thinkers, like Russian composers, love the strong chorus.

Zenkovskii writes that the end of the nineteenth century was the time of great systems in Russian thought. Chaadaev had raised the basic questions early in the century. Between Chaadaev and the end of the century, individual thinkers and groups of thinkers had taken these questions in many various directions. Speculation was often audacious and original, but no one had achieved a unified system. Individual insights, passionate examination of isolated questions, and profound but one-sided treatment of fundamental problems characterized most of the century of thought. Much was written about each of the major questions Chaadaev had raised, but no thinker had incorporated them all into a single, coherent system.[37]

Fedorov's great contribution was to unite all the opposed positions, all the divergent tendencies into a new whole, into a single project. Solov'ev offered an ideal synthesis of all previous idealist tendencies in Russian thought—but Fedorov unified more. In Fedorov we find a synthesis not only of the various idealist tendencies, but also of the materialist and anti-idealist tendencies. In Solov'ev, we find the culmination and unification of both Slavophilism and Westernism, but not of nihilism, scientism, populism, Marxism, and all the other isms that developed in the second half of the century. As a synthesizer of Russian *and* European thought, Solov'ev has no equal. He unified the best from both the Russian and European traditions. Fedorov, on the other hand, rejected the entire European tradition. But as a synthesis of *Russian* thought, Fedorov's system has no equal. His great contribution was to gather, to reorganize, and, if only for a brief moment, to hold up together to the light more of the apparent contradictions, opposed principles, and divergent tendencies that characterize the entire history of Russian thought than probably any of his compatriots has held together before or since.

Fedorov And The Twentieth Century

Fedorov published so little during his own lifetime, and his posthumously published works were printed in such small editions, were so poorly distributed, and appeared at such an inopportune moment that is is a wonder that his ideas had any impact at all on the Russia of our century. The first edition of the first volume of *The Philosophy of the Common Task* appeared in 1906, not in one of the great cultural centers of Russia, but in the remote town of Verny, now Alma-Ata (capital of Kazakhstan) in an edition of only 480 copies. And following Fedorov's principle that ideas were not one person's property and that truth should not be bought and sold, but freely exchanged, Kozhevnikov and Peterson had each copy stamped "Not for Sale" and distributed them without charge to libraries, institutions of learning, and to any individual who requested a copy by mail. Moreover, the editors renounced all copyright, and invited any interested person to copy and distribute the books at will. Judging from Peterson's correspondence with Tolstoi, and from the invitation to write for copies that accompanied his articles on Fedorov, it appears that not all the copies could even be given away, and that many that were sent were either lost or never looked at by the recipient. Subsequent editions of Fedorov's writings, and most of the early commentary on him, reached an equally small audience. Nevertheless, his ideas became known and did have a certain impact on twentieth century Russia.

Traces of Fedorovism, as mentioned earlier, have been noted in the works of Russians as different in mind and talent and sphere of activity as: the poets Valerii Briusov, Andrei Belyi, Vladimir Maiakovskii, Velimir Khlebnikov, Boris Pasternak, Nikolai Zabolotskii, and Anna Akhmatova; the biologist V. I. Vernadski; the composer Alexander Scriabin; the proponents of the *émigré* "Eurasian' movement of the thirties and of the "local studies" movement in the USSR; and even, Joseph Stalin [38],—all in addition to the writers, thinkers, and theologians whose comments on Fedorov have been cited earlier. Somehov, then, knowledge of Fedorov's idea did get around. The question is how.

In the 1890's, as we have seen, Solov'ev had proposed that he and Fedorov together issue a joint call to the common task. But nothing had come of this idea. After the publication of the first volume of Fedorov's works, Peterson asked Tolstoi to write something that would draw general attention to Fedorov and his idea, but Tolstoi did not respond the the suggestion. The obituaries that appeared in the Moscow newspapers after Fedorov's death talked much about his eccentricities and saintly devotion to his job, but said little about his ideas. So at the time of the appearance of *The Philosophy of the Common Task*, perhaps no more than a dozen people knew much about Fedorov's thought. The publication of Fedorov's works and the first commentaries on him by Kozhevnikov and Peterson drew some attention. Berdiaev and Bulgakov were the first respected thinkers to take Fedorov seriously and to write extended commentaries on his idea. Through them, Fedorov's ideas became well know to the circle of young theologians, many of them former Marxists, who would soon lead the extraordinary revival of spirituality that has been called "The Russian Religious Renaissance of the Twentieth Century." Fedorov's idea of a Christianity of action, and of man's duty to accomplish on this earth ideals that had traditionally been awaited in the next world probably had more influence than has been recognized on the emerging systems not only of Berdiaev and Bulgakov, but also of other members of this remarkable group, especially Father Pavel Florenskii and Father Giorgii Florovskii.[39] Even those thinkers, such as S. L. Frank and N. O. Losskii, who would not incorporate Fedorovian or antiFedorovian elements into their systems, nevertheless were thoroughly familiar with his work and took it into account.

But the first known group of committed "Fedorovists"

was a band of unknown poets who wrote for *Novoe Vino*, a small Kiev magazine started in 1909 by Vera Kuznetsova. The magazine was not well known, but nevertheless drew some attention to itself for its militant stand against "art for art's sake." Kuznetsova apparently brought Fedorov's ideas to the attention of her writers and assistants, and in 1912 the group decided to put together a special miscellany devoted to Fedorov and his thought. The publication was scheduled to appear in December of 1913 to commemorate the tenth anniversary of Fedorov's death. But the miscellany, called *Vselenskoe Delo* (The Universal Task) did not appear until 1914, just as the First World War was starting. The printers, who happened to be Germans, were immediately arrested, the print shop was sealed, and the copies of the miscellany stored there were apparently confiscated and destroyed. Thus the only copies distributed were the few that the editors had collected from the printers before the shop was closed.[40]

More notable for the editors' enthusiastic endorsement of Fedorov's ideas than for the intrinsic literary or philosophical value of most of the works included, the miscellany announced as its slogan "Mortals of the world—unite!" and urged the immediate and total adoption of Fedorov's project. *Vselenskoe Delo I* was intended to be only the first issue of a monthly publication devoted entirely to the propagation of Fedorov's teachings. But twenty years passed before the second (and so far last) issue of the miscellany appeared.[41] Between 1914 and 1934, many of the contributors worked their way into responsible positions within the Soviet government[42] and thus enabled some—but of course not all—of Fedorov's ideas to be incorporated into Soviet policy. As S. V. Utechin has shown, "Fedorovism" was one of several ideological strains existing within Bolshevism until heterodoxy in party thought was finally hammered into a single orthodox party ideology.[43] The "Fedorovist" Bolsheviks were primarily the technocrats and scientists within the party who wanted to carry through many of Fedorov's radical proposals for restructuring society and regulating nature, but who of course ignored the theological base underlying Fedorov's projects. Meteorological regulation—one of Fedorov's favorite projects—was considered an important task for Soviet scientists. One of the Fedorovian ideas then being seriously discussed was a project for melting the polar ice to provide water for drought-stricken areas. Also, some of Fedorov's ideas on rainmaking apparently contributed to the ambitious attempts undertaken in the late twenties and early thirties to produce rain by artificial means over the deserts of Soviet Turkestan.⁴⁴ Fedorov's ideas of labor armies to fight nature, and of the need to combine thought and action through the creation of special "task forces" of worker-intellectuals may have been put to perverse use as part of the inspiration and rationalization for Stalin's labor camps. A number of contemporary observers saw Fedorovism as the guiding principle behind the construction of the now notorious White Sea Canals.⁴⁵

The center of organized Fedorovism in the first decades of Soviet power was the Commission for the Study of the Natural Productive Forces of Russia. This agency was established by the Academy of Sciences in 1915 as a part of the war effort and retained a degree of autonomy until 1929 when it was merged into other agencies of the Communist administrative system. This Commission, chaired by the scientist and thinker V. I. Vernadskii (whose debt to Fedorov has often been mentioned but never fully explored), proposed a number of extraordinarily far-sighted projects for developing solar and electro-magnetic energy sources. At this time, even the most futuristic projects were welcomed by the new regime. And Vernadskii, who was not a Marxist, but whose far-reaching theory of a biosphere and its relationship to the structure of the earth qualified him as a "revolutionary" scientist, was permitted to head one of the major agencies assigned to offer blueprints for the Promethean future.⁴⁶

Another branch of organized Soviet Fedorovism was the Regional Studies movement. Fedorov's idea was that each village should have its own research station, its own local museum, and its own local task force for the collection of data about the ancestors and for exploration of the means to restore life to them. After the Revolution, and during the Civil War years, adverse political and material conditions forced many scientists to seek refuge elsewhere, and many settled in small towns and villages where they put their training to use by organizing societies and institutions for the scientific study of local regions. This movement, which grew from 160 institutions in 1917 to 516 by 1923, established museums throughout provincial Russia and, just as in Fedorov's project, set local residents to the task of gathering data on their localities. This movement fit in perfectly, at first, with the new government's plans to replace traditional religious education with universal scientific education. An All-Russian conference on regional studies was convened in 1921, and the following year the Academy of Sciences established a Central Bureau for Local Studies. The journal of the movement, *Regional Studies*, [*Kraievedenie*] remained a forum for the discussion of Fedorovist projects until, with the movement itself, it was suppressed in the purges of the thirties.[47]

Fedorov's name was not included in the lists of official "Fathers" of Bolshevism. By the middle thirties, in fact, as Solzhenitsyn tells us, Fedorov had become one of the "non-persons" whose ideas were generally understood to be in disgrace.[48] But if, even in the early years of Soviet power, Fedorov's name was usually not mentioned in public, people who endorsed at least the non-religious sides of his project were in responsible positions and were able to incorporate certain of his projects into Bolshevik policy. Even his call to resurrect the dead found some support among Soviet officials. L. B. Krasin, a high Communist Party official, a former Comissar of Trade and Ambassador to Britain and France, stated publicly at the funeral of a high party colleague his belief that "science would achieve the resurrection of the dead"[49]—but Krasin, contrary to Fedorov's teachings, held that not all, but only an elite few, those most valuable to the state, would be deemed worthy of resurrection. From Setnitskii, we learn that in the early years of Soviet rule medical scientists directed considerable energy to the problem of "resurrecting corpses"[50]—and one wonders, given Krasin's belief in the resurrection of the elite and Setnitskii's testimony that Soviet scientists had begun work toward this end—if the decision to preserve Lenin's body might not have been prompted by Fedorovistic anticipations.

For a while, Soviet Fedorovists pressed for a Soviet edition of Fedorov's writings. The plan, which in effect would have amounted to a tacit Soviet approval of at least some parts of Fedorov's project, came to nothing, even though it had the support of Maksim Gor'kii. But if the word "samizdat" is new, the phenomenon is not. Since Pushkin's "Gavriliad" government proscription has not prevented the wide circulation of works that Russians want to read. Thus, despite the fact that only 480 copies of Fedorov's works had been printed in the first place, and despite the rejection of proposals for a Soviet edition, the general outline of Fedorov's idea became, and to this day remains, common knowledge among Soviet intellectuals. N. V. Ustrialov, who in his day was a popular chronicler of current events and intellectual trends, reported that in a 1925 visit to Moscow he found that Fedorov was a leading topic for discussion among intellectuals.[51] René Fülop-Miller, after a visit in the mid twenties, reported that a strong, if clandestine, revival of Fedorov's thought was underway.[52] Gor'kii was still able to mention Fedorov in a favorable context in two of his articles in the twenties, and conducted an interesting debate on the question of Fedorov's relationship to Bolshevism in his correspondence with the young writer Sergei Grigor'ev. That Fedorov's idea was common knowledge among writers and intellectuals of the twenties and early thirties is indicated by Gor'kii's correspondence with two other young writers, Mikhail Prishvin and Ol'ga Forsh. In his letters Gor'kii recommends that they read Fedorov, but both Prishvin and Forsh reply that they have already long been acquainted with his works. Prishvin admits that at one time he had been quite carried away by Fedorov's ideas but later lost much of his interest. Forsh, in 1926, was deeply engrossed in her study of Fedorov's writings and was eager to exchange ideas about him with Gor'kii.[53]

But, for all the interest being shown in the Soviet Union, the world center for Fedorovism in the late twenties was not in Russia, but in Manchuria. There, at the Harbin School of Law, a young professor, N. A. Setnitskii had gathered a circle of true believers who were prepared to devote everything to the common task. In 1926, this circle published a strange, anonymous pamphlet called *The Apotheosis of Death* [*Smer-*

tobozhnichestvo] in which the authors call upon all men to accept the common task, announce that the project of resurrection must replace the worship of death practiced by all present branches of Christianity today, and anathematize in advance all who would turn away from the common task.[54] The long string of anathemas that conclude the work could only have seemed ridiculous to readers who were not Fedorov fanatics. And, indeed, the philosopher Lev Shestov, in an article written in 1933, noted that many of Fedorov's most enthusiastic supporters were doing him a disservice by spreading "Fedorovian" doctrines that were not in harmony with his original teachings.[55] Especially extreme were the claims made by A. K. Gornostaev (real name Gorskii) for Fedorov's influence on Dostoevskii, Tolstoi, and Solov'ev.[56] As we have seen in earlier sections of this discussion, Fedorov's ideas did, in varying degrees, stimulate and tantalize each of the three great thinkers, and in some instances Fedorov's ideas were incorporated into works by his famous contemporaries that remain better known than anything written by Fedorov. But Gornostaev leaps far beyond the evidence he presents, and arrives, nose first, at conclusions that shatter his entire argument and leave only scattered observations intact.

Setnitskii published under his own name in the *Proceedings of the Harbin School of Law* several treatises on economic and philosophical problems that included lengthy discussions of Fedorov's ideas.[57] Indeed, thanks to the influence of Setnitskii and to the sympathy of the editorial board, the official publication of the Harbin School of Law remained for several years a major (and respectable) outlet for Fedorovian thought. Nearly every issue of the *Proceedings* between 1926 and 1930 carried at least one article on Fedorov.

In addition to his academic treatises, Setnitskii, working under the pseudonym A. Ostromirov, launched a series of publications devoted entirely to the reprinting and elucidation of Fedorov's works.[58] Although plans for a complete second edition of Fedorov's collected works were not realized, (only three of twelve projected issues appeared) enough of the long "Brotherhood" essay was reprinted to offer many readers at least a direct source for ideas that they had long known second hand. But since the second edition circulated more widely than the first, most subsequent commentary focused only on the approximately three hundred pages reprinted, and whatever ideas could be found only in the nine hundred remaining pages of the first edition remained unknown. Thus, while a few of Fedorov's ideas were widely discussed, many more were not. But as Ostromirov, Setnitskii also published a biographical essay which has served until now as the basic source for everything written about Fedorov's life. And, also as Ostromirov, he wrote three articles, published as separate pamphlets under the general title *Fedorov and Our Time*, in which Fedorov's ideas are related to new developments in the arts and sciences and to major events in recent history. In these articles, Fedorov is depicted as a great prophet who anticipated the discoveries made by Einstein and Freud, and who foresaw the coming of the First World War. The difference between Setnitskii's work under his own name and his work as Ostromirov is chiefly one of emphasis. As Setnitskii, he tries to make Fedorov relevant to the construction of a new order in the Soviet Union. In these works, Setnitskii emphasizes the materialist side of Fedorov's thought and underplays the religious side. As Ostromirov, he writes as one sympathetic to Fedorov's religious views, and emphasizes the worldwide significance of the common task. But in the end, apparently Setnitskii won over Ostromirov. For sometime in the mid thirties Setnitskii returned to the Soviet Union, and although nothing is known of his fate, his commitment to Fedorovism was so firm, and, probably, so well known that it is unlikely that he survived the great purges that had begun even before his return. But fortunately, before leaving Harbin, he sent important documents in his possession to the philosopher Berdiaev and to the literary critic D. S. Mirskii, who published them in the respective Russian language journals they edited in Paris.[59] Setnitskii also passed a number of materials on to the writer K. A. Chkheidze, who, with the help of the Director of the Czech National Museum, Novotny, established *Fedoroviana Prahensia*, a Fedorov archive still maintained at the national museum in Prague.[60]

One of the most interesting of the known Fedorovians was a young thinker named Valerian Murav'ev. The son of Count

Nikolai Murav'ev, Nicholas II's Foreign Minister, Valerian Murav'ev was educated in England and later attempted to publish his own translations of his works there. But in October 1917, he was arrested and sentenced to death for having aligned himself with the Constitutional Democrat (Cadet) opposition. Trotskii, with whom he had conducted a lively political correspondence, commuted the death sentence to a five year prison term. After his release in 1922, Murav'ev drew close to a circle of Moscow Fedorovians, and in 1924 published *Control Over Time* [*Ovladenie vremenem*], a short book whose thesis is that man could and should overcome time by scientific means, and should use control over time as a means for resurrecting the dead.[61] Although no reviews of the book appeared in the Soviet press, the idea provoked much debate in Moscow, and the work was reviewed with extreme interest by the leading *émigré* journals. After the publication of *Control Over Time*, Murav'ev was appointed to responsible positions first in the Ministry of Foreign Affairs, and then in various domestic ministries. But in 1929 he was again arrested, and died in 1932, at the age of thirty-seven, in Western Siberia. In recent years interest in Murav'ev's theory of time has reportedly revived among Soviet scientists. But Murav'ev himself has not been "rehabilitated", and scientists interested in his theories are reluctant to allow their names to be identified with this revived interest.

The most important *émigré* political movement of the twenties and thirties was the "Eurasian" [*Evraziistvo*] movement based in Paris. Leading members of the group included the linguist Prince N. S. Trubetskoi, the economist and geographer P. N. Savitskii, the historian G. Vernadskii, the philosopher V. N. Il'in, and the literary critic Prince D. S. Mirskii, all among the most prominent figures in their disciplines at the time. Their basic idea was that the greatest problem facing mankind was how to resolve the East-West conflict, how to unite the best of Europe with the best of Asia. The future of Russia would decide this question for all men and for all time. But Bolshevism was not the answer. Bolshevism combined not the best, but the worst of both Europe and Asia. And as the only alternative to Bolshevism, the Eurasians offered themselves. During the twenties they actually sought recognition as a government in exile and support from the major European countries in their campaign to replace the Bolsheviks. As their hopes for the collapse of Bolshevism faded, and as their own dreams of governing a new Eurasian Russia also dissipated, some, like Vernadskii, settled for academic positions in the West, and others, like Mirskii, opted for suicidal returns to Russia. From the start, all the Eurasians viewed Fedorov as the prophet of the new Russia, but some also saw value in Marx. The ideological problem that the Eurasians never overcame was how to reconcile Fedorov and Marx. They viewed the two thinkers as equals, but differed on the question of whether Fedorov and Marx were also opposites. The pure Fedorovists rejected Marx, while the rest persisted in futile efforts to reconcile the two. In the end, the Eurasians experienced a "schism" [*raskol*] on the question of whether their position should be "Fedorov and Marx" or "Fedorov against Marx." The pure Fedorovists insisted that Fedorov was more radical than either Marx or Lenin because he wanted to remake the world entirely while Marx and Lenin merely wanted to destroy the past. Those who argued for Fedorov and Marx took the position that both had developed philosophies of action, rather than philosophies of contemplation, and that as the two main sources of the new philosophy both must be treated with respect. The final, compromise position— and even this was rejected by the pure Fedorovists—was that the Eurasian movement should begin as Marxist and end as Fedorovist, for Marx seemed more relevant to current circumstances, but Fedorov would be more relevant in the future. From the letter of a Soviet friend of the Eurasians, we learn that M. I. Kalinin was one of the high party officials favorably disposed toward Fedorovism. The assumption that Fedorovism and Marxism could mix, and indeed were mixing under Stalin, was probably a major factor in the decision of Mirskii and other Eurasians to return to the Soviet Union.[62]

The question of Fedorov's impact on twentieth century Russian art and literature has often been addressed but has not been answered to anyone's satisfaction. One difficulty that anyone who approaches this question faces is that not even all the creative works, much less the letters and other biographical materials, of those writers and artists most likely to have been interested in Fedorov have been published. So while Western scholars have pointed out Fedorovian motifs in the works of a number of major and minor figures, no one, in the absence of biographical materials, can conclusively state that someone like Khlebnikov or Scriabin actually knew the works of Fedorov. We know that Briusov once met Fedorov and was, for a while, deeply interested in his teachings.[63] We know that Andrei Belyi, Aleksander Blok, and perhaps others in the Symbolist group, spent some time wrestling with "the problem of combining Vladimir Solov'ev and Fedorov with the philosophy of Russian social thought (with Lavrov and with Herzen.)"[64] We are told by Nadezhda Mandelshtam that "Akhmatova, without knowing it herself, was a disciple of Fedorov."[65] A. Kiselev has noted echoes of Fedorov in Khlebnikov's entire, ambitious "cosmogony," in Platonov's long story *The Foundation Pit* [Kotlovan], and throughout the work of the poet Zabolotskii.[66]

But until firmer evidence is presented, the question of Fedorov's "influence" on such writers as Platonov and Zabolotskii must remain problematical. What does seem clear is that Fedorov's idea of restructuring not only society but man himself and indeed the entire cosmos, what George L. Kline has called Fedorov's "theurgical Prometheanism"[67] prefigured and probably contributed to the Promethean ethos that dominated Russian culture and intellectual life between 1905 and 1925. The idea that we must reshape everything found its way into every kind of activity, from art (cubism, futurism, etc.) to zymurgy (the introduction of *mesimaria*, etc.)[68] This was not all, of course, Fedorov's doing. The first decades of this century were years of "revolutionary" change everywhere, and Russia's cultural and political revolution was, in part, only a particularly dramatic instance of a worldwide phenomenon. What Fedorov contributed to Prometheanism in Russia was a detailed blueprint for the total reshaping of a world that almost everyone assumed needed reshaping. Fedorov's was not the only blueprint—but it was bolder and more comprehensive than any other, and it pointed Russians in a direction that they had long been predisposed to take. Thus, while we cannot say that Fedorov had as clear an influence on Russian Futurism as Solov'ev had on Russian Symbolism, he did offer a philosophical basis for the "projective" art not only of the Futurists, but of the Constructivists, the Suprematists, the Cosmists, and other groups who took for their task the transformation of the physical world. Historians of literature and art usually view the emergence of Futurism, Acmeist, etc. as a reaction against the preceding "ism", in this case, Symbolism. The difference between Futurism and Symbolism, however, is as much philosophical as literary. The Symbolists believed that the task of the poet was to "attune" himself to vibrations, transcendent visions, emanations—or whatever—that filtered through to us from "other worlds" (Solov'ev's *inye miry*), from "other shores" (the constant motif in the early Blok). The Futurists took as their task the transformation of the given world, and viewed the artist not as a receptacle of higher truth but as an engineer of a better world. This was essentially the difference between Solov'ev and Fedorov. Hence, the Futurists, whether they realized it or not, were, in their reaction against Symbolism, giving artistic embodiment to the philosophical position that Fedorov had taken against Solov'ev. In this sense, then, Fedorov was as much the unrecognized "father" of Russian Futurism, Constructivism, etc. as Solov'ev was the recognized "father" of Russian Symbolism. Just as we understand Blok and Ivanov better when we know something about Solov'ev, so we also get a better idea of what some of the post-Symbolists were doing when we know something about Fedorov. The Futurist emphasis on victory over nature, on technological achievement, and on the cosmic reach of the human hand takes on special meaning in the context of Fedorov's project. Scriabin's conviction that certain chords could effect radical transformations in the physical universe, the attempt by Kruchenykh, Matiushin, and Malevich to "integrate" their arts into a single spectacular "Victory Over the Sun," and Malevich's designs for *planity*, architectural structures to house life beyond the planet earth, all can be seen as conscious or unconscious efforts to realize projects formulated by Fedorov.[69] The Cosmist poet Kraiskii ("Extreme," pseudonym for Alexei Kuzmin), could have been echoing Fedorov in his proclamation: "We shall arrange the stars in rows and put reins on the moon;" and: "We shall erect upon the canals of Mars the palace of World Freedom." [70] Malevich formulated the aesthetic equivalent of Fedorov's summons to overcome nature. Like Fedorov's "man as he ought to be" Malevich's artist must free himself from subservience to nature: "The artist can be a creator only when the forms in his picture have nothing in common with nature"—the canvas and the drawing board become, in Malevich, the first battleground in our struggle to win life from nature.

But if all these artists shared Fedorov's idea that we must reshape the cosmos, they did not share the most important part of his idea, namely that all this must be done in order to resurrect the dead. In contradistinction to Fedorov, most of the Prometheans regarded the creation of forms independent of nature as merely a grand affirmation of man's creativity, or, if they thought further, as a means for transforming this world into a better one. They either did not know or did not share Fedorov's idea of just what kind of world was to be created.

But one famous poet and one obscure artist did know and share Fedorov's idea that through science and technology we shall be able to resurrect our ancestors. The linguist Roman Jakobson tells us that in 1920, on returning to Moscow from a visit to Europe, he called on Maiakovskii. "Maiakovskii made me repeat several times my confused account of the general theory of relativity and the discussion that was growing around it at that time. The liberation of energy, the problem of time, the question of whether there might exist a velocity greater than the speed of light, that might reverse the movement of time—all this intrigued Maiakovskii. I had rarely seen him so attentive and animated. 'But don't you think,' he suddenly blurted, 'that that's how immortality will be achieved?' I looked amazed and mumbled something about my doubts. Then with the hypnotizing pertinacity with which all who knew him closely are acquainted, he began to move his cheekbones: 'But I am absolutely convinced that there will be no death. They will resurrect the dead.'.... For me at that moment an entirely different Maiakovskii was revealed: the demand that death be conquered possessed him."⁷¹ Jakobson appears to have been surprised that Maiakovskii's ideas could have "converged with the materialistic mysticism of Fedorov."⁷² And Edward J. Brown concludes his discussion of Maiakovskii and Fedorov: "The position Maiakovskii had reached in 1923 has implications inconsistent with his earlier views: instead of throwing the past 'overboard from the steamship of modernity,' he now looks forward to the possibility of resurrecting and preserving it."⁷³ The works in which Maiakovskii puts Fedorov's ideas to artistic use are "About That" (*Pro Eto*) and *The Bedbug*. Brown is probably correct in suggesting that "the utopian passages in the poem ["About That"], not only where they tell of the future resurrection of the dead but also where they touch upon the necessity for universal love and brotherhood, derive in part from Fedorov."⁷⁴ But in the poem, the idea of resurrection is presented in the hyperbolic, half-comic tone characteristic of Maiakovskii, and in *The Bedbug* the idea serves more nearly as a framework within which to juxtapose satirical images of both the present and the future than as a vehicle for the direct presentation of a philosophical position. In both the poem and the play, Maiakovskii uses Fedorov's idea for his own artistic purposes and does not here try, through art, to win converts to a particular doctrine. Maiakovskii is, of course, serious here as always in his play, but at least in these works he remains a philosophical poet and does not try to become a poetic philosopher.

But V. N. Chekrygin, the obscure artist from whom Maiakovskii probably learned about Fedorov, tried his best to make his art a vehicle for the expression of Fedorov's idea. Brown and Jakobson were right to note the incongruity of Maiakovskiis' belief in resurrection. His commitment was to an all-new future, not to the resurrection of the past, and his brief interest in Fedorov did not essentially alter his commitment. He took what he could from Fedorov, (and from Einstein, Pushkin, and whomever he read or heard about, as any creative artist does) but he did not become a confirmed Fedorovian. Chekrygin did. This young, gifted, but now forgotten artist, who took his own life in 1922 at the age of twenty-five, completed over a thousand works in his short career, the most important of which are a series of illustrations to Maiakovskii's poems, and a grand attempt to embody Fedorov's idea in a cycle of drawings entitled "Resurrecting the Dead." In the last years of his life, Chekrygin devoted full attention to the task of picturing the act of resurrecting. Those who viewed the canvases in a posthumous exhibition were impressed by the power with which he had expressed the moment of resurrection. In the lower part of the intended fresco were to be the faces and bodies of those whose resurrection had just begun—fear, weight, and disfigured flesh dominate the sketches for this section. But higher up, the figures become lighter, the faces calmer, and spiritual qualities become more obvious than the flesh. The work was never completed. Like the nineteenth century artist Aleksander Ivanov, whose ambition to paint the face of Christ became such an obseession that he feared he could not complete the painting until he himself became Christlike, Chekrygin found himself unable to put on canvas the vision of resurrected faces that would complete the work, and his suicide suggests that he could not live with his failure. Among the works he left, besides the resurrection series, is a drawing for a temple-museum that was to serve as a resurrection center.[75]

What is clear, then, is that through the early thirties, individual parts of Fedorov's project stimulated Russians in many fields, both in the Soviet Union and in emigration, to incorporate Fedorovian themes into works of their own. Fedorov's religious ideas found echoes in the works of *émigré* theologians, while social, scientific, and artistic sides of his project were incorporated into various Promethean undertakings begun in the early years of Soviet power. But in each of these instances, only one side, or at most a few sides, of Fedorov's enormous single project, attracted support. Those who believed that the entire project should be undertaken were, apparently, very few and very fanatical. The group in Harbin that published *The Apotheosis of Death* has already been mentioned. But Fedorov had other equally fanatical and equally mindless followers. Berdiaev tells us of an early encounter with "Fedorovism" at a debate he attended in Moscow in 1918 or 1919. As a recent convert from Marxism to Russian Orthodoxy, Berdiaev was invited to a meeting of an anarchist club to join proponents of other doctrines in a discussion about Jesus Christ.

> A number of Tolstoyans, followers of Nikolai Fyodorov, professing a mixture of Fyodorov's ideas and anarchist communism, some straightforward anarchists and communists also took part in the debate. As I entered the crowded hall, I had an almost physical sensation of terrific tension in the air. The crowd contained a great many Red Army men, sailors and workers. The whole atmosphere was significant of the elemental forces behind the Revolution, exalting in the downfall of intolerable restraints, wanton, unbridled, ruthless, and frank to the point of naked shamelessness. One worker read a paper on the Gospel, in which he affirmed as scientifically proved that the Mother of God was a prostitute and Jesus Christ the illegitimate son of a Roman soldier—a statement which was greeted with wild applause from the audience. He also dwelt incessantly on the "contradictions" and "inconsistencies" in the Gospels. He was followed by a Tolstoyan who made a sharp attack on the church. A follower of Fyodorov, who described himself as a "biocosmist," produced, in what sounded like unprintable slang, some incredible hotch-potch of science, gnosticism, and the Gospels. He finished by proclaiming that, since the maximum social programme had already been put into practice, "the cosmic resurrection of the dead" will occur any moment. This statement provoked an uproar of laughter in the audience.[76]

Fedorov's ideas, then, on the one hand stimulated and enlarged the creative imagination of a number of men of genuine talent, such as Maiakovskii, Chekrygin, Vernadskii, Tsiolkovskii, and even Berdiaev himself; on the other hand, his ideas also inflated the rhetoric and expanded the confusion of many a featherbrained enthusiast. His bold project attracted bold followers, not all of whom possessed qualities that justified such boldness.

The purges put an end to both the creative and degenerative sides of Soviet Fedorovism. For more than thirty years, Fedorov's name was one of the many that could not be mentioned in print. It even took courage not to burn whatever Fedorov materials had been kept. As Solzhenitsyn writes: "And in that awful time, when in apprehensive loneliness precious photographs, precious letters and diaries were burned, when every yellowed piece of paper in the family cupboard all of a sudden gleamed out like a fiery fern of death and could not jump into the fire fast enough, in that awful time, what great heroism was required *not* to burn things up night after night for thousands and thousands of nights and to preserve the archives of those who had been sentenced (like Florensky) or of those who were well known to be in disgrace (like the philosopher Fedorov)!" [77]

The first writer to mention Fedorov again, after the long silence, was Viktor Shklovskii, who in his memoirs, *Once Upon A Time,* [*Zhily-byli,* 1964] wrote that Fedorov had been Tsiolkovskii's teacher. Once the ice had been broken, Fedorov's name began to appear again regularly: in books about Tsiolkovskii and Dostoevskii, in histories of Russian philosophy, and even in original essays on man's destiny. The scientist-thinker I. M. Zabelin wrote, in 1966, in a long article entitled "Mankind—what is it for?," that the human task is to counteract entropy, and that Fedorov understood this a century ago.[78] In a more recent work, *Physical Geography and the Science of the Future,* (1970), Zabelin again discusses Fedorov's project and develops ideas of his own that are very much in the Fedorovian spirit. Another Soviet writer, a dissident who writes under the pseudonym Viktor Velskii, acknowledged in 1966 that Fedorov was his precursor, and develops his own idea of immortality against the background of Fedorov's resurrection project.[79] And although Velskii is the only recent dissident writer to have discussed Fedorov's idea at length in print, apparently he is not alone in his interest. Circles of Fedorovists (as well as followers of Berdiaev and Solov'ev) exist in many parts of the country. One hopes that someday these circles will find it possible to make their ideas and researches known.

In the West, knowledge of Fedorov's idea has been limited to circles of Russian *émigrés* and to specialists in Russian literature and thought. The unavailability of Fedorov's works has forced even many of those interested in his thought to rely on summaries found in secondary sources or on incomplete editions of his writings. Only recently, when both volumes of the first edition of *The Philosophy of the Common Task* were reprinted in full by an English publisher, did Fedorov's works become readily accessible to readers of Russian. Translations of excerpts of one of his essays have been available since 1965, and efforts to translate all his major works into English have begun. It is possible, then, that readers of English will soon be able to wrestle with Fedorov's own account of the ideas discussed here, and to reach their own conclusions about a writer who has fascinated Russians for a century but whose ideas remain generally unknown in the West.

The emphasis of the present discussion has been on Fedorov as a *Russian* thinker. And surely he was that. But as important as Fedorov's contributions to Russian philosophy are, his contributions to the future of thought elsewhere may prove to be even greater. For Fedorov pondered longer, and probed deeper, into problems whose significance is only now beginning to be apparent than perhaps any thinker the world has known. The question of just where technological advance is taking us, and just where it should take us, has never seemed so urgent as now. The degree to which we can and should have control over death is now a matter of general concern. As this page is being written, a court of law is trying to decide whether the life of a young girl in a coma is to be prolonged indefinitely or to be cut short. The advance of technology has put us face to face with a moral problem that formerly might have seemed inconceivable. And this may be merely the beginning. The question of whether, and if so toward what end, we should attempt to alter the natural structure of organisms, including ourselves, is another problem that can only become more important in the future. All accounts of recent scientific developments written for laymen indicate that we are now on the verge of a new age in which it will be possible for us to restructure, if not actually to create, life itself. Just what we should do with this Godlike power is a question that someone is going to have to answer. Fedorov's answer may not be the best one that will ever be proposed, but so far it seems the most thorough and deepest attempt at one.

In philosophy before Fedorov the inevitability of death is accepted as a given. How we face this inevitability, or what other modes of life may lie beyond this one, has been the chief concern of philosophy. And Christian thought, while accepting the idea of our immortality, has looked beyond man and beyond this world for the power through which this immortality is to be accomplished. But Fedorov turns the inevitability of death into a conditional hypothesis and turns immortality from a divine gift into a human project. To accept Fedorov's philosophy and theology means, essentially, to reject the fundamental assumptions inherent in all previous systems of thought and belief. Fedorov's idea is that radical. He has not only given the world a new idea, but forces anyone who would accept his idea to reject all others. Fedorov knew that no one could either "prove" or "disprove" his idea by mere argument. So we shall never know who was right—Fedorov or all previous philosophers—unless Fedorov's task is undertaken. The chief objection raised in the course of this study is that Fedorov asks us to restructure the world in order to eliminate something that neither Fedorov nor we can claim to know. As people of limited intelligence and limited experience, as inhabitants of a very small planet in a very large universe about most of which we know absolutely nothing, we are in no position to say, as Fedorov does say, that the principle of nature everywhere is death and that nature must be reshaped so that death is excluded. For death may not be our enemy. We do not know where death takes us, what it does with us, or why it exists. Traditional Christian thought celebrates, rather than tries to eliminate, this awesome mystery. Our tradition of faith tells us that only by passing through this terrifying unknown may we reach eternal life. The faith that Christ, in ways that we cannot yet know, has already "trampled death by death", that He has already broken death's hold on us, may have been dismissed as "mysticism" by Fedorov, but still seems to offer better hopes for our future than Fedorov's faith that we can somehow by our own efforts become what we have never been: perfectly integrated individuals, loving brothers and sisters, dutiful sons and daughters who will live forever in perfect harmony with all others. If we had to choose between Fedorov and the collective wisdom and experience of all past ages, and if the choice had to be made today, I think it would have to go against Fedorov. But as Fedorov's idea becomes better known, the objections that are raised here and that have been raised against him in the past may not prove to be final. Our present may still confirm the wisdom of the past, but the future may yet belong to Fedorov.

NOTES

NOTES TO PREFACE

[1] *Filosofiia obshchago dela: stat'i, mysli, i pis'ma Nikolaja Fedorovicha Fedorova*, [The Philosophy of the Common Task: Articles, Reflections, and Letters of Nikolai Fedorovich Fedorov], edited by V. A. Kozhevnikov and N. P. Peterson, Volume I, Verny (now Alma-Ata), 1906, 731 pp.; Volume II, Moscow, 1913, 473 pp., as reprinted by Gregg International Publishers, Ltd., Westmead, Farnborough, Hants, England, 1970. This is the text used and referred to throughout this study. Hereafter, this text will be referred to by only volume and page number within parentheses. A translation of the table of contents for each volume is included as an appendix to this study. The first volume was printed in an edition of only 480 copies, and, in accordance with Fedorov's conviction that ideas should not be bought and sold, each copy was marked "not for sale" and distributed without charge to libraries, institutions of learning, and to individuals who requested copies. The second volume, also printed in an extremely small edition, did not bear the injunction prohibiting sale, and was apparently distributed through normal commercial channels. This edition, fortunately reprinted in its entirety in 1970, remains the best primary source for Fedorov's writings. A few short articles published anonymously during Fedorov's lifetime were not included in the two volumes, and a few materials apparently intended for a possible third volume of Fedorov's works have appeared in various journals (see Bibliography, pp. 248-250). But most of Fedorov's known writings can be found in the two volume collection. A second edition of Fedorov's works was begun in 1928, in Harbin, Manchuria. But only approximately one quarter of the works published in the first edition were reprinted in the second edition. A small fraction of Fedorov's work has been translated into English. See: *Russian Philosophy*, edited by J. M. Edie, J. P. Scanlan, M. B. Zeldin, with the collaboration of G. L. Kline, Chicago, 1965, II, pp. 16-54. And: *Ultimate Questions: An Anthology of Modern Russian Religious Thought*, edited by A. Schmemann, New York, 1965, pp. 175-223.

[2] Vladimir Aleksandrovich Kozhevnikov (1852-1917) was the author of over twenty works on religion and philosophy, the most important of which are: *Filosofiia chuvstva i very* [The Philosophy of Feeling and Faith], Moscow, 1897; and a two volume *Buddizm v sravnenii s khristianstvom* [Buddhism in Comparison with Christianity], Moscow, 1916. The son of a wealthy merchant, and the brother of two distinguished academicians, Vladimir Kozhevnikov came under Fedorov's influence while still a university student, and remained Fedorov's best friend and most sophisticated and intelligent

disciple for the rest of his life. He co-edited, with N. P. Peterson, the two volume collection of Fedorov's works cited above. In addition, he wrote the first and probably still most lucid extended account of Fedorov's thought. This work first appeared serially under the title *Nikolaj Fedorovich Fedorov* [Nikolai Fedorovich Fedorov] in the prestigious journal *Russkii Arkhiv:* 1904, No. 2, pp. 315-25; No. 3, pp. 390-401; No. 4, pp. 545-54; No. 5, pp. 2-26; No. 9, pp. 106-24; No. 10, pp. 225-61; 1905, No. 1, pp. 180-200; No. 2, pp. 333-65; No. 7, pp. 417-70; 1906, No. 1, pp. 63-102; No. 2, pp. 269-301. Hereafter this work will be referred to as K., *R. A.*, and the numbers following will refer to the year, issue, and pages cited. This study was later published as a monograph: *Nikolai Fedorovich Fedorov: opyt izlozheniia ego ucheniia po izdannym i neizdannym proizvedeniiam, perepiske i lichnym besedam,* [Nikolai Fedorovich Fedorov: An Attempt at an Exposition of his Teachings on the Basis of Published and Unpublished Works, Correspondence, and Personal Conversations], Moscow, 1908, 320 pp. The monograph is identical in content to the serialized study, with letters from Dostoevskii, Solov'ev, and Fet appended. But since the monograph is a great bibliographical rarity, I have referred the reader in this study to the more accessible *Russkii Arkhiv* version. During his time, Kozhevnikov was highly respected by leading Russian philosophers, scholars, and religious thinkers. Zenkovskii mentions his work favorably in his history of Russian philosophy (see note 17 below). But Kozhevnikov's works, like Fedorov's, were published in very small editions, and have become rarities. As a religious philosopher, he is ignored in the USSR today. A complete list of his published works can be found in *Izvestiia Iuridicheskogo Fakul'teta v g. Kharbine* [Proceedings of the Harbin School of Law], Harbin, 1927, Vol. IV. An obituary notice appeared in *Vselenskoe Delo II*, Riga, 1934, pp. 178-9.

[3] Nikolai Pavlovich Peterson (1844-1919), Fedorov's other chief disciple, was, for most of his life, more nearly a propagandist and a polemicist than a thinker. The adopted son of a Swedish woman, Peterson received a nobleman's education and was graduated from Moscow University in 1864. But even before receiving his degree, Peterson had served as a teacher in one of the peasant schools established near Iasnaia Poliana by Tolstoi. After Tolstoi's marriage in September 1862, the school in which Peterson had taught was disbanded, and Peterson moved to Moscow where he prepared for his university examinations and began to associate with a group of socialist radicals later known as "The Organization." (In 1866, Dmitri Karakozov, one of the group, would attempt to assassinate the Tsar). In 1864, having received his degree, Peterson moved from Moscow to the village of Bogorodsk, where he met and fell under the influence of Fedorov. For the rest of his life, he served as Fedorov's chief advocate, scribe, and agent. It was only at Peterson's insistence and with Peterson's help that Fedorov began to write. Peterson introduced Fedorov's thought to Dostoevskii, Tolstoi, Solov'ev, and others, co-edited the two volume edition of Fedorov's works, and wrote a number of articles in support of Fedorov's ideas. These articles were collected under the title: *N. F. Fedorov i ego kniga 'Filosofiia obshchago dela' v protivopolozhnost' ucheniiu L. N. Tolstogo 'o neprotivlenii' i drugim ideiam nashego vremeni* [N. F. Fedorov and his Book 'The Philosophy of the Common Task' in Opposition to the Teachings of L. N. Tolstoi 'On Non-resistance' and to Other Ideas of Our Time], Verny, 1912, 183 pp. Henceforth this book will be referred to by the initial P., followed by the numbers of the pages cited. From 1869 until his death, Peterson served in various administrative posts in the Ministry

of Justice: as a justice of the peace in such towns as Spassk (1869), Kerensk (1870). In 1891 he was appointed municipal judge for the city of Mokshansk, in 1894 for Voronezh; and from 1899 he served as a member of the circuit court for Askhabad, for Verny (1904), and finally for Zaraisk (1912). After the 1917 Revolution, the circuit court system was eliminated, and Peterson moved to Zvenigorod, where he died in 1919. An obituary and a list of his publications and unpublished manuscripts can be found in *Vselenskoe Delo II*, Riga, 1934, pp. 179-181.

⁴ N. A. Setnitskii, who also published under the pseudonym A. Ostromirov (information supplied to Taras Zakydalsky by K. A. Chkheidze), was probably too young to have known Fedorov personally. In a group portrait taken of the faculty of the Harbin School of Law in 1929 and published in *Izvestiia Iuridicheskogo Fakul'teta v g. Kharbine*, Vol. —III, 1938, **Setnitskii appears to have been in his early thirties**. He probably left Russia not long after the revolution and settled in the large émigré community in Harbin, and eventually joined the faculty of the law school which had been established there in 1920. In 1928, using the pseudonym Ostromirov, he began to issue a second edition of Fedorov's works and to publish **a series of pamphlets devoted to Fedorov's** life and thought: A Ostromirov, *Nikolai Fedorovich Fedorov, 1828-1903-1928: Biografiia* [Nikolai Fedorovich Fedorov, 1828-1903-1928: Biography], Harbin, 1928, Issue I, 20 pp. This biography was also printed as an introduction to the first issue of the second edition of Fedorov's works. The three other pamphlets in the series appeared under the general title: *Nikolai Fedorovich Fedorov i Sovremennost'* [Nikolai Fedorovich Fedorov and Our Times), Harbin Issue II, 1928, 51 pp.; Issue III, 1932, 40 pp.; Issue IV, 1933, 51 pp. Henceforth these works will be referred to as: 0, *Biografiia*; 0, II; 0, III; and 0, IV. Under his own name, Setnitskii also published a number of articles and essays in which Fedorov's ideas are summarized and discussed. These articles first appeared in the *Proceedings* for the Harbin School of Law, and were also published as separate pamphlets. A complete list will be found in the bibliography. After the deaths of Kozhevnikov and Peterson, the materials intended for the third volume of Fedorov's works were apparently passed on to Setnitskii. Before his return to the Soviet Union in the mid or late thirties, Setnitskii sent some of these materials to leading émigré journals in Paris, where they were published, and may have passed others on to friends who may or may not have preserved them in archives. Setnitskii was apparently at one time close to Andrei Belyi and Maksim Gor'kii, for he tells us in 0, IV, that *Fedorov and Our Times* was originally to have appeared in Belyi's journal *Epopeia*, and that the second edition of Fedorov's works was supposed to have been scheduled for publication in one of the Soviet organs with which Gor'kii was connnected. But Setnitskii's efforts to get Fedorov's works published in the USSR came to nothing, and we do not know what fate awaited Setnitskii on his return to Russia.

⁵ These letters, frequently cited in the secondary literature on Fedorov, were first published together as an appendix to Kozhevnikov's monograph (see note 2 above). Dostoevskii's letter to Peterson, dated March 24, 1878, was first published, with a preface by Fedorov, in *Don*, No. 80, 1897, apparently with some deletions. Peterson claimed to be publishing the entire text of the letter in *Russkii Arkhiv*, No. 3, 1904. But Peterson's version is shorter than the version now considered authoritative in Dolinin's collection of Dostoevskii's letters: *F. M. Dostoevskii, Pis'ma v chetyrekh tomakh*, ed. A. S. Dolinin Moscow, 1959, IV, pp. 9-10. The letter, with Fedorov's preface, also appeared

in *Vselenskoe Delo, I,* Odessa, 1914. An English version, with some omissions, is available in J. Coulson, *Dostoevskii: A Self-Portrait,* New York, 1962, pp. 216-17. Solov'ev's remarks are from his first, undated letter to Fedorov, published in *Pis'ma Vladimira Sergeevicha Solov'eva,* ed. E. L. Radlov, St. Petersburg, 1909, II., p. 345. The letter from Fet (real name Shenshin, 1820-92), quoting Tolstoi's remark, has often been cited by commentators on Fedorov, but has not appeared in any collection of Fet's letters. The Kozhevnikov monograph, then, remains the only source for this letter.

[6] K., *R.A.,* 1904, No. 2, p. 315.

[7] N. V. Ustrialov, *Nashe Vremia* [Our Time], Shanghai, 1934, p. 197. Ustrialov was the author of several books on Russian intellectual life during and immediately after the revolution. He was a colleague of Setnitskii's on the faculty of the Harbin School of Law, and probably learned of Fedorov from Setnitskii. While not an outright Fedorovian, he was well acquainted with Fedorov's ideas and in most of his books devotes a paragraph or two to Fedorov's project. Although his dates of birth and death are unknown, he appears to have been in his late forties in the group portrait taken of the Harbin law faculty in 1929 (see note 4 above).

[8] D. S. Mirskii, "Some Remarks on Tolstoi," *London Mercury,* XX, June, 1929, p. 174. Prince Dmitriii Sviatopolk Mirskii (1870-?) was the author of the classic, *A History of Russian Literature* (N.Y., 1949) and of a good, brief, introduction to Pushkin. In the 1930's he edited the *émigré* journal *Versty,* which published some materials from the third volume of Fedorov's works, and was one of the members of the "Eurasian" movement, which for a time attempted to present itself as an alternative to Bolshevism. Like Setnitskii and others who were interested in both Fedorov and Marx, Mirskii returned to the USSR sometime in the thirties and probably became a victim of Stalin's purges.

[9] A. L. Volynskii (real name: Akim Lvovich Flekser, 1863-1926), a leading literary and art critic of the time, was the author of a two volume work on Russian literary criticism, and of several works on Dostoevskii. Religious, and philosophically idealistic in his orientation toward literature, Volynskii sharply attacked the radicals of Russian literary criticism and has subsequently been assigned to the reactionary camp by Soviet historians of Russian literary criticism. His remarks on Fedorov are cited in O., *Biografiia,* p. 7.

[10] Father Sergei Nikolaevich Bulgakov (1871-1944) was a leading figure in the twentieth century revival of Russian religious thought. Closer to Solov'ev's system than to Fedorov's, he nevertheless incorporated some of Fedorov's activism into his own "Philosophy of Economics." His article on Fedorov, "Zagadochnyi myslitel'" [The Enigmatic Thinker] first appeared in the periodical, *Moskofskii ezhenedel'nik,* Dec. 5. 1908, was later reprinted in his book, *Dva Grada* [Two Cities], Moscow, 1911, II, pp. 260-77. The remarks quoted are from the first page of the article.

[11] Nicholas Berdiaev, "N. F. Fedorov", *The Russian Review,* IX, New York, 1950, p. 124. Berdiaev, who remains perhaps the best known of twentieth century Russian religious thinkers, wrote frequently and extensively about Fedorov. His first and longest work on Fedorov appeared in the journal *Russkaia Mysl'* in 1915. The article translated for the *Russian Review* was first published as part of a longer article on Tolstoi, Ibsen, and Fedorov, in the journal *Put',* No. 11, Paris, 1928.

[12] Konstantin Eduardovich Tsiolkovskii (1857-1935) worked closely with

Fedorov for three years during the 1870's. His relationship to Fedorov will be discussed in the first chapter of this study. The quotation is from: Konstantin Altaiskii, "Moskovskaia iunost' Tsiolkovskogo" [Tsiolkovskii's Time of Youth in Moscow], *Moskva*, No. 9 (Moscow, 1966), p. 82.

[13] For traces of Fedorovism in early twentieth century Russian art and literature, see: A. Kiselev, "Uchenie N. F. Fedorova v svete sovremennosti" [N. F. Fedorov's Teachings in the Light of Our Times], *Grani*, No. 81, Frankfurt, 1971, pp. 122-23. For Fedorovism in Soviet domestic policies, see: S. V. Utechin, "Bolsheviks and their Allies After 1917: The Ideological Pattern", *Soviet Studies*, X, Oxford, 1958/59, pp. 113-35. For a discussion of Fedorov's ideas in relation to subsequent advances (and sometimes backward steps) in Russian medical science, see: Peter Wiles, "On Physical Immortality," *Survey*, No.No. 56, 57, London, 1965, pp. 125-43, 142-61.

[14] Solzhenitsyn's calls for decentralization, a return to village life, and a return to theocracy, and, at the same time, his concern for redintegrating religion and science, seem to me closer to Fedorov's particular brand of neo-Slavophilism than to the various other versions of Slavophilism. But until Solzhenitsyn writes more on the question of resurrection and on other questions that Fedorov treats in detail, we cannot be certain just how close or how far apart the two thinkers are.

[15] Most of the items listed in the bibliography are extremely rare, but attempts are being made to collect microfilm or xerox copies of all available Fedorov materials. When collected, these materials will be available for the use of Fedorov scholars at Baker Library, Dartmouth College, Hanover, New Hampshire.

[16] In *Dream and Reality* (N.Y., 1951, p. 233) Berdiaev describes an encounter with one of the mindless enthusiasts who preached "Fedorovism" in the second decade of the century. The philosopher Shestov (real name Lev Isaakovich Shvartsman, 1866-1938) mentions in his book, *Umozrenie i otkrovenie* [Speculation and Revelation], Paris, 1964, pp. 127-30, that Fedorov's supporters are distorting Fedorov's teachings. Those particularly guilty of distortion include the authors of a curious booklet of 1926 called *Smertobozhnichestvo* [The Apotheosis of Death], and the writer A. K. Gornostaev, author of several short works that attribute to Fedorov enormous influence on the works of Dostoevskii, Tolstoi, and Solov'ev. These works are discussed at appropriate points in this study, and are listed in the bibliography.

[17] For harsh critiques of Fedorov's teachings, from a theological standpoint, see: Georgii Florovskii, *"Proekt mnimogo dela"* [The Project of an Imaginary Task], in *Sovremennye Zapiski*, No. 59, Paris, 1935, pp. 399-414 (later reprinted in his book, *Puti russkogo bogosloviia*); and S. Golovanenko, who wrote first a review and then a series of articles on Fedorov for *Bogoslovskii vestnik*, Moscow, 1913, No. 12, pp. 832-44; 1914, No. 4, pp. 664-88; No. 5, pp. 83-109; No. 7-8, pp. 569-92; 1915, No. 3, pp. 498-516; No. 6, pp. 294-315; 1916, No. 1, pp. 119-135. For criticism from a Marxist point of view, see: "Fedorov, Nikolai Fedorovich" in *Filosofskaia Entsiklopediia*, ed. F. V. Konstantinov, 1970. V., pp. 308-9; and "N. F. Fedorov" in *Istoriia Filosofii v SSSR*, [The History of Philosophy in the USSR], ed. V. E. Evgrafov and others, Moscow, IV, 1971, pp. 57-64. For fair, balanced assessments of Fedorov's ideas, see: N. O. Lossky, *History of Russian Philosophy*, London, 1952, pp. 75-80; and especially: V. V. Zenkovskii, *Istoriia Russkoi Filosofii*, Paris, 1950, II., pp. 131-47 (available in English: V. V. Zenkovsky, *A History of Russian Philosophy*, tr. G. L. Kline, New York, 1953, II., pp. 588-604).

[18] Even before the reprinting of Fedorov's works in 1970, a number of students and scholars had begun to devote fresh attention to Fedorov and his thought. Emong the more recent articles listed in the bibliography, Pletnev and Lord offer the most interesting analyses, though Lord's studies contain some misinformation and a few highly questionable conclusions. Of the dissertations listed, Grunwald's offers the best discussion of Fedorov's relationship to subsequent Russian religious thinkers, mine offers the fullest previous general account of Fedorov's life and thought, and Zakydalsky's presents the most rigorous philosophical analysis yet attempted of Fedorov's idea of resurrection.

NOTES TO CHAPTER I

[1] V. F. Lazurskii lived with the Tolstois between 1894 and 1898 as tutor to the children. His memoirs, "Dnevnik V. F. Lazurskogo" (The Diary of V. F. Lazurskii) appeared in *Literaturnoe Nasledstvo* [Literary Heritage], Vol. 38, 1939, pp. 443-509. The quotation is from pp. 465-66.

[2] According to Fedorov, the evolution of handwriting, from the old, upright, carefully and lovingly calligraphed *ustav* and gothic scripts of medieval times, through the *poluustav*, half upright scripts of more recent times, to the *skoropis'*, cursive, "speedwriting" of the present tells the story of man's degeneration. Speed and ease have replaced care and loving effort. (I, 23-26).

[3] Fedorov's universal history, written in part to counter Hegel's idea of history, tells the story of the dissolution of the human family. Essentially, the task of the Tsar (international father) is to bring the children back together in the task of returning life to their parents. See the section of "Brotherhood" entitled "What History Is" (I, 128-247).

[4] The woman's smile tempts sons to abandon their fathers, makes men compete to win her wavor, and encourages them to create luxuries to please her instead of living with bare essentials. The smile of an attractive woman calls men to abandon their self-control and to give themselves wholly to nature and death. (I,9, 31, 84, 315, 552) The newborn infant cries as he enters the unnatural cycle that will lead him to death. Childbirth must eventually be replaced by the restoration of life to the dead. The goal is not to bring more people into the world of death, but to extend life backward until there is no more death. (I, 312-317) Dante's paradise is only for the immature, for those who want to receive eternal life without giving it. Dante's paradise is also an individual fantasy rather than a common task. Man is sent to Dante's paradise as he is, without having remade himself into what he should be. In Dante, only some are awarded eternal life, others are consigned to eternal punishment, living death. (I, 420-421, 534).

[5] For more about the Gagarin line, see O., *Biografiia*, pp. 8-9. Before Ostromirov, no one had definitely stated which Gagarin was Fedorov's father. Ostromirov tells us that he got his information from N. P. Chulkov, a colleague of Fedorov's at the Ministry of Foreign Affairs.

[6] Ostromirov, and, following him, all others, have incorrectly stated that Nimforoda Semenova was I. A. Gagarin's second wife. Elisabeth Koutaissoff, in her article "Some Futurological Aspects of Fedorov's "Philosophy of the

Common Cause", *Russian Literature Triquarterly*, Ann Arbor, No. 12, Spring 1975, p. 406, corrects this mistake.

[7] Cited in O., *Biografiia*, p. 9.

[8] See O., *Biografiia*, p. 8. P. B. Bartenev, a longtime acquaintance of Fedorov's, and editor of *Russkii Arkhiv*, was the first to propose the Circassian hypothesis. The author of the article in *Filosofskaia Entsiklopediia* (see Preface, note 17), who apparently had access to the Fedorov archive at the Lenin Library, also says that the mother was Circassian. The normal assumption would probably be that the mother was a Russian or Ukrainian peasant woman. To have suggested that she was Circassian, someone must have known something. Until evidence is found to settle the question one way or another, the Circassian hypothesis seems to me the one more likely to be true.

[9] Fedorov's birthdate is still a matter of controversy. Ostromirov's date of January-April 1828 is, he says, (O., *Biografiia*, p. 8) based on documents in the Rumiantsev Museum. But he does not specify what these documents are. And Peterson claims (P., pp. 77, 78) that Fedorov was four years older than Tolstoi, which would mean that Fedorov's birthdate would be closer to 1824 than to 1828. Moreover, Tolstoi constantly assumed that Fedorov was older than he, and often refers to Fedorov as "an old man", and, at the age of fifty four, writes that Fedorov is "about sixty" (L. N. Tolstoi, *Polnoe sobranie sochinenii*, Moscow, 1934, Vol. 63, p. 83). And, finally, Tsiolkovskii, in 1873, judged Fedorov to be "a man of about fifty" (see page 180 of the Altaiskii interview referred to in note 12 to the Preface). So, from much testimony, it is clear that Fedorov at least looked like a man who had been born around 1824 instead of in 1828. But, in 1824, P. I. Gagarin, the supposed father, was still in the foreign service and may well have still been in the U.S.A. It is usually assumed that Gagarin began his liaison with Fedorov's mother after his "retirement" in 1826. Moreover, if Fedorov had been born in 1824 he would have been four years older than most of his classmates if Ostromirov's dates for his graduation from the Tambov gymnasium and attendance at Richelieu Lyceum are correct. Moreover, again, the author of the *Filosofskaia Entsiklopediia*, who apparently had access to the archive materials, gives his birthdate as 1828. So, unless contrary evidence is discovered, I will continue to accept Ostromirov's date of 1828, and assume that Fedorov merely looked older than he was.

[10] K., *R.A.*, 1904, No. 9, p. 109.

[11] O., *Biografiia*, p. 8. This was common practice. The poet V. A. Zhukovskii (1783-1852) was given the patronymic Andreevich after his godfather.

[12] O., *Biografiia*, p. 9.

[13] In 1891 Russian newspapers were full of commentary on recent American rainmaking experiments. Russia was then experiencing a severe drought, and at a technical conference in Odessa, A. Starkov, editor of a technical journal, called for Russian experiments in rainmaking. (I, 659) But a clergyman, Father Amvrosii of Kharkov, in a speech at Kharkov University, objected that to shoot cannons at heaven would be an act of unforgivable hubris. (I, 3) Fedorov believed that to shoot cannons into the air to bring rain would be a start toward regulating nature, and was, therefore, a sacred-scientific act. Fedorov's proposal for disarmament was not to disband standing armies, but to turn them into armies whose task was to fight for control over nature. (I, 656-668). See Peterson's interesting comparison and contrast of Fedorov's disarmament project to William James' "moral equivalent to war" (P., 14-20).

[14] By shifting his orientation from horizontal (the death position) to vertical (the life position) man transforms himself from an earthbound creature to a heaven-dweller. The horizontal position is the position in which man is most obedient to the laws of gravity, and in which he is closest to the four-legged animals. The horizontal is the position of man in the grave. The first funeral monuments were vertical slabs, signifying the wish to stand the deceased upright again (resurrect him). By assuming the vertical, two-legged position, man differentiated himself from other animals and obtained a higher, broader view of his surroundings. Art and architecture should celebrate the vertical. Space exploration would be a logical extension of man's vertical orientation. By mastering nature and the forces of gravity, we should be able to restore all who are now in the horizontal position (the dead) to the vertical position of life. Hence the shift in the aim of a cannon to vertical from horizontal represents exactly the kind of shift that we ought to try to achieve in our orientation to everything in the world. (II, 253-254; 260-270).

[15] For a discussion of Chernyshevskii's book in a literary context, and for a general discussion of the question of the "new man" in Russian literature, see Rufus W. Mathewson Jr., *The Positive Hero in Russian Literature*, New York, 1958, especially pp. 94-107. For a detailed description of the nihilist milieu, see Charles A. Moser, *Antinibilism in the Russian Novel of the 1860's*, The Hague, 1964, pp. 23-61.

[16] P., 88-89.

[17] "The Organization" [*Organizaciia*] was started in 1863 by a group of eight young men, (most from the nobility) who wanted to transform Russia into a socialist society. They talked, rather grandly, about opening the prisons and seizing Moscow, but confined their activities to discussing plans and distributing propaganda. The group grew, and apparently lost whatever organized structure it might have had at the beginning. When questioned, Peterson and other members did not even know that the group they had belonged to was "The Organization." But in 1865, the inner circle of the group decided to form a harder core, and the name that they gave themselves was "Hell" [*Ad*]. The chief goal of this inner group was to assassinate the Tsar. Other, secondary assassination targets included Count Murav'ev, who as Governor of Vilna had crushed the Polish uprising of 1863, and M. N. Katkov, the publisher of the conservative *Moskovskie Vedomosti*. Members of "Hell" were to avoid respectable society (so not to compromise their revolutionary purity), to spy on all members of "The Organization", and, in the event of revolution, were not to become leaders or public figures but to remain the hidden watchdogs of the movement, ready to eliminate any revolutionary leader who appeared to be wavering in his convictions. Members of "Hell" were to carry on their persons at all times explosive devices so that they could strike at a moment's notice, or destroy themselves to avoid capture. But all of this was little more than revolutionary fantasy. In fact, when Karakozov went to Petersburg, the other members of "Hell', fearing that he might try something drastic, sent an emissary to retrieve him. From his own testimony, we learn that Karakozov was seriously ill, that he acted without the group's knowledge or agreement, and that his main idea was to do something spectacular for "the cause" before dying of his (unspecified) grave illness. Although all the leaders of the group were sentenced to death, Karakozov was the only one actually executed. Peterson, sentenced to six months in prison, was released after serving only a part of his sentence.

Never a member of the inner group, Peterson, after meeting Fedorov, attempted to persuade his former associates that their revolutionary activities were irrational, immoral, and would be futile. In testimony he freely admitted that he had not reported having seen a fugitive from Siberia in the room of one of Peterson's acquaintances who had given the fugitive asylum. He denied all other charges brought against him, including that he had participated in a plot to free Chernyshevskii from a Siberian prison, and was found innocent of all charges save the one he admitted. For more details on the Karakozov episode, "The Organization," "Hell," and Peterson's involvement, see the trial transcripts published in: "Pokushenie Karakozova 4 aprelia 1866 g." (Karakozov's Attempted Assassination on April 4, 1866) ed. A. Shilov, *Krasnyi Arkhiv*, No. 17, Moscow, 1926, pp. 91-137; and *Pokushenie Karakozova* [Karakozov's Attempted Assassination], eds. M. M. Klevenskii & K. G. Kotelnikov, Moscow, 1928-30, 2 vols. For short biographies of the participants (including the information on Fedorov), see: *Deiateli Revoliutsionnogo Dvizheniia v Rossii. Bio-Bibliograficheskii Slovar'* [Participants in the Revolutionary Movement in Russia: A Bio-Bibliographical Dictionary], eds. A. A. Shilov & M. G. Karnaukhova, Moscow, 1928, Volume I, Part II—*Shestidesiatye gody* [The Sixties]: Peterson, p. 311; Fedorov, p. 427. I am grateful to Taras Zakydalsky for having referred me to these sources.

[18] For information about the Rumiantsev Museum and the Lenin Library, including a complaint that during Fedorov's time many books taken out were never returned, see: *Istoriia Gosudarstvennoi Ordena Lenina Biblioteki SSSR Imeni V. I. Lenina Za 100 Let: 1862-1962* [The History of the Lenin and Order of Lenin State Library for 100 Years: 1862-1962], eds., K. R. Kamenetskaia & E. V. Seglin, Moscow, 1962. Fedorov is mentioned on pp. 48-49. The quotation about Lenin is from page 10.

[19] O., *Biografiia*, p. 12.

[20] I. A. Linnichenko, *Rechi i Pominki* [Events and Recollections], Odessa, 1914, p. 315. Professor Linnichenko, a frequent visitor to the library, was a close friend of the director, the Shakespearean scholar N. I. Storzhenko. He witnessed a number of unusual encounters between Fedorov and Tolstoi, which will be discussed at a later point in this study.

[21] We learn in an 1874 letter from Peterson to the dramatist Chaev that Fedorov had established a repository for local documents in Kerensk, and had gone to Moscow to seek documents pertaining the Kerensk region, leaving Peterson in charge of the repository. See: "Pis'mo N. Petersona k N. A. Chaevu o N. F. Fedorove" [A Letter from N. Peterson to N. A. Chaev about N. F. Fedorov] *Russkii Arkhiv*, No. 3, Moscow, 1915, pp. 28-81.

[22] For more details on Fedorov's projects for museums, see his article: "Muzei, ego smysl 'i znachenie" [The Museum: its Meaning and Importance], in II., 398-463. Also, Kozhevnikov's article: "Nikolai Fedorovich Fedorov: Muzeiskii Deiatel' " [Nikolai Fedorovich Fedorov: Museum Worker], in K., R.A. No. 3, 1904, pp. 390-491.

[23] Peterson tells us (P., 78) that during his years of fulltime work, Fedorov received a salary of 498 rubles per year. He refused to accept more because those who earned more than 500 rubles a year had to serve jury duty, and Fedorov was in principle opposed to passing judgment on his fellow men. After his retirement, he received 17 rubles and 51 kopecks per month. The Gogol' scholar V. I. Shenrok tells us that the library director, at that time M. I. Venevitinov, once asked Fedorov if he would like a raise. When Fedorov refused, the director asked: "And if my position were offered to you?" "And

I would refuse that too!" Fedorov replied. See: V. I. Shenrok, "Pamiati N. F. Fedorova i A. E. Viktorova" [Memories of N. F. Fedorov and A. E. Viktorov], *Istoricheskii Vestnik*, St. Petersburg, 1904, No. 2, pp. 663-670. The quoted conversation is from page 667.

[24] Altaiskii (see preface, note 12), p. 180.

[25] *Ibid.* Tsiolkovskii deliberately used the word "enchanted", saying that it was the only word for the effect that Fedorov produced on him and others. He says that he didn't dare ask Fedorov about himself and his life, but he soon became acquainted with a student named Volodia, who told him a great deal about Fedorov's life. This "Volodia" was probably Kozhevnikov.

[26] Altaiskii, p. 181.

[27] *Ibid.*

[28] V. L'vov, "Priamoe Voskhozhdenie" (Direct Ascent), *Neva*, No. 2, Moscow, 1966, p. 130. In this article, Lvov tells us that Tsiolkovskii told Viktor Shklovskii that he learned about space travel from Fedorov.

[29] Altaiskii, p. 182.

[30] Viktor Shklovskii, "K", in "Kosmonavtika ot A do Ia" [Cosmonautics from A to Z], *Literaturnaia Gazeta*, No. 15, Moscow, April 7, 1971, p. 13.

[31] For a description of his plan, see L'vov, *op. cit*, p. 131.

[32] Cited in O., *Biografiia*, p. 17

[33] Since Dostoevskii is known to have used the library on visits to Moscow, he may have seen or even spoken to Fedorov without knowing who he was.

[34] F. M. Dostoevskii, *Dnevnik Pisatelia za 1876 god.* [Diary of a Writer for 1876], Berlin, 1922, pp. 131-132. Both the except he prints from Peterson's article and Dostoevskii's comments on the excerpt can also be found in the English translation: Fedor Dostoevskii, *Diary of a Writer*, tr. Boris Brasol, N.Y., 1949, II, pp. 247-8. Verification that Dostoevskii received the manuscript from Peterson is found in "Neizdannyi Dostoevskii: Zapisnye Knizhki i Tetradi 1860-1881 gg." [Unpublished Dostoevskii: Workbooks and Notebooks, 1860-1881], in *Literaturnoe Nasledstvo*, Vol. 83, Moscow, 1971, pp. 450, 452, 508-509. Peterson, who at that time was living in the town of Kerensk, had sent the article to a local periodical, "Spravochnyi listok raiona Morshansko-Syzranskoi zheleznoi dorogi" [Bulletin of the Morshansk-Syzransk Railroad Region], but the editor had refused to print it.

[35] Dostoevskii's letter of March 24, 1878, in F. M. Dostoevskii, *Pis'ma c chetyrekh tomakh* [Letters in Four Volumes], ed. A. S. Dolinin, Moscow, 1959, IV. No. 620, pp. 9-10. For the publication history of this letter, see Preface, note 5.

[36] In commenting on Dostoevskii's letter, Fedorov writes: "We don't know anything about an 'abyss' or about what 'vanquished death' will 'vanquish', but we do submit that it is possible for us—as instruments of the God of the fathers, who has breathed life into us—that it is both possible and necessary, on the one hand, to attain through, ultimately, all people knowledge of and control over all the molecules and atoms of the external world, in order to collect what has been dispersed, to redintegrate what has disintegrated, i.e. to synthesize [dispersed particles of matter] into bodies of the fathers, like those they had at the time of their demise; and, on the other hand, we submit that it is both possible and necessary, that, having also attained internal control by psychophysiological development, to replace the birth of children similar to their fathers and forefathers (atavism) with a restoration of life to the fathers from whom life was received." (II, 442) This is one of the

clearest statements of what Fedorov means by "resurrection." Problems that arise from his formulation will be discussed in the second part of this study.
[37] P., 106.
[38] A. K. Gornostaev's study of Fedorov's influence on Dostoevskii (see Preface, note 16), the title of which in English would be *Paradise on Earth,* contains a great many wild speculations and a few genuine insights. By a long series of quotations, Gornostaev establishes that Dostoevskii was deeply interestted in the problem of resurrection, and that he indeed gave this idea an important place in *The Brothers Karamazov.* But Gornostaev exaggerates the similarities between Dostoevskii's and Fedorov's ideas of resurrection, and ignores the differences. He so overstates the case for Fedorov's influence that one is tempted to react by taking the opposite stand: that Fedorov had no influence whatsoever on Dostoevskii. But V. L. Komarovich, who first published Dostoevskii's notebooks for *The Brothers Karamazov,* in German, and who was the first to discuss Fedorov's thought in detail in a language other than Russian, presents all the evidence and arrives at reasonable conclusions about what Dostoevskii learned from Fedorov: W. Komarowitsch, "Der Vatermord und Fiodoroffs Lehre von der 'Fleischlichen Auferstehung'" [Patricide and Fedorov's Doctrine of 'Physical Resurrection'], in *F. M. Dostojewski: Die Urgestalt der Brüder Karamasoff:* Dostojewskis Quellen, Entwürfe und Fragmente, Erläutert von W. Komarowitsch mit einer einleitenden Studie von Professor Dr. Sigm. Freud [*F. M. Dostoevskii: The Prototype of The Brothers Karamazov:* Dostoevskii's Sources, Drafts and Fragments, with Commentary by V. Komarovich, and With an Introductory Essay by Professor Dr. Sigmund Freud] Munich, 1928, pp. 3-58. Komarovich's position is essentially that Dostoevskii, by his own admission, was no philosopher, that he sought a philosophical basis for the idea of resurrection, and that he found that basis partly in Solov'ev, but primarily in Fedorov. In *The Brothers Karamazov,* we find not direct statements of Fedorov's philosophy, but Dostoevskii's own artistic treatment of ideas that he accepted from Fedorov's philosophy. In two essays on Fedorov and Dostoevskii, Robert Lord takes a position similar to Komarovich's: R. Lord, "Dostoevskii and N. F. Fedorov," *The Slavonic and East European Review,* XL, London, 1961-62, pp. 409-430; and "Resurrection and Applied Science" in Robert Lord, *Dostoevskii: Essays and Perspectives,* Berkeley, California, 1970, pp. 175-200. In both essays, Lord misstates a number of details pertaining to both Fedorov's life and thought, but also offers a number of interesting, original observations on Fedorov's idea. His position on Fedorov's influence is that Dostoevskii accepted Fedorov's ideas to a point (and Lord carefully marks the limits) and that he shared the spirit, if not the letter, of Fedorov's project. Dostoevskii did not include direct statements of Ferodov's ideas in his novel because, as an artist, he found it more effective to cloak his own thoughts in ambiguity than to present them directly and thereby antagonize ideological opponents. Rostislav Pletnev, in his two articles, takes a rather different position: Rostislav Pletniow, "Grundlinien der philosophischen Lehre N. F. Fiodorows" [The Basic Outlines of Fedorov's Thought], *Der Russische Gedanke,* (Festschrift N. O. Losskii), Bonn, 1934, pp. 133-140; and R. Pletnev, "N. F. Fedorov i F. M. Dostoevskii" [N. F. Fedorov and F. M. Dostoevskii], *Novyi Zournal,* No. 50, September, 1957, pp. 220-246. Pletnev emphasizes the similarities and differences between Dostoevskii and Fedorov, and argues that Dostoevskii had arrived at his ideas on resurrection long before he read Fedorov, and that *The Brothers Karamazov* contains no trace of Fedorov's influence. In his article on Fedorov

and Dostoevskii, "Lichnost' Dostoevskogo" [Dostoevskii's Personality] first published in *Zvezda*, No. 12, Moscow, 1969, and later reprinted in his book, *Lichnost, Dostoevskogo*, Leningrad, 1974, pp. 7-79, the Soviet critic B. Bursov argues that Fedorov and Dostoevskii reached most of their conclusions independently, but that Fedorov's manuscript did have a certain influence on *The Brothers Karamazov*. But the "influence" that Bursov seems to have in mind does not fit into our usual notions of "influence." Bursov attempts a tricky explanation. Fedorov's ideas were "mystical" and these "mystical" ideas appear at the end of *The Brothers Karamazov*. But Dostoevskii, here as in all Soviet criticism, must somehow come out a "realist." Bursov gets around his dilemma by arguing that Dostoevskii was interested in the phenomenon of mysticism more nearly from the standpoint of a clinical analyst than from that of a person attempting to discover and express his own views. Taras Zakydalsky, in an as yet unpublished paper delivered at the October, 1975 American Association for the Advancement of Slavic Studies conference in Atlanta, argues that Fedorov had no influence on Dostoevskii, but on the question of mysticism takes a view opposite Bursov's. According to Zakydalskii, Fedorov is a materialist and Dostoevskii is a mystic. Dostoevskii's idea of resurrection is so different from Fedorov's that Dostoevskii could not have been deeply influenced by Fedorov. I find some truth in all of these positions, and see no contradiction between the idea that Dostoevskii learned much from Federov, and the idea that he didn't leave many obvious traces of that learning in his art. Moreover, it seems clear to me that Dostoevskii cannot be pinned down to any single *ism*, whether it be realism, mysticism, or even "mystical realism." Dostoevskii was not a simple man, and the question of "influence" is not a simple question. In my discussion of Dostoevskii and Fedorov I deliberately avoid trying to prove or disprove Fedorov's "influence." More interesting and fruitful, it seems to me, is to explore the many ways in which Dostoevskii and Fedorov do and do not agree on resurrection.

[39] Dostoevskii's notebooks for *The Brothers Karamazov* were first published in German by Komarovich (see note 38, above). They first appeared in Russian in: *F. M. Dostoevskii: Materialy i issledovanie* [F. M. Dostoevskii: Materials and Research], ed. A. S. Dolinin, Leningrad, 1935. The text that I have quoted is the readily available English translation: F. M. Dostoevskii, *The Notebooks for The Brothers Karamazov*, ed. & tr. by Edward Wasiolek, Chicago, 1971, pp. 26, 30, 32.

[40] As cited by Lord, *op. cit.*, 423-427.

[41] Pletnev, "N. F. Fedorov i F. M. Dostoevskii," op. cit., pp. 242-243.

[42] The newspaper in which the preface appeared, *Don*, is unavailable in the West. I have quoted from the preface as it appears in *Vselenskoe Delo, Sbornik*, I, Odessa, 1914, p. 24

[43] It is possible that Peterson was responsible for the tone of the *Don* preface. But since it was first published while Fedorov was still alive, Fedorov must have approved it before it was sent to the newspaper. All of Fedorov's writings were, to a certain extent, joint efforts in which either Peterson or Kozhevnikov or both participated. But even a letter or article intended to be published anonymously would probably not have been released without Fedorov's approval.

[44] Quoted from Dostoevskii's "Notes from Underground" in the translation by David Magarshack, *The Best Short Stories of Dostoevsky*, Modern Library, New York, p. 131.

[45] See pp. 43-44, above.

[46] "Chteniia o Bogochelovechestve (1877-1881)" (Lectures on Godmanhood: 1877-1881) in *Sobranie sochinenii Vladimira Sergeevicha Solov'eva* [Collected Works of Vladimir Sergeevich Solov'ev] 10 Vols., ed. S. M. Solov'ev & E. L. Radlov, second edition, Vol. III, St. Petersburg, pp. 3-186. These lectures have been translated into English: *Lectures on God-Manhood*, tr. with an introduction by P. P. Zouboff, New York, 1944. A more recent translation of selections from the lectures by George L. Kline is available in Edie, Scanlan, Zeldin, & Kline's *Russian Philosophy, op. cit.*, III, pp. 62-84. In the Godmanhood Lectures, we can see the main outlines of Solov'ev's system, and can find that, even before he learned of Fedorov's thought, Solov'ev had already formulated his own ideas of a free theocracy (similar to Fedorov's "autocracy") a nature pervasively evil (similar to Fedorov's idea of the blind natural force that now governs the universe) and the idea of "total unity" (analogous to Fedorov's "all-unifying task"). Solov'ev would later add Fedorovian themes (such as the task of resurrection) to his already developed system, but he would not radically alter the structure of his system itself.

[47] The best commentary on Solov'ev and Fedorov is: Kn. Evgenii Trubetskoi' "Zhiznennaia zadacha Solov'eva i vsemirnyi krizis zhizneponimaniia" [The Life Task of Solov'ev and the Universal Crisis in the Understanding of Life], *Voprosy filosofii i psikhologii*, No. 114, Moscow, Sept-Oct. 1912, pp. 224-87, reprinted as a chapter in his *Morosozertsanie VI. S. Solov'eva* [Solov'ev's World-Conception], Moscow, 1913. I, pp. 35-93 (on Solov'ev & Fedorov, 78-85). Prince Trubetskoi's remarks, that Fedorov's influence is to be found in the middle, but not in the first period of Solov'ev's development, provoked a letter of protest from Peterson. See: "Polemika" [A Polemic], *Voprosy filosofii i psikhologii*, No. 118, Moscow, May-June, 1913, pp. 405-426 for both sides of the polemic between Peterson and Trubetskoi. In his letter, Peterson tells how much of Fedorov's writing Solov'ev saw, and argues that Solov'ev was Fedorov's disciple from the late seventies on. Trubetskoi refutes Peterson's claim, and establishes that from the start each thinker had his own system, and that Solov'ev was never Fedorov's absolute disciple. Gornostaev's essay on Fedorov and Solov'ev, (see Preface, note 16) is a very weak attempt to argue that Fedorov was the decisive influence in Solov'ev's life. As in his Dostoevskii essay, Gornostaev overstates the case, exaggerates Fedorov's influence, and attempts to build up Fedorov's reputation at the expense of Solov'ev's. Most recently, Taras Zakydalsky, in his paper mentioned above (see note 38) argued that Fedorov did have an inportant influence on Solov'ev in turning Solov'ev's attention from progress to the redemption of the past and in forcing him to make room in his system for the salvation of all the dead at the end of history. Zakydalsky concluded that Solov'ev's idea of resurrection is very different from Fedorov's, but the importance of this idea in Solov'ev's works written in the late eighties and early nineties reveals a Fedorovian influence. I agree with Zakydalsky conclusion.

[48] The letter is undated, but Trubetskoi (see above) places it in the early eighties. It is included in: *Pis'ma Vladimira Sergeevicha Solov'eva* (See Preface, note 5), II., 0. 345.

[49] Peterson, in "Polemika" (see note 48, above), p. 409.

[50] S. L. Frank, "Introduction" *A Solov'ev Anthology*, Arranged by S. L. Frank, tr. Natalie Duddington, N. Y., 1950, p. 24. This anthology offers a good introduction to Solov'ev's philosophy. S. L. Frank, (1877-1950), the

editor, was considered by Zenkovskii to have been the most significant and profound of Russian philosophers.

[51] *Pis'ma ... Solov'eva, op. cit.*, pp. 346-7.

[52] Noted by Kozhevnikov in his monograph on Fedotov, (see Preface, note 2), cited by Bulgakov, (see Preface, note 10), *Dva Grada*, p. 271.

[53] See especially *La Russie, et l'église universelle*, St. Petersburg, 1889, pp. 330-336. (This book first appeared in French, and did not appear in Russian until 1911. It is available in English: *Russia and the Universal Church*, H. Rees, tr., London, 1948.) As Zakydalsky has pointed out, one of Solov'ev's last works, "Kratkaia povest ob antikhriste" [A Short Story about the Antichrist] in *Sob. soch.*, X., pp. 193-221, available in *A Solov'ev Anthology, 229-248,* contains a parody of Fedorov's philosophy. Constantinople (as in Fedorov) is the world center, Antichrist is the master-scientist (Fedorov's autocrat) who performs miracles and who reconciles the churches by using museums.

[54] Solov'ev's letter to Tolstoi of July 28-Aug. 2, 1894, in *Pis'ma ... Solov'eva*, III., pp. 38-42. In this letter he seeks to elucidate the differences between his philosophy and Tolstoi's, and sees that the most important difference is that Tolstoi does not accept the idea of resurrection. Solov'ev then gives a clear account of his own idea of resurrection.

[55] N. P. Peterson, "Pis'mo k Izdateliu *Russkogo Arkhiva*" [Letter to the editor of *Russian Arkhive*], *Russkii Arkhiv*, No. 6, Moscow, 1904, pp. 300-301.

[56] N. H. Gusev, *Lev Nikolaevich Tolstoi: Materialy k Biografii s 1881 po 1885 god* [Lev Nikolaevich Tolstoi: Materials toward a Biography, from 1881 to 1885], Moscow, 1970, contains a number of interesting anecdotes about Fedorov and Tolstoi. In 1878, Tolstoi was doing research toward a sequel to *War and Peace*, set in the period of the Decembrist uprising (1825). He eventually abandoned this work, but, apparently, in the course of his research did make the acquaintance of Fedorov. (Gusev, p. 75).

[57] This diary entry for October 5, 1881, is Tolstoi's first mention of Fedorov. L. N. Tolstoi, *Polnoe Sobranie Sochinenii* [Complete Collected Works], 90 Vols., Moscow, 1928-1958, Vol. 49, 1952, p. 58. Hereafter Tolstoi's collected works will be cited as Tolstoi, *Polnoe*, volume and page. In the eighties and nineties, his diaries and letters contain many references to Fedorov. See Tolstoi, *Polnoe*, Vol. 49, pp. 58, 73, 89, 90; Vol. 50, pp. 23, 33, 65, 72 for diary and notebook entries. For letters, see: Vol. 63, p. 81; Vol. 66, p. 85; Vol. 68, p. 247; Vol. 78, p. 48; Vol. 82, pp. 179-80; Vol. 83, p. 314.

[58] Tolstoi, *Polnoe*, Vol. 63, p. 80.

[59] Ernest J. Simmons, *Leo Tolstoi*, N.Y., 1960, II., pp. 366-7.

[60] Linnichenko, (see note 20 above), p. 317.

[61] Cited by Gornostaev, (see Preface, note 16), p. 6.

[62] "Tolstoi v 1880-m gody: Zapiski I. M. Ivakina" [Tolstoi in the 1880's: the Notebooks of I. M. Ivakin], in *Literaturnoe Nasledstvo*, Moscow, 1961, Volume 69, Book II pp. 21-124. Ivakin first met Tolstoi in 1880, when, as a young philologist, he took a position as tutor to the Tolstoi children. His memoirs contain much material on Fedorov. But unfortunately, the editors of *Literaturnoe Nasledstvo* viewed Ivakin's memoirs as a work of interest primarily to students of Tolstoi, and therefore deleted passages, including many devoted to Fedorov, which did not bear directly on Tolstoi.

⁶³ See Gusev (note 56 above), p. 64; and Ostromirov, (Preface, note 4), p. 16.

⁶⁴ Linnichenko (note 60 above), p. 317.

⁶⁵ V. F. Lazurskii, (see note 1 above), p. 466. This is the continuation of the quote used at the beginning of this chapter.

⁶⁶ Cited by Gornostaev (see Preface, note 16), p. 16.

⁶⁷ Cited by Gornastaev, p. 8.

⁶⁸ N. P. Peterson, "Razgovor s L. N. Tolstym" [A Conversation with L. N. Tolstoi], Askhabad, 1899, No. 285, as cited by Gornostaev, *op. cit.*, p. 8.

⁶⁹ From a manuscript of reminiscences, G. P. Georgievskii, *L. N. Tolstoi i N. F. Fedorov* [L. N. Tolstoi and N. F. Fedorov], in the manuscript division of the Lenin Library, as cited by Gusev (note 57 above), p. 78. Georgievskii (who also wrote under the pseudonym P. Ia. Pokrovskii) published what is apparently a shorter version of this manuscript in a leading Russian newspaper just after Fedorov's death: P. Ia. Pokrovskii, "Iz vospominanii o Nikolae Fedoroviche" [From My Recollections of Nikolai Fedorovich], *Moskovskie Vedomosti*, No. 23-26, Moscow, Jan. 23-26, 1904, pp. 4-5, 4-5, 5, 4.

⁷⁰ Tolstoi, *Polnoe*, Vol. 68, p. 247. Shenrok (see note 23 above) tells us that Fedorov was reluctant to attend the celebration in his honor. He did not want to have speeches made about him and tried to discourage the festivities. in his honor.

⁷¹ See Peterson, "Moia perepiska s gr. L. N. Tolstym" [My Correspondence with Count L. N. Tolstoi] in P., 94-120. At one point, in 1909, Peterson adopted such a hostile tone that Tolstoi had to ask him not to write any more. Later, in 1910, Tolstoi forgot or forgave Peterson's earlier hostility, and they resumed their correspondence.

⁷² In 1908, Peterson sent Tolstoi a copy of the first volume of Fedorov's works and asked him to write something that might bring the book to the attention of the general public. (P., 96). Tolstoi did not reply to this request. On October 5, 1910, not long before his death, Tolstoi wrote that he did not have a copy of Fedorov's book and asked Peterson to send him one. (P., xi). From this letter, it would seem that either the first copy that Peterson sent did not reach Tolstoi, or that it reached him and he misplaced it without having read it.

⁷³ See Strakhov's letter of October 19, 1881, in *Perepiska L. N. Tolstogo s N. N. Strakhovym. 1870-94.* [L. N. Tolstoi's Correspondence with N. N. Strakhov: 1870-94], St. Petersburg, 1914, pp. 284-285.

⁷⁴ Simmons, *op cit.*, II., pp. 125-126.

⁷⁵ Sir Isaiah Berlin begins his famous study of Tolstoy, *The Hedgehog and the Fox*, New York, 1957, by quoting a fragment from Archilochus: "The fox knows many things, but the hedgehog knows one big thing." Thinkers are then divided into hedgehogs and foxes, those who relate everything to a single, universal, organizing principle, and those who pursue many ends which are often unrelated and even contradictory. He finds that Pushkin as an arch-fox, and that Dostoevskii and Dante are supreme hedgehogs. Tolstoi was a natural fox who tried all his life to become a hedgehog. Fedorov, whom Sir Isaiah does not discuss, seems to me an even better example of a "hedgehog" than Dostoevskii.

⁷⁶ One of the popular legends that Fedorov collected and prepared for

print was: "Skazanie o postroenii obydennago khrama v Vologde 'vo izbavlenie ot smertonosyia iazvy'" [The Legend of the Building of the Common Church in Vologda 'For the Sake of Salvation from a Deadly Plague'], in *Chteniia v imperatorskom obshchestve istorii i drevnosti Rossii pri Moskovskom Universitete*, CLXVI, Moscow, 1893, pp. 1-21. The foreword that Fedorov wrote (anonymously) for this legend appears in his collected works, (I, 650-655). Fedorov finds implicit in this legend the idea that true Christianity is a collective task to save all men from death. Another legend that Fedorov prepared for publication, and which was published after his death, is: "Bytie krestnago syna" [The Life of a Godson], *Russkii Arkhiv*, No. 11-12, Moscow, 1915, pp. 296-303.

[77] For his ideas about what ought to be included in a card catalogue, see his articles on library science (I, 677-680, and 681-684). For details of his project for an exchange, see his two articles: "Vopros ob obmene izdanii mezhdu Parizhem i Moskvoiu" [The Question of a Book Exchange between Paris and Moscow], *Moskovskiia Vedomosti*, No. 52, Moscow, Feb. 22, 1892, pp. 2-3, unsigned; and, "K voprosu ob ustanovlenii postoiannago pravilnago nauchno-literaturnago obmena mezhdu Frantsiiu i Rossieiu" [On the Question of Establishing a Permanent Regular Scientific-Literary Exchange between France and Russia], *Russkiia Vedomosti*, No. 67, Moscow, Mar. 9., 1892, p. 3., signed: "D".

[78] Letter to Kozhevnikov of September 8, 1899, "Iz perepiski N. F. Fedorova s V. A. Kozhevnikovym o Turkestane" [From the Correspondence of N. F. Fedorov with V. A. Kozhevnikov about Turkestan], *Versty*, No. 3, Paris, 1928, p. 180.

[79] From letters to Kozhevnikov written June 17, 1901, June 28, 1901, July 15, 1902, and August 15, 1899, cited in K., *R.A.*, 1906, I., pp. 65-66.

[80] K., R. A., 1904, II., p. 66.

[81] Pasternak desoribes how be made the sketch in: "Iz zapisok Leonida Pasternaka" [From the Notes of Leonid Pasternak], *Novyi Zournal*, No. 77, New York, 1964, pp. 190-214. Pasternak's drawing is reproduced in *Literaturnoe Nasledsttvo*, Volume 37-38, *L. N. Tolstoi*, II., Moscow, 1939, p. 273. The drawing itself is in the Tolstoi Museum in Moscow, and a full color painting, from the drawing, is privately owned in England. Pasternak's death mask of Fedorov is reproduced in *Vesy*, No. 6, Moscow, 1906.

NOTES TO CHAPTER II

[1] See note 1, preface.

[2] Quoted in K., R.A., 1905, No. 1, p. 184, note 2.

[3] Zenkovskii, *op. cit.*, p. 588.

[4] Bulgakov, *Dva Grada, op. cit.*, p. 261.

[5] Berdiaev, *Russian Review, op. cit.*, p. 125.

[6] Lord, *Slavonic Review, op. cit.*, p. 409.

[7] John G. Kemeny, in *A Philosopher Looks at Science*, (N.Y., 1959, pp. 3-13) argues that the language of philosophy should approach the mathematical ideal, in which one word would stand for one and only one idea,

and all ambiguity would be eliminated. But, in poetry, as William Empson has admirably demonstrated in his 1930 book, *Seven Types of Ambiguity,* several—and sometimes contradictory—senses of a word can make ambiguity a virtue rather than a defect. Fedorov's use of ambiguous words seems to me to enrich, rather than to impoverish, his writings. It is in this sense that his philosophy is closer to poetry than to science.

⁸ For the essay's full title, see p. 41 above.

⁹ "The people are silent" [*narod bezmol'stvuet*] are the closing words (stage directions) in Pushkin's *Boris Godunov.* This formula was often used by later radical critics to refer to the smoldering but unspoken call to revolution which they attributed to the Russian peasants.

¹⁰ K., *R.A.*, 1904, IV, 107-109.

¹¹ Kozhevnikov, in K., *R.A.*, 1904, Iv., p. 109 tells us that Herzen was an early influence. Both Soviet commentators, in *Entsiklopedia ...* and *Istoriia ... op. cit.*, note the influence of Fourier. James Billington, in "The Intelligentsia and the Religion of Humanity," *American Historical Review,* LXV, (1959/60), pp. 814, 820, includes Fedorov in his list of Russian thinkers influenced by Comte.

¹² In the main, my account follow's Kozhevnikov's in K., *R.A.*, IV, pp. 106-124. But I have omitted much from his discussion and have changed several of the examples.

¹³ Fedorov's interpretations of oriental thought probably owe something to Khomiakov's discussion of the differences between the "Iranian" and the "Cushite" casts of mind. According to Khomiakov, the Iranian type was distinguished by his quest for freedom, while the Cushite sought to submit to necessity. Fedorov's distinctions between the "Indian" and "Iranian" principles are more complex. Fedorov's Indians are essentially pantheists, who either accept all phenomena as divine and good, as in Hinduism, or reject the entire phenomenal world as an illusion and as evil, as in Buddhism. Fedorov's Iranians, whose principle he believes the Slavs share, neither deify nor reject the natural world, but struggle to transform evil into good, as taught in the *Avestas.* (I, 265-277, 346-347). New translations of the *Zend-Avesta* (into French by C. de Harlez, 1881, and into English by J. Darmesteter, 1880-87) brought much fresh attention to the beliefs of the ancient Iranians during the very years in which Fedorov was putting his ideas into writing.

¹⁴ Zakydalsky has correctly pointed out, in his dissertation, that Fedorov does not explain what he means when he says that we shall see God "face to face." How can we "see" an immaterial Being? One speculation, which Fedorov does not attempt to make, might be that by the time we are ready to "see" God, "face to face" might mean "aura to aura."

¹⁵ Golovanenko, *op. cit.*, 1914, No. 4, pp. 666-71.

¹⁶ *Ibid.*, p. 666.

¹⁷ Fedorov says surprisingly little about the role of the mother. Contrary to the traditional Russian veneration of the Mother of God, Fedorov usually subsitutes the daughter for the mother in his trinity of kinship.

¹⁸ Zakydalsky classifies Fedorov's "projectivism" as a form of pragmatism. But it seems clear that Fedorov's theory of knowledge includes an element of absolutism foreign to most versions of pragmatism.

¹⁹ Dostoevskii's letter is discussed on page 40 above.

[20] Zakydalsky's attempt to analyze and defend Fedorov's project within the framework of reductive materialism seems to me a valiant attempt at the impossible. Fedorov tries to include materialist arguments within his system, but his system is not limited to and cannot be contained by any materialist conception of the universe. Too much of Fedorov has to be cut out to fit him into a materialist framework.

[21] See page 57 above.

[22] Losskii, *op. cit.*, p. 79.

[23] For a detailed analysis of the problem and for a possible solution, see Zakydalsky's dissertation.

[24] P. S. Boronetskii, "O iurodivyx chudachestvakh Fedorovstva i o zamysle preodoleniia smerti" [On the Fool-for-Christ Eccentricities of Fedorovism and the Idea of Conquering Death], *Tret'ia Rossia*, No. 8, (Paris, 1938), p. 80.

[25] Florovskii, *op. cit.*, p. 404.

[26] *Ibid.* p. 405.

[27] See Losski, *op. cit.*, p. 77.

[28] The classic defense of the idea of the divine rule of the Russian autocrat can be found in Ivan IV's letters to the defector, his former best friend, Kurbskii. See J. L. I. Fennell, *The Correspondence Between Prince A. M. Kurbskii and Tsar Ivan IV of Russia, 1564-5179*, Cambridge, England, 1955.

[29] According to the Primary Chronicle, the Slavs invited the Varangians to send them a ruler: "Our whole land is great and rich, but there is no order in it. Come to rule and reign over us." Serge A. Zenkovsky, *Medieval Russia's Epics, Chronicles, and Tales*, Revised edition, New York, 1974, p. 50.

[30] See Solov'ev's article, "Chto takoe Rossiia" in *Rus'*, 1897, No. 37, (noted in I., 355).

[31] See the fifteenth century narrative, "The Tale of the White Cowl" in Serge A. Zenkovsky, *op. cit.*, pp. 323-333.

[32] Essentially, what Fedorov seems to have been attempting here, and elsewhere in his essay on history, would be to offer a Slavophile alternative, a "dialectical spiritualism" to the dialectical idealism of Hegel's popularizers and the dialectical materialism already being propounded even in Fedorov's time by Russian followers of Marx. For an account of Hegel's impact on 19th century Russia in general, see D. I. Chizhevskii, *Gegel' v Rossii*, Paris, 1939.

[33] Fedorov might have been too quick to find nothing of value in Eastern religious thought. For instance, he understood the need for gradual spiritual development, but failed to recognize some of the very practical guidelines offered toward this development by Indian yogis and sages. The unfolding of human consciousness as projected by Fedorov has more in common than Fedorov realized with Indian (especially Buddhist) meditation techniques.

[34] The conditionality of freedom is a basic theme in Russian thought. Even in the standard Russian dictionaries, *svoboda* [freedom] is defined first in terms of the conditions that make it possible, and the definition offered first in most Western dictionaries ["exemption from external control"] is placed near the bottom of the list.

[35] A good discussion of the basic Russian traits valued by the Slavophiles can be found in Peter K., Christoff's *An Introduction to Nineteenth Century Russian Slavophilism: A Study in Ideas, Volume I: Xomjakov*, The Hague, 1961, especially pp. 121-244.

[36] Fedorov's notions of Russia's mission in world history follow the pattern established in "The Tale of the White Cowl" and the doctrine of "Moscow—the Third Rome." See Serge A. Zenkovsky, *op. cit.*, pp. 323-333.

[37] The question of whether Fedorov is or is not an Orthodox Christian thinker has often been asked by Russian theologians. Fathers Florovskii and Golovanenko insist that he is not. Losskii calls him "an uncanonized saint" (Losskii, *op. cit.*, p. 75), and following Solov'ev, assigns Fedorov an important place in the evolution of Christian thought. Kozhevnikov tells us that Fedorov regularly attended Orthodox services, prayed, and lived by the Orthodox calendar. It is clear, then, that Fedorov was a devout believer. His intention was to restore meaning to the idea of resurrection, not to depart from Christian doctrine.

NOTES TO CHAPTER III

[1] Kozhevnikov lists dozens of contemporary writers and thinkers whom Fedorov probably had read. See especially K., *R.A.*, 1906, No. 1, pp. 63-102; and No. 2, pp. 269-301. For Fedorov's views on the very newest major Russian writers that appeared near the end of his life (Chekhov, Gor'kii', and others) see his letter of April 2, 1896 to Kozhevnikov, published in *Evraziia*, No. 24, May 4, 1929, p. 8, For more on Fedorov and his day see Appendix II.

[2] See Peterson's statement on pp. 21-22 above.

[3] For example, in the article for *Istoriia filosofii v SSSR* (*op. cit.*, p. 59), we read: "The utopianism of Fedorov's social theory, its conservative and reactionary character does not, however obviate the fact that his sincere concern for the need to establish justice in social relationships prompted him to true critical observations and fruitful speculations on a number of problems." The article concludes that the "fruitful hypotheses, original ideas, contained in Fedorov's reflections on life and people, suffered from the corrupting, influence of religious, monarchic and other superstitions. This influence tied the wings of his utopia and deprived his idea of the actual 'projectivity' he dreamed about." (*Ibid.*, pp. 645).

[4] See especially E. N. Vodovozova, *Na zare zhizni* [At the Dawn of Life], Petersburg, 1911; N. Strakhov, *Iz istorii literaturnogo nigilizma, 1861-1865* [From the History of Literary Nihilism, 1861-1865], St. Petersburg, 1890; and V. Peresvetov, "O zamechatel'nom, no ne blagotvornom napravlenii nekotorykh sovremennykh pisatelei," [On the Remarkable, but Unsound, Tendency of Certain Contemporary Writers], *Russkaia rech'*, No. 60, July 27, 1861, pp. 126-7. All these cources, and others, are cited and discussed in Moser, *op. cit.*, pp. 23-57. Other good sources for information about the radical *milieu* of the 1860's are the documents concerning the Karakozov trial. See especially the description of "The Organization" given by the members who testified at the hearings in *Pokushenie Karakozova*, Moscow, 1928-30 and in "Pokushenie Karakozova 4 aprelia 1866 g.", *Krasny Arkhiv*, No. 17, Moscow, 1926, pp. 91-137. The picture of the intelligentsia that emerges from these documents differs somewhat from the standard Marxist picture of the intelligentsia as the voice of the people's aspirations.

[5] D. I. Pisarev, "Pushkin i Belinskii," *Sochineniia*, III.

[6] Cited by James H. Billington in *The Icon and The Axe*, New York, 1968, p. 388.

[7] Dmitri Pisarev, "Nineteenth Century Scholasticism," *Selected Philosophical, Social, and Political Essays*, Moscow, 1959.

[8] Dmitri Pisarev, "Thinking Proletariat," *Selected Philosophical, Social, and Political Essays*, Moscow, 1959, p. 646.

[9] Johann Friedrich Blumenbach (1752-1840) was a German physiologist and anthropologist who first divided mankind into five great families or races: Caucasian, Mongolian, Malayan, Negro, and American. He attributed to each race certain anatomical, cranial, and psychological, characteristics. Arthur de Gobineau (1816-1882), author of the 1853-55 *Essay on the Inequality of the Human Race*, was the major nineteenth century spokesman for the myth of Aryan unity and superiority. Although Fedorov does not share Gobineau's fears of the pollution of Aryan purity, he does accept the general nineteenth century concept of a once unified Aryan family that has regrettably broken into disparate factions.

[10] Jacob Ludwig Carl Grimm (1785-1863) formulated his famous law in *Deutsche Grammatik* (first edition, 1819; second edition, 1822-1840), but was probably assisted by the previous work of the Danish philologist, Rasmus Christian Rask (1787-1832). But before the definitive studies by Rask and Grimm, Sir William Jones had in the 1780's established a connection between Sanskrit, Greek, Latin, Persian, Celtic, and Germanic languages, and had posited the existence of an original Aryan mother tongue.

[11] From E. N. Vodovozova, *Na zare zhizni*, cited in Moser, *op. cit.*, p. 27.

[12] For Chernyshevskii's view of education as a cure for all ills, see N. G. Chernyshevskii, *Polnoe Sobranie Sochinenii* (Moscow, 1939), XI, pp. 124-125. The quotation from Pisarev is from D. I. Pisarev, "Realisty" (1864), *Sochineniia*, Moscow, 1956, III, p. 122, cited in Moser, *op cit.*, p. 46. For other statements and projects by radicals, including P. V. Pavlov's sunday schools, see Moser, pp. 46-47.

[13] Cizhevskii, *op. cit.*

[14] See Fedorov's article, "Chemu nauchaet drevneishchii khristianskii pamiatnik v Kitae" [What is the Significance of the Oldest Christian Monument in China?], *Russkii Arkhiv*, No. 4 (Moscow, 1901), pp. 631-637, later reprinted in Setnitskii's *"Russkie mysliteli o Kitae"* [Russian Thinkers on China].

[15] Nicholas Berdiaev, *The Russian Idea*, tr. R. M. French, Boston, 1962, p. 212.

[16] *Ibid.*, p. 209.

[17] See Zenkovskii, *op. cit.*, p. 601.

[18] George P. Fedotov, *The Russian Religious Mind*, I, Cambridge, Mass., 1946, I., pp. 15-20.

[19] Iuri Krizanich (or Crisanius) was a Croatian Catholic priest who came to Russia with a Polish diplomatic mission in the mid seventeenth century, and later returned to spend more than two decades in Russia. His goal was to convert Russia to Catholicism, and, at the same time, to encourage in Russia the development of a new united Slavdom. He introduced Russians to the ideas of Machievelli, advocated an absolute autocracy, and fanned the first

NOTES TO CHAPTER III

fires of Panslavism. For more information, see S. Belokurov, "Iurii Krizhanich v Rossii" in *Iz dukhovnoi zhizni moskovskago obshchestva XVII veka*, Moscov, 1902.

[20] For Ivan's correspondence with Kurbskii, see J. I. L. Fennell, *op. cit.* Chaadaev's letters are quoted here as translated by M.-B. Zeldin from Edie, Scanlan, Zeldin, and Kline, Vol. I., *op. cit.*, M.-B. Zeldin has edited and translated a complete edition of Chaadaev's philosophikal letters.

Belinskii's "Letter to Gogol'" and Vyacheslav Ivanov and Mikhail Gershenzon's "A Corner to Corner Correspondence" are available in English in Marc Raeff, *Russian Intellectual History: An Anthology*, New York, 1966.

[21] Zenkovskii, *op. cit.*, p. 5.

[22] Chaadaev, "First Letter", Edie, Scanlan, Zeldin & Kline, *op. cit.*, I., p. 115.

[23] In addition to Christoff's work on Khomiakov noted above, his more recent study of Kireevskii offers excellent discussion of the basic ideas of the Slavophiles. See: Peter K. Christoff, *An Introduction to Nineteenth-Century Russian Slavophilism: A Study in Ideas, Volume II: I. V. Kireevskii*, 1972, The Hague.

[24] Berdiaev, *The Russian Idea*, see especially Chapter IX, pp. 193-218.

[25] Chaadaev, "First Letter", *op. cit.*, p. 119.

[26] The Very Rev. Alexander Schmemann, *Orthodox Holy Week: A Liturgical Explanation for the Days of Holy Week*, St. Vladimir's Seminary Press, Tuckahoe, N.Y., (no date), p. 45.

[27] Fedor Dostoevskii, *Crime and Punishment* (Garnett tr.), N.Y., 1927, p. 554.

[28] Leo Tolstoi, *Resurrection*, (Maude tr.), N.Y. 1963, p. 507.

[29] Peter Wiles, "On Physical Immortality", *op. cit.* Wiles traces the idea of physical immortality from its religious sources through twentieth century attempts by Russian scientists to discover the means of prolonging life. Among the various attempts discussed are Mechnikov's theories of orthodosis, Metalnikov's work with "immortal" cells, and Voronov's efforts to prolong life and virility by grafting upon human testicles certain parts of the testicle of an ape. (One of the many gullible celebrities who submitted to Voronov's "treatment" was the aging W. B. Yeats). Other Russian born scientists sought the key to longevity, and perhaps even immortality, in the pituitary gland, the connective tissue, and in frequent soda baths.

[30] Wiles, *op. cit.*, July, 1965, p. 125.

[31] *Ibid.*, p. 126.

[32] Chaadaev, "First Letter," *op cit.*, p. 107.

[33] *Ibid.*, pp. 122-123.

[34] *Ibid.*, "Third Letter," p. 125.

[35] *Ibid.*, p. 129.

[36] *Ibid.*

[37] Zenkovskii, *op. cit.*, pp. 469-472.

[38] See preface, note 13, above.

[39] For a brief note of Fedorov's influence on Bulgakov, see the review of *Filosofiia khoziaistva* in *Bogoslovskii vestnik*. Dec. 1913, pp. 844ff. Berdiaev discusses his own debt to Fedorov in *Dream and Reality*, Chapter XIV. A brief

note on Berdiaev's points of agreement and disagreement with Fedorov can be found in C. S. Calvin, *Berdiaev's Philosophy of Hope*, Minneapolis, 1968, p. 99. Florenskii, like Fedorov, is a controversial religious thinker. Active as both a scientist and a theologian, Florenskii combines mysticism and scientism, develops his own peculiar literary manner, places "total-unity" at the top of his list of values, and shared many ideas with the Slavophiles—all of which indicates at least some intellectual kinship with Fedorov. But so little has been written about Florenskii that it is difficult to assess the extent and depth of his kinship with Fedorov. Florovskii appears to have developed many of his positions in reaction to, or in opposition against, Fedorov. His critique of Fedorov is one of the harshest ever written. Florovskii's own ideas about Christ and the Resurrection, his reaffirmation of the mystical tradition, may owe something to the strong but negative influence of Fedorov. But both Florenskii and Florovskii are thinkers whose relationship to Fedorov would merit investigation by future students of Russian theology.

[40] A copy of *Vselenskoe Delo I* can be found in the library of Helsinki University, but information about its contents and contributors can be found in the slightly more accessible *Vselenskoe Delo II*, a copy of which is located at Columbia University. See especially, pp 107-115, and 182-183.

[41] *Vselenskoe Delo II* contains poems by A. Nesmelov, P. Luchitskii, and A. Gornostaev; articles by G. G. Gezhelinskii, D. S. Kononov, K. A. Chkheidze, V. Aleksandrov, R. Manovskii, and S. Chuev. Documents printed here include an article by Setnitskii, a letter from Solov'ev to K. Leont'ev in which Fedorov is mentioned, Letters from Fedorov to Peterson and Kozhevnikov, a letter from I. M. Ivakin to Tolstoi about the need to bring Fedorov's ideas to the attention of the public, and letters from Peterson and N. V. Ustrialov on Fedorov. Further items include a review of Komarovich's edition of the notebooks for *The Brothers Karamazov*, a note on the Fedorov archive in Prague, obituaries of Kozhevnikov, Peterson, Murav'ev, and Kuznetsova (editor of the first *Vselenskoe Delo*). Also printed here is an annotated bibliography (actually a series of brief review notices) of works by and about Fedorov through 1934. In general, the poems in both issues are weak, the articles are more hortatory than astute, and only a few items in each issue are of either intrinsic or historical value.

[42] Among the contributors to the first issue of *Vselenskoe Delo* who eventually occupied positions of responsibility in the Soviet Government were: the poet Valery Briusov, who exercised some influence over emerging literary schools and offcial publication policies; the physicist P. Bakhmetev, who headed a laboratory that conducted experiments in anabiosis and the preservation of life under extremely low temperatures; A. Pankratov, a library administrator who completed an unpublished biography of Fedorov. Since many of the poems and articles were written under pseudonyms, the identity of some contributors who later occupied important government posts (according to the editors *of Vselenskoe Delo II*) are not known. But among those known the editors name: I. Brikhnichev, a poet who became a party member, rose to secretary of Central Committee [*Pomgol*] and was the first to mention Fedorov in the Soviet press. He was either shot or died in a concentration camp in 1931. M. N. Pokrovskii, a well-known historian, party member, and high official in the Zamnarkompros. B. Shmankevich, a poet who was never a high government official but who talked about Fedorov with everyone and was close to the Maiakovskii circle.

⁴³ S. V. Utechin, "Bolsheviks and their Allies After 1917: The Ideological Pattern," *Soviet Studies*, X, Oxford, 1958/59, pp. 113-35.

⁴⁴ Setnitskii tells us (in O., IV, pp. 2-3) that Fedorov's influence was particularly strong on P. Ivanitskii', who wrote about rainmaking experiments in 1925: "Iskusstvennoe vyzyvanie dozhdia i upravlenie pogodoi posredstvom reguliatsii atmosfernogo i zemnogo elektrichestva" [Artificial rainmaking and the control of the weather by means of the regulation of atmospheric and terrestrial electricity], *Novaia Derevnia*, Moscow, 1925. Losskii sees Fedorov's influence on Stalin's plan to warm Siberia by changing the direction of the Gulfstream "and diverting polar icebergs toward England in order to freeze that country which is the embodiment of hated capitalism." (Losskii, *op. cit.*, p. 79.) More recently, Elisabeth Koutaissoff notes in her article "Some Futurological Aspects of Fedorov's 'Philosophy of the Common Cause," *Russian Literature Triquarterly*, No. 12, Spring, 1975, pp. 393-407, that a recent *Izvestia* article by Iurii Sedunov ["Weather to Order", Fe. 23, 1974] issued an appeal "for legislation and international cooperation in the field of meteorological regulation." (p. 407). So Fedorov's ideas, on regulation at least, continue to find supporters.

⁴⁵ "Voluntary labor" is the Soviet euphemism for the manner in which the canals were built. But political prisoners and ordinary convicts were the volunteers. Leading writers were called upon to describe the construction, and Solzhenitsyn, in *Gulag*, discusses the hymns of praise they wrote. Although the idea for building such canals originated with Peter the Great, the suggestion that the immediate impetus for the Soviet project may have been Fedorov's ideas can be found in Setnitskii, *O konechnom ideale*, pp. 82 ff.

⁴⁶ For more information about the Commission and Vernadskii', see Utechin, *op. cit.*, pp. 132-33.

⁴⁷ *Ibid.*

⁴⁸ Alexander Solzhenitsyn, *The Gulag Archipelago: Two*, New York, 1975, p. 641.

⁴⁹ Utechin, *op. cit.*, p. 130.

⁵⁰ Setnitskii, *O konechnom ideale*, p. 83.

⁵¹ N. V. Ustrailov, *Rossiia: u okna vagona* (Russia: From a Train Window), Harbin, 1926, p. 46.

⁵² R. Fülop-Miller, *The Mind and Face of Bolshevism*, tr. F. S. Flint, and D. F. Tait, New York, 1929, pp. 261-2.

⁵³ See Gor'kii's correspondence with Grigor'ev, Prishvin, and Forsh, in *Gor'kii i sovetskie pisateli: Neizdannaia perepiska* [Gor'kii and Soviet Writers: Unpublished Correspondence], *Literaturnoe Nasledstvo*, No. 70, Moscow, 1963, pp. 133-136, 335-338, 584-597.

⁵⁴ *Smertobozhnichestvo* [The Apotheosis of Death] Anonymous, Harbin, 1926. A review and a number of quotations from this work can be found in *Vselenskoe Delo II*. Fedorov's name is not mentioned once in the work, but the task urged on all men is clearly his Common Task.

⁵⁵ L. Shestov, *Umozrenie i otkrovenie* [Speculations and Revelations], Paris, 1964, pp. 127-30.

⁵⁶ A. K. Gornostaev (real name Gorskii) argued, in his work on Tolstoi, [*Pered litsom smerti*], Harbin, 1928) that the great writer figuratively hid his face from the world and allowed his contemporaries to see him only from

the rear. He accepted Fedorov's project, but after his attempts to propogate Fedorov's ideas met with ridicule, Tolstoi grew bitter and began to preach nihilism. In *Rai na zemle*, Gornostaiev argues that Dostoevskii had searched all his life for the meaning of the idea of resurrection. He found this meaning in Fedorov, began to present Fedorov's project in *The Brothers Karamazov*, and, had he lived longer, would have given full artistic embodiment to Fedorov's philosophy. In *Tiaga zemnaia*, Gornostaiev argues that Solov'ev became Fedorov's disciple in the late seventies, considered Fedorov his only master, and died ruing that he had strayed from the true Fedorovian path. There is a kernel of truth in each of Gornostaev's assertions, but he constantly overstates the case and arrives at conclusions far beyond those warrented by the evidence.

[57] The titles of Setnitskii's treatises, all published first in the *Proceedings* of the Harbin School of Law and then issued as separate pamphlets, are: "Kapitalisticheskii stroi v izobrazhenii N. F. Fedorova" [The Capitalist System as Depicted by N. F. Fedorov], Harbin, 1926; "Russkie mysliteli o Kitae" [Russian Thinkers on China], Harbin, 1926; "Eksploatatsiia" [Exploitation], Harbin, 1928; "O konechnom ideale" [On the Ultimate Ideal], Harbin, 1929 (later incorporated into a large book of the same title). Generally these works present useful and interesting comments on Fedorov and his thought, but Setnitskii's own sociological, political, and philosophical speculations are not of great intrinsic merit.

[58] The Eurasian writer, K. A. Chkheidze, who lived in Prague until his recent death, and who was in charge of the Fedorov archive at the National Museum, told Taras Zakydalsky that "A. Ostromirov" was in fact Setnitskii. In the works published under the general title *Nikolai Fedorovich Fedorov i Sovremennost'*, Setnitskii—Ostromirov offers interesting speculations on the relationship between Fedorov's ideas and Freud's theories of the death wish and the destructive nature of sex; on Fedorov's view of the unity of space-time, and Einstein's theory of relativity; on Fedorov's concept of particles of matter and Bohr's theories on the composition of atoms; on Fedorov's speculations on electro-magnetism and recent scientific work on that problem; and on Fedorov's relationship to Symbolist and Futurist and Imaginist art. Ostromirov argues that Fedorov predicted the First World War, as well as the Russo-Japanese War. In general, Ostromirov attempts to cast Fedorov in the light of prophet for every major advance in civilization in this century.

[59] See the articles published in *Put'* and *Versty* listed in the bibliography.

[60] For an account of the founding of *Federoviana Prahensia* see *Vselenskoe Delo II*, pp. 176-178.

[61] Valerian Murav'ev, *Ovladenie vremenem*, Moscow, 1924. Basing his argument on Einstein's theory that time is not absolute but relative, Murav'ev argues that by extending our control over the physical universe, we can eventually control time. And by controlling time, we can restore the past and resurrect the dead. A sympathetic review of Murav'ev's book, by V. Sezeman, appeared in *Versty*, No. 3, 1928. An obituary of Murav'ev was published in *Vselenskoe Delo II*.

[62] For a discussion of Fedorov's influence on the Eurasians, by an anonymousmember of the movement, see "Put' Evraziistva" [The Path of Eurasianism] *Evraziia*, No. 8, Paris, Jan. 12, 1929, p. 1. Letters discussing Fedorov's relationship to Eurasianism and Fedorovism in the USSR appeared in No.No. 3 (Dec. 3, 1928), 22 (April 20, 1929), and 24 (May 24, 1929). From advertisements in the newspaper for the movement, we learn that the Eurasian publishing

house served as a European distributor for the second edition of Fedorov's works and for the Harbin works written about him. Basic position papers for the movement were: *Iskhod k Vostoku* [The Eastward Turn], 1921; *Evraziistvo: opyt sistematicheskogo izlozheniia* [Eurasianism: An Attempt at a Systematic Analysis], 1926; and *Evraziistvo: Deklaratsiia, Formulirovka, Tezisy* [Eurasianism: Declaraction, Formulations, Theses], 1932, all issued by the Eurasian Publishing House in Prague. In these works, the political, economic, cultural, and religious positions are defined, and many of these positions are restatement of Fedorov's ideas.

[63] Valerii Briusov (1873-1924) a leading Symbolist theorist and poet, and one of the best critics of Russian literature, became, after the Revolution, an important figure in literary politics, a convert from Symbolism to Bolshevism. In his diary, *Dnevniki, 1891-1910*, Moscow, 1927, he describes (p. 85) a meeting with Fedorov in 1900. At the request of the editors, he also sent a letter outlining his response to Fedorov's ideas for publication in *Vselenskoe Delo I*.

[64] Andrei Belyi (Boris Bugaev, 1880-1934), another leading Symbolist poet, theorist, critic, and novelist, was well acquainted with Fedorov's project. See his "Vospominanie o Bloke" [Reminiscences of Blok], *Epopeia*, No. 2, Moscow-Berlin, Sept. 1922, p. 119.

[65] Nadezhda Mandelshtam, *Mozart and Salieri*, tr. Robert A. McLean, Ann Arbor, 1973, p. 19. Nadezhda Mandelshtam does not mention whether her husband, the poet Osip Mandelshtam (1891-1938) also knew of Fedorov's works. Her own objection to Fedorov's idea is that in the resurrection we may not be able to re-establish the human relationships, the close ties with people we love, that make this limited, fated, present life worth living. She believes that poets, who mentally resurrect and enter into conversation with their long dead predecessors (Mandelshtam and Dante), practice a higher form of resurrection than that advocated by Fedorov.

[66] See A. Kiselev, "Uchenie N. F. Fedorova v svete sovremennosti" [The Teachings of N. F. Fedorov in the Light of Our Times], *Grani*, No. 81, Frankfurt, 1971, pp. 122-53.

[67] George L., Kline, "Religious Motifs in Russian Philosophy" Studies on the Soviet Untion, Vol. 9, No. 2 (1969), p. 90.

[68] Mesimaria, an exotic drink distilled from a rare berry that grows only in Finnish Lapland and ripens under the midnight sun of the Arctic summer, replaced wine and vodka for a brief time as the most popular drink in silver age Russia. See Billington, *op. cit.*, p. 472.

[69] See Billington, *op. cit.*, pp. 478-492.

[70] *Ibid.*, p. 490.

[71] Roman Jakobson, "O pokolenii rastrativshem svoikh poetov" [On a Generation that Squandered its Poets], *Smert' Vladimira Maiakovskogo*, Berlin, 1931, pp. 24-25.

[72] *Ibid.*, p. 24.

[73] Edward J. Brown, *Maiakovskii: A Poet in the Revolution*, Princeton, 1973, p. 256.

[74] *Ibid.*, p. 254.

[75] For more information on Chekrygin, see: A. Bakushinskii, "V puti k velikomu iskusstvu" (On the Path to Great Art), *Zhizn'*, No. 3, Moscow,

1922, pp. 132-5; and A. Saltykov, "Pervyi illiustrator Maiakovskogo" [Maiakovskii's First Iluustrator], *Tvorchestvo*, No. 12, Moscow, 1965, p. 15. The Saltykov article includes a photograph from Chekrygin's Resurrection cycle.

[76] Nicolas Berdiaev, *Samopoznanie*, [Self-Knowledge], Paris, 1949, pp. 256-257. A loose translation, by Katherine Lampert, appeared under the title *Dream and Reality*, N.Y., 1951. For critical commentary on this translation, see the review by George L. Kline in Vol. 50 (1953) of *The Journal of Philosophy*, pp. 441-446.

[77] Solzhenitsyn, *op. cit.*, p. 641.

[78] I. M. Zabelin, "Chelovechestvo—dlia chego ono?" [Mankind—What is It For?], in *Moskva*, No. 8, 1966, and No. 5, 1968, pp. 172-86; 147-61 The article has been included in his *Chelovek i chelovechestvo* [Man and Mankind], Moscow, 1970.

[79] *Otkroveniia Viktora Velskogo* [The Revelations of Victor Velskii], Anonymous, *Grani*, No. 75, Frankfurt, 1970, pp. 3-114.

APPENDIX I

Since even the Gregg reprint edition of Fedorov's works is lacking in many public and university libraries, I have translated here the table of contents to both volumes so that those interested may obtain a clearer idea of the scope of Fedorov's work. Exact dates of composition are, in most cases, unknown. Many of the articles and essays were not written by Fedorov himself, but were written by Peterson from Fedorov's dictation, then reworked by both into final form. Most of the items included in the second volume were put together from the various manuscripts, drafts, and scraps of paper that the editors found after Fedorov's death. Roughly half of these articles were prepared for print by Peterson, and the other half by Kozhevnikov. So the problem of fixing dates of composition is a difficult one. A scrap of paper written in 1887 may have been added to a scrap of paper written in 1899 to make an article that was not put together until 1910. When internal evidence for dating exists, then, that evidence can be confusing. References by Fedorov to current events are accompanied by parenthetical editorial references to events (such as publication dates) that may have occurred later or even after Fedorov's death. Furthermore, the editors do not always indicate which dates were mentioned in the original manuscripts and which dates were later inserted by the editors. So the scholar who would hope to settle questions of "influence" by comparing dates of composition would have to have access to the original manuscripts—if they still exist. So for now we cannot give specific dates, but only approximate periods of composition. We know that Fedorov had already developed much of his idea by the time he met Peterson in 1864. We further know that most of the "Brotherhood" essay was first written between 1878 and 1881 in response to questions from Dostoevskii, and from internal evidence it is clear that much of the present first section of this essay was added after the famine of 1891. From internal evidence and from biographical information, we also know that most of the other articles were written during the last ten years of Fedorov's life. What complicates even very rough attempts to determine the time of composition is that Fedorov apparently considered nothing finished, and continued to rework his previous efforts right up until the time of his death. Whenever possible, then,

I have indicated parenthetically in the translation of the table of contents the approximate date or period of composition. A plus sign after the date indicates that the article was written either during or after the year indicated.

CONTENTS OF *THE PHILOSOPHY OF THE COMMON TASK*

Volume One, Gregg Reprint of 1906 edition.

English Introduction by N. Zernov
Russian Forewords by V. Kozhevnikov and N. Peterson.

1. The question of brotherhood, or kinship, of the reasons for the unbrotherly, unkindred, i. e. unpeaceful state of the would, and of the means for the restoration of kinship. A note from the unlearned to the learned: clergy and laity, believers and unbelievers. (1878-1891+)

　a) Part 1. An appeal to the learned clergy and military men on the occasion of the famine of 1891, and of experiments in rainmaking by means of explosive substances, (the regulation of the meteorological process as a beginning, a step toward the control of nature's blind forces, in general, and as a task that would unify the human race in the image of the Holy Trinity), and on the occasion of the jubilee of the venerator of the Holy Trinity St. Sergius, who venerated in the Trinity the model and commandment for those who gather in oneness 1-41

　b) Part 2. The cult of ancestors as the one true religion. The Trinity as a commandment. The test of faiths. Faith, as unification in the task of the fathers, or in the restoration of fidelity to the fathers and to the God of the fathers. On the criterion by which the path of The Lord and the image of God is to be determined 42-127

　c) Part 3. What history is. How it is to be understood that universal resurrection did not follow Christ's resurrection. The Protestant, and in general, western concept of Christ's feat, or the religion of those not yet mature. True Christianity in Orthodoxy, understood as a lament on disunity and as unification in the task of all the fathers 128-247

　d) Part 4. In what our task consists. The problem of food and sanitation.—Together with this one all three of the above parts stand as appeals to the learned laity, western and Russian, and include an indication of the duty of the learned, who have realized that the division into learned and unlearned is the root of all divisions—the division into rich and poor, the division of one reason into two, theoretical and practical, which leads to two kinds of ignorance: to the ignorance of the doers, the people, who acknowledge themselves to be dark; and to the ignorance of the thinkers, i.e. the learned, who do not recognize objective truth in knowledge. In the division, expressed in society according to the type of the organism, in evolution and progress, is also contained the immaturity of the human race; but unification in the common task of controling the blind forces of nature, in the task of the fathers, will lead the human race to maturity, i.e. to unity in the image of the Holy Trinity, indivisible and infusible ... 248-352

2. *Autocracy* a) The historical significance of the Tsar's title; b) What Russia is and what Orthodoxy is; c) The autocrat as the one who stands in the place of the fathers and of the First Father (1895+) 353-398

3. *Supramoralism*, or the universal synthesis (i.e. universal unification). The synthesis of the two kinds of reason, and of the three objects of knowledge and action (God, man and nature; man as an instrument of Divine reason and himself as the reason of the universe); the synthesis of science and art in religion (1894-1902+) 399-468

4. *The project of church unity*, inviting the clergy of all faiths to cooperate in turning the military into an instrument of salvation from famine; and indicating, in an analysis of V. S. Solov'ev's paper "On the Reasons for the Collapse of the Medieval Worldview", that a reconciliation of the churches in matters of dogma and ritual must precede the reconciliation or unifying of believers and unbelievers in the common task (1898+) 469-491

5. *The Exhibition of 1889*—which reveals the meaning of progress—the centennial jubilee of bourgeois rule; what an exhibition of the last year of the 19th century or the first year of the 20th century should be; what the 19th century bequeathes to the 20th. (1893+) 492-519

6. The question of the restoration of universal kinship. The means for the restoration of kinship. The *Sobor*. On the one *sobor*, universal but incomplete, in connection with the fall of Constantinople and on the renewal of the *sobor* in connection with the liberation of Constantinople as the

center—the *sobor* as holy synod and congress of all science, for the implementation of the project of the transformation of our life as it now is (history as fact) into what it ought to be (history as project) (1887+) 520-598

7. The paintings on the outer walls of a temple housing a museum or a library (1892+) 599-616

8. The paintings inside a temple (1893+) 617-626

9. Two celebrations—clergy and laity, Saint Sergius and V. N. Karazin, as two early forms of activity whereby sons might realize the task of all the fathers (1894+) 627-655

10. *Disarmament.* How instruments of destruction can be turned into instruments of salvation (1901) 656-668

11. On the conversion of weapons, i.e. of instruments of destruction into instruments of salvation. On the conversion of the army, that is, of the people as a whole, of the entire human race—by means of universal and lifelong military duty—into an experimental science force, into a force to control the blind forces of nature (1902+) 669-676

12. What is the significance of a file card for a book? Toward the actualization of V. N. Karazin's idea that the expansion of knowledge is inseparable from the spreading of enlightenment (1896) 677-680

13. *Bibliography.* Popular knowledge, encyclopedic knowledge, imaginary knowledge, and real knowledge; the transition from imaginary knowledge to real knowledge (1893+) 681-684

14. On the significance of *temples built by the community* [*obydennye khramy*] in general and in our time in particular. Temples built by the community as the highest manifestation of the principles of assistance [*pomoch'ii*] God help us! [*Bog v pomoch'*] and joint effort (*toloka*) and as an expression of religious uplift [*religioznye pod'emy*] (1898) 685-731

Volume Two, Gregg reprint of 1913 edition.
Foreword by V. Kozhevnikov and N. Peterson.

I. *Articles on Religion*

1. Faith, action [*delo*] and prayer 3
2. Religion—the cult of ancestors and the task of resurrection 5
3. The Jewish Sabbath and the Christian Sunday 7

APPENDIX I

4. On Orthodoxy and the Symbol of faith 7
5. Orthodoxy and what distinguishes it from egoism and altruism 8
6. —"— 9
7. The meaning of the Gospel of John and of the Gospels in general 10
8. Prayer for universal salvation 12
9. Heaven and hell? Or purgatory? 13
10. On the conventional character of prophecies of the end of the world (1898+) 13
11. Temptation in relation to the problem of capital punishment 16
12. Meteoric regulation as the fulfilment of the prayer, "Give us (i.e. all of us) this day our daily bread (i.e. earned by our labor)" 17
13. The day-to-day destruction of the temple 18
14. St. Lazarus week 19
15. Bethany 23
16. What is our Messianic hope? 27
17. Buddha's "great demise" and Good Friday 28
18. The gifted thief 29
19. The hundred in Capernaum and at the Cross 31
20. On Renan 32
21. "Man is the creature who buries his dead" 33
22. The Orthodox funeral rite and its meaning 34
23. On religious folk-art, or "according to the learned"—on "local inventions." 35
24. Concerning the question of the celebration of Holy Trinity day 36
25. On secularization as profanation 36
26. Why is a calendar needed? 38
27. The daughter of man as reconciler 40
28. The enslavement of the Creator to the Creation in the latest Protestantism (1899) 40
29. —"— 41
30. In justification 42
31. The verdict and a few words of justification 42

II. *Articles on Philosophy*

1. Creation and re-creation 47
2. What is freedom? (1902) 47
3. Two historical types of worldview 48
4. On the limitations of western "enlightenment" 49
5. On the teleology of the world 49
6. Metaphysicians and agnostics 51
7. —"— 52

8. The Last Judgment of Philosophy 53
9. The yoke of Kant 54
10. A variant of the article "The yoke of Kant" 55
11. On the two "Critiques": the urban, bourgeois; and the rural, peasant 57
12. Kant's axioms 58
13. —"— 59
14. Kantianism as the essence of Germanism 59
15. Knowledge and action—On the two kinds of reason and the two social classes, or, more accurately, on the class that has separated itself from the people 60
16. On the boundaries of the "outer" and "inner" 61
17. What is a postulate of practical reason? 62
18. Phantom autonomy (1893) 63
19. Three kinds of reason and one kind of reason 63
20. Criticism as play or diversion 64
21. "Back to Kant!" 65
22. Kant and the child of the Gospels or the son of man 65
23. Why practical reason has not fulfiled in fact what theoretical reason has recognized to be unfulfiled in thought ... 67
24. On Kant's categories 68
25. Concerning the question of two kinds of reason 69
26. On unifying the two kinds of reason 70
27. More on the question of two kinds of reason 72
28. The idea of universal bourgeois history 72
29. The same. Second essay 73
30. Kant's legacy 75
31. In what does the universal categorical imperative consist? 77
32. Kant's false democratism 77
33. Regarding Kant's view of the autonomy of the will 78
34. Letter to N. P. Peterson 80
35. Kant's moral casuistry 81
36. Panlogism or illogism 82
37. The reform of Hegel's "Logic." 85
38. The philosopher-bureaucrat 86
39. Supramoralism and Hegelianism 87
40. The last philosopher—"thinker" 88
41. Regarding Schopenhauer 89
42. Regarding V. Kozhevnikov's book, "The Philosophy of Feeling and Faith" (1897+) 91
43. On Hamann 92
44. Hamann and the 18th century "Enlightenment" 95
45. On Jacobi 96
46. "I" and "Not-I" from the philosophical and human point of view 97
47. On the Neo-Kantians 89
48. The philosopher of the Dark Kingdom 100

APPENDIX I

49. Pertaining to the article "The Philosopher of the Dark Kingdom" 102
50. The Dark Prophet and the Dark King 104
51. How did "Zarathustra" originate? 105
52. The positivistic element in Nietzsche's development 107
53. The last philosopher 107
54. The end of philosophy 109
55. An infinite number of involuntary recurrences or a single, conscious and voluntary recurrence? 113
56. Arbitrariness—the creator of the doctrine of involuntary recurrences? 116
57. The Polish aristocrat as philosopher 117
58. Lackey aristocratism 119
59. Supermanhood, as a vice and as a virtue 121
60. Immortality as the privilege of supermen 122
61. Morality—not brotherhood, but kinship 127
62. The superman as adolescent 128
63. On morality and mysticism in Nietzsche 129
64. "Beyond good and evil." 131
65. What is left unsaid in the ethics of the "superman" 132
66. Christianity against "Nietzschianity" [*nichsheanstvo*]... 133
67. Beyond compassion, or the superman's laughter 135
68. Love of power or love of the fathers? 137
69. The "learned, all-too learned" thinker, that is, the learned Philistine 140
70. On "excessiveness" [*chrezmernost'*] and the inadequacy of history 143
71. "Excessiveness" or the inadequacy of history? 144
72. Thoughts on Nietzsche's aesthetics (1898+) 144
73. The philosophy of stupefaction 148
74. The tragic and the Bacchic in Schopenhauer and Nietzsche 151
75. On the unification of the arts (with regard to the ideas of Wagner and Nietzsche on the task of art) 153
76. Life as intoxication or as sobriety (1898+) 154
77. World tragedy 155
78.   —"—   157
79. What does it mean "to become oneself?" 158
80. The prodigal son of philosophy 159
81. Birth or re-creation? 161
82. "Amor fati" or "Odium fati?" 162
83. On the two kinds of morality: theo-anthropic and zoo-anthropic. (with regard to V. S. Solov'ev's book, "The Justification of the Good") 163
84. Solov'ev's Agathodicy and Leibniz's Theodicy 177
85. On the philosophy of V. S. Solov'ev 178
86. Kant and Ritschl 181
87. On Ritschl 183

88. Thoughts on Ritschl	184
89. The Ritschl school of theology	185
90. Lotze's practical philosophy or the science of the value of existence	189
91. The founding father of the Slavophiles	191
92. On the Slavophile-Pharisees and the Westernizer-Sadducees	192
93. The vagueness of Slavophile ideas of unity	193
94. On some of Kireevskii's ideas	194
95. Son, Man, and their synthesis—The Son of Man	198
96. Neither egoism nor altruism, but kinship	201
97. To live not for oneself, nor for the sake of others—the negation of both altruism and egoism	201
98. Physical and moral chastity—an indispensable condition of immortality	202
99. On mortality	203
100. On the great future of the family, and on the insignificant future of current "social action"	204
101. The end of orphanhood; limitless kinship	205
102. Concerning university, or neo-pharisaic, morality	206
103. What are "intellectuals?"	207
104. Mephistopheles as spokesman for "secular culture"	208
105. A "boulevard" apology for death	208
106. One of the contradictions in "sons of this age"	210
107. The lively and deathly apprehension of history	211
108. The relationship of commercial-industrial "civilization" to the monuments of the past	212
109. On the beginning and end of history	213
110. Where is the beginning of history?	215
111. What is Russianly-Universal and Universally-Russian history? (1898)	216
112. Russian history is international history	217
113. Concerning the argument about the three Romes	219
114. Two contraries	220
115. The significance of the bowing down of the three kings (1896)	221
116. To bow or not to bow (1897+)	222
117. On ideographic writing	223
118. Art, its meaning and importance (1881+)	224
119. Science and art	238
120. How did art begin, what has it become, and what ought it to be?	239
121. The art of imitation and the art of reality	241
122. Copernican art	243

APPENDIX I

III. *Articles on the regulation of nature and on pacification*

1. Who is our common enemy, our single enemy, everywhere and always present, living within and without us, but, nevertheless, an enemy who is only temporary? 247
2. The heavenly sciences, as fact and as project 248
3. The future of astronomy 251
4. Falling worlds and the being that counteracts the fall (1895+) 253
5. The horizontal position and the vertical—death and life 260
6. So long as there is death there will be hunger and there will be disease; and conversely, so long as there is disease and hunger there will also be death 271
7. Parents and resurrectors 273
8. Karazin, as a meteorurgist rather than a meteorologist (1892+) 275
9. On the misuse of the words "dominion over nature" and of the world "brotherhood" 279
10. Pertaining to the article "Disarmament" (1898) 280
11. On the means of restoring universal kinship. Duty and obligation, or freedom? (1882+) 283
12. The common cause of common misfortunes and the common duty to struggle with it 287
13. Sacredly scientific militarism 288
14. On the tasks of the Disarmament Conference. An address from starving Old Russia (*Rus'*) 292
15. On two conferences 297
16. The problem of gathering 299
17. War in its broader meaning, external and internal 299
18. On the unity of meteoric and cosmic processes 301
19. On the human race's attainment of maturity; on its physical and intellectual immaturity 301
20. On the distribution of the tasks of the world-wide regulation of nature 303
21. The union of the two Britains 305
22. Pacification—the sacred task of Russian autocrats 306
23. The two roads of the Peace Conference 308
24. The meaning and goal of universal military duty 311
25. The supralegal task of man in society and in nature 313
26. The duty of the universal restoration of life 314
27. The question of sanitation 316
28. A conversation for the new year, 1899 318
29. Strikes and the Peace Conference 321
30. What does the Peace Conference have in common with the icon of the Archpriest's prayer? (1898) 322
31. On the Marxists 322
32. The task of the Peace Conference 323

33. The conversion of the armed forces into an experimental science force 343
34. How can the contradiction between science and art be resolved? 347

IV. *Miscellaneous Articles*

1. Is brotherhood possible? Under what conditions is it possible? What is necessary to bring it about? (Concerning L. N. Tolstoi) 355
2. Tolstoi and brotherly unity 356
3. "Non-action," or the task of the fathers and brothers? (1884+) 362
4. The museum, its meaning and importance 398
5. Notes to the article, "The Museum" 463

APENDIX II

Fedorov in Askhabad

(Summary of a talk delivered at the Annual Meeting of the New England Slavic Association, April 16, 1977, Harvard University. General remarks on Fedorov and his thought included in the talk for the benefit of those unfamiliar with Fedorov are here omitted, and remarks which I thought would be of interest only to fellow Fedorov specialists, deleted from the talk, are here presented.)

Previous commentary on Fedorov, my own included, has often repeated the claim originally presented by Peterson and Kozhevnikov that Fedorov published almost nothing during his lifetime, and that his ideas were known to only a handful of friends, disciples, and library acquaintances. But last summer in Leningrad, working in the Biblioteka Akademii Nauk, I found a complete run of *Askhabad*, one of the provincial newspapers in which works by Fedorov were known to have appeared during his lifetime. In the course of attempting to check and verify that the known *Askhabad* articles (Razoruzhenie, Otvet na vopros 'Chto takoe Rossiia', Samoderzhavie, and Ob obrashchenii oruzhiia, t.e. orudii istrebleniia v orudiia spaseneiie) appeared there exactly as reprinted in FOD (which they did), I came upon some forty-five other articles by and about Fedorov, none of which have appeared in previous Fedorov bibliographies. Since all the articles were printed under pseudonyms, and since at least one of the authors, Peterson, wrote under more than one pseudonym, it was not always easy to tell who had written what. But my best guess is that of the forty-five previously unlisted items, six were by Fedorov himself, sixteen were by Peterson, and the rest were by local columnists, regular and irregular contributors, and ordinary writers of letters to the editor. In the enclosed bibliography, the articles, letters, etc. are listed chronologically, articles reprinted in FOD are marked **, and articles by Fedorov are marked *. It should also be noted that No. 50, Peterson's article on Gorkii, was reprinted in Peterson's book on Fedorov. In addition, someone writing under the pseudonym "Sigma" published an attack on Fedorov's *Ashkhabad* articles in a rival Askhabad newspaper: Sigma, "Po povodu stat'i 'Samoderzhavie' ", *Zakaspiiskoe Obozrenie*, No. 164, (Askhabad,

26 July 1901.) The newspaper *Askhabad* was a daily, four pages, edited by Z. D. Dzhavrov, and Fedorov's articles—and commentary about them—usually appeared on page three—exceptions were the long articles, Samoderzhavie, and Razoruzhenie, which appeared in installments usually beginning on page one. While in Leningrad it was impossible for me either to photograph or to copy by hand all the articles on the list. But I did have time to take notes on all but a few of the items listed, and on my return I placed an order through Dartmouth Library for a microfilm of all issues of Askhabad from 1899-1903. Until the microfilm arrives, the following account of the articles, based on notes, is the best that I can give.

We know from Kozhevnikov (*Russkii Arkhiv* 1904, No. 3, p. 398) that Fedorov spent a year in Askhabad, and from a collection of letters from Fedorov to Kozhevnikov ("Iz perepiski N. F. Fedorova s V. A. Kozhevnikovym: O Turkestane," *Versty*, No. 3 (1928), 278-288) that he began his stay at the end of the summer of 1899. A few years earlier he had visited Peterson in Voronezh, where in 1897 his preface to Dostoevskii's letter was printed in the local newspaper *Don*. A check through the issues of *Don*, 1896-1898, might turn up other articles by Fedorov and/or Peterson, but so far the preface to the Dostoevskii letter is all that we know he wrote then. But not long after his arrival in Askhabad, where Peterson was serving as judge of the circuit court, Fedorov materials began to appear in *Askhabad*.

Looking back, we can reconstruct the sequence of events roughly as follows. Not long after Fedorov arrived, he and Peterson renewed their collaboration on works that would eventually appear in FOD, such as Samoderzhavie and Razoruzhenie. Fedorov as always took a deep interest in the locality, and began to think about the significance of Turkestan, its meaning as a symbol of devastation, and its place in the project of resurrection. Writting under pseudonym "K-nev" Peterson, as a member of the local circle of amateur archeologists, put some of these ideas into the first Askhabad article (1). In this article, we do not find any specific mention of the task of resurrection, or indeed of any of the more radical or far-flung sides of the common task. No space travel, no reconstitution of matter. What we do find are hints at the importance of the museum as the repository of traces of the ancestors, the significance of the Pamirs as the original homeland of the Aryan forefathers and perhaps even the abandoned site of Eden, and the role of Russia as the regulator and peace-maker of land and people savage by nature. We have Fedorov's idea that Russia is the new Iran, carrying on the Zarathustrian task of overcoming dark with light, evil with good. And we have here the first published formulation of the Pamirs and the Russian autocrat as the one who stands in the "father-place" [otsov-mesto.] Looking back, we can see exactly where the article was pointing, but contemporary readers could have taken this article as little more than a slightly eccentric call for Rus-

APPENDIX II

sians to take a greater interest in local history and geography, and for Russians to feel not exiled but in a privileged location while stationed in the wilds of Turkestan. This article provoked (so far as I can tell) not a single response. So a month later Peterson tried again, this time under his own name (2) in an article on Tolstoi. Although this article is not reprinted in his book on Fedorov contra Tolstoi, it covers many of the same points covered there: Tolstoi's love of death versus the idea of overcoming death. He uses Tolstoi's novel *Resurrection* as an opportunity to discuss the need for some kind of active task of resurrection, but he does not spell out the details of that task. From the first two articles, it is clear that Peterson (and perhaps Fedorov as well) did not want to spring the radical ideas first, but instead wanted to introduce the idea of resurrection gradually, starting with the familiar and conventional, and gradually working toward the bolder and more original parts of the common task.

A week after the Tolstoi article, Peterson, again under his own name, published a long serialized book review on the history of popular education in Turkestan (3.) And at about the same time, in another Askhabad newspaper, *Turkestanskii Vestnik* (No. 79, 1899—I was not able to locate this item but found it referred to) he published a speech he had delivered at a meeting of the local archeological society. In the book review he treats the book under consideration as a point of departure for an exposition of Fedorov's ideas about education—the ideas are essentially those presented by Kozhevnikov in the section of his study devoted to Fedorov as educator. The book review, and the ideas about education, provoked no reaction, but the speech to the archeological society apparently did. In the October 22 issue of Askhabad, an anonymous commentator (Peterson?) draws attention to the speech, writes that it was followed by "heated objections," but urges that readers support the suggestion that Askhabad become a center for scientific congresses and fieldwork by specialists in all disciplines. Behind this article (4) is a clearly Fedorovian understanding of precisely why Askhabad would be an ideal place for scientific gatherings, that Askhabad is already an important center rather than the out-of-the-way place it might at first appear to be.

But the real controversy had not yet begun, and wouldn't for another year. In the October 26 issues of Askhabad there appeared, under the initial "N" an article on November Falling Stars (5). The article is pure Fedorov and presents more of his ideas than any of the previous Askhabad articles. We have here the idea that earth, properly viewed, is a heavenly body, and that man is a "heaven-dweller" [nebozhitel'] whose scope of activity is not limited to this small planet. Indeed, most of the ideas on the nature and future of astronomy in FOD can be found here. And still, no reaction.

For a year, no new articles by Peterson or Fedorov appeared in *Askhabad*. But early in 1901, their works, and commentary on them, began to appear regularly. On January 9, Peterson wrote a short article on the need for fresh approaches to the study of the ancient orient, and the next day, without mentioning either Peterson or Fedorov (who was never mentioned by name in *Askhabad*) a local archeologist named K. Sidorovich began a long series of articles on the history of the transcaspian region, in which a number of Fedorov's ideas found partial expression. In June of the same year *Razoruzhenie* was published in two installments, and two weeks later a regular columnist named Tsirkunov, who wrote under the initials P. Ts. discussed *Razoruzhenie* in his column. Here, as in all the articles he would write on Fedorov's ideas, P. Ts. finds the ideas stimulating, original, and profound, but wonders if the goals are attainable. In his discussion of *Razoruzhenie* he cites an article "by the same author" on the Holy Trinity, indicating that he had either met Fedorov personally or had received unpublished manuscripts from Peterson. And in later articles P. Ts. and other columnists refer to other unpublished Fedorov materials, indicating that Peterson was circulating manuscripts to anyone who indicated interest in the idea of resurrection.

Evidently encouraged by P. Ts.'s response, Peterson quickly published two more of the articles that would eventually appear in FOD (10 & 11). And even before the last installment of *Samoderzhavie* had appeared, reactions began to pour in. P. Ts., with some reservations, considered the idea of resurrection probably the best solution yet proposed to the fundamental problems of human existence. Like Solov'ev, P. Ts. endorsed the idea that we should take as our task the resurrection of the dead, but doubted that scientific technology could and should be the means. But another technology could and should be the means. But another regular commentator, who used the pseudonym "Pensoso" found Fedorov's ideas utterly absurd. In his article of July 3, Pensoso makes fun of Fedorov's writing style, says that Fedorov belongs to the class of writers who try to masquerade as philosophers merely by couching their ideas in strange terminology, and asks what new horizons Fedorov thinks he is opening by calling a constitution a *vrag* and citizens *bludnye syny*. At the first opportunity, (August 2, No. 15) Peterson write the first of what would become a long series of counterattacks. "Mr. Pensoso does not discuss the article itself, but simply indulges in abuse." Peterson says that he would not have allowed publication of the articles if he had known that the editor would permit them to be subjected to the kind of frivolous treatment accorded them by Pensoso. In his next column, two days later. Pensoso responded to Peterson's letter, refusing to retract his previous criticisms and pointing out that he had merely used against Fedorov the same words and the same loose arguments that Fedorov had used against his own opponents (philosophers.)

And so it continued for two more years. Peterson would outline another of Fedorov's ideas, P. Ts. would respond with qualified endorsement, Pensoso would ridicule both Fedorov and Peterson, and

Peterson would counterattack. And soon others joined in the polemics. A lady who signed her articles "E. M. Kras-skaia" offered the opinion that both sides were partly right and partly wrong, and one "G. R." wrote articles critical of both sides, but generally preferring Fedorov's idealism to Pensoso's cynicism. A certain "Z. Z." expressed the fear that Fedorov's project might result in the loss of freedom of conscience, and a columnist who signed his articles "Rubio" attempted a weak parody of Fedorov in one of his columns, concluding that to become a philosopher one merely needed to stand in the "Philosophy-place" [filosofii-mesto] and spout any kind of nonsense. In a rival paper, "Sigma" took a long, jaundiced look at Fedorov's ideas and found them pretentious, incomprehensible, and/or decadent.

In replying to all these critics, Peterson used more than one pseudonym, permitting himself the privilege of referring to materials he hod written earlier under other pseudonyms without appearing to promote himself. Thus, writing as Mr. $*_{**}$ he was able to find much to praise and agree with in articles he had written earlier as Mr. N. P. and Mr. K-nev. But Pensoso was not fooled. In an article entitled "Krugom da okolo" Pensoso suggests that Peterson changed his pseudonym so that he would not have to answer all the difficult questions that had been addressed to "Mr. N. P."

But as more of Fedorov's idea emerged, respect for it grew and criticisms turned milder. Even Pensoso, at the end, was willing to admit that the ideas may not be absurd but simply needed clear systematic presentation. What troubled Askhabad commentators most was the idea that Fedorov's project threatened freedom of thought and belief. The idea that an autocrat would serve as everyone's taskmaster, that all would have to participate, and that all diversity of opinion and belief would be ended, horrified not only Pensoso but most of the Askhabad writers. Pensoso and others insisted that diversity of mind, even discord [rozn'] was necessary if men were to remain free. Peterson replied that the project of resurrection would bring freedom from death, freedom to live as brothers and sons in absolute harmony, and that this freedom was more valuable than Pensoso's freedom of each individual to go his own way and fragment the whole. It was at this point that Fedorov himself joined the polemic. On February 14, 1902, Peterson wrote a letter (28) to the editor explaining that he had just received a new article from Moscow which corrected some misconceptions that Peterson had unintentionally allowed to enter his previous writings on resurrection. The unsigned work, obviously ledorov's, entitled "Concerning the polemic on 'The Blissful Life' " (29) offers a much more detailed and forceful defense of the idea of universal harmony through the common task, and a sharper attack on the idea of individualistic freedom, than Peterson had managed. A week later another article by Fedorov, this one signed "Y" was printed under the title "The Poetess of 'Pensive Sorrow' ", a reference to an earlier citation by Pensoso of the works of the Italian poetess Aga Negri. According to Fedorov, Aga Negri's poems of sorrow contain within them a hidden appeal for the resurrection of the dead. The next issue of the paper contained three responses, by various persons, to Fedorov's idas, including Pensoso's assertion that Fedorov's interpretation of Negri's poems idiosyncratic and at worst perverse. On March 3, another article by Fedorov criticizing earlier articles by Pensoso appeared accompanied by a cover letter from Peterson. This article is chiefly an attack on the shallowness of Pensoso's arguments, and points out many of Pensoso's deliberate misunderstandings and misinterpretations of the teachings on resurrection. Three days later, Pensoso, in an article "To the Authors of the Articles on Resurrection" wrote that everything written by Peterson and Fedorov was interesting and challenging, but confused, and suggested that what was needed was a clear and systematic account of the ideas expressed piecemeal in the articles for *Askhabad*.

On March 19, again writing under the initial "Y" Fedorov published "A Last Word to Mr. 'Penoso' ", charging that Penoso has understood nothing, is not interested in the idea of resurrection, and writes only from fondness for polemics. And on March 31, his last appearance for 1902, Fedorov published a general article on polemics as war (42). Here he argues that argument itself is a manifistation of nature's power over men, and that instead of submitting to the forces of nature—in polemics as in war—we should seek reconciliation and agreement in a single common task. The last entries by Fedorov and Peterson in Askhabad (49 & 50) are items later reprinted in FOD and Peterson's book.

Generally, these rediscovered articles by Fedorov offer little that cannot be found in FOD. Of the six new Fedorov articles, four are trivial, and only two—the articles on falling stars and polemics as war—might have been worth reprinting in FOD. Peterson's articles also offer little that cannot be found elsewhere, either in Peterson's book on Fedorov or in Kozhevnikov's *Russkii Arkhiv* series. The fact that the articles were published and did have a considerable impact on readers of *Askhabad* is new information—the contents of the articles themselves cover territory already well known to students of Fedorov.

The reactions of Askhabad readers to the idea of resurrection offer a capsule preview of the commentary that has followed the posthumous publication of FOD. Readers appreciated the scope, the originality, and the boldness of Fedorov's idea, but had reservations about the feasibility and even the desirability of universal adoption of the common task. The two points most frequently and strenuously criticized were the question of freedom and Fedorov's writing style. Some of the responses (especially Tsirkunov's) gave Fedorov reason to hope for the future of his project, others (especially Pensoso's) offered grounds for despair. We know from Fedorov's letters to

Kozhevnikov (cited above) that he feared that neither was his project ready for the world nor was the world ready for his project. The reactions of Ashkabad readers to what they had seen of his idea may have been a factor in Fedorov's pessimism and may have contributed to his reluctance to attempt to publish a collection of his works in the last years of his life.

One question that the Askhabad series raises is why Peterson never did mention most of the articles in his later writings, and why he did not reprint at least the two best shorter articles (5 & 42) in the second volume of FOD. And one would think that the fact that Fedorov's articles had made a strong impression on a number of general readers is something that Peterson should have mentiond either in his preface to FOD or in his book. Perhaps when doing his later work, Peterson no longer had copies of the Askhabad articles, or forgot about them. But a more likely answer might be that as a loyal disciple he wanted to present Fedorov's ideas in only the most favorable light, and to ignore or even suppress all criticism of his master. Since most of the responses of Askhabad readers contained at least some criticism of the project, and some contained almost no favorable remarks, Peterson may have preferred simply to let the Askhabad series remain forgotten, remain—as it were—unresurrected. As a result, students of Fedorov and his work today still have much to uncover. We know that Fedorov was read and discussed in Askhabad—indeed, for a while the project of resurrection seems to have been the major issue of the day—and we know that he wrote a number of articles that were neither reprinted nor mentioned later by his disciples. A search through other publications in which Fedorov's writings are known to have appeared, or through periodicals in towns where Fedorov is known to have lived or spent vacations, a search through such obscure periodicals as *Don* (Voronezh), *Penzenskiia eparkhialniia vedomosti* (Penza), and through such better known publications as *Nauka i zhizn'*, *Russkiia vedomosti*, and *Moskovskiia vedomosti* might well turn up as many, or even more, unsuspected Fedorov materials as were buried in the pages of *Askhabad*.

FEDOROV IN ASKHABAD

Articles in *Askhabad*. Listed chronologically.

1. K-nev. [Peterson] 'Askhabadskii Muzei', No. 273, 30 September 1899.
2. N. Peterson, 'Razgovor so L. N. Tolstym', No. 285, 12 October 1899.
3. _____. 'K istorii narodnogo obrazovaniia v Turkestanskom krae', Nos. 290, 303, 332; 17 October, 30 October, 28 November, 1899.

4. Anonymous. [Peterson?] 'Gde byt' nauchnym zvezdam v Turkestane', No. 295, 22 October 1899.
* 5. N. [Fedorov] 'Neskol'ko predpolozhenii po povodu noiabr'-skikh padaiushchikh zvezd.' No. 298, 25 October 1899.
6. K-''. 'Po povodu stat'i K. Sidorovicha: "K voprosu ob uchrezhdenii zakaspiiskogo obshchestva liubitelei vostochnykh drevnostei" v No. 5 *Askhabad'*, No. 9, 9 January 1901.
** 7. Anonymous. [Fedorov] 'Razoruzhenie: kak orudie razoruzheniia obratit' v orudie spaseniia.' Nos. 154, 156; 3, 5 June 1901.
8. P. Ts. [Petr Iakovlevich Tsirkunov], 'Po povodu stat'i "Razoruzhenie" ' No. 170, 19 June 1901.
9. N. P. [Peterson] 'K peresmotru sistemy nashego obrazovaniia' No. 186, 5 July 1901.
** 10. Anonymous. [Fedorov] 'Otvet na vopros "Chto taket Rossiia" ', No. 187, 6 July 1901.
** 11. _____ 'Samoderzhavie', Nos. 191, 192, 200, 202, 203; 10, 11, 19, 21, 22 July 1901.
12. P. Ts. 'Zametki po povodu stat'i: "K peresmotru sistemy nashego obrazovaniia" i "Samoderzhavie" ', No. 199, 18 July 1901.
13. N. P. Letter in response to P. Ts's article in No. 199; No. 203, 22 July 1901.
14. Pensoso. 'Avtoru "Samoderzhaviia." ' No. 212, 31 July 1901.
15. N. P. letter in response to Pensoso's article in No. 212; No. 214, 2 August 1901.
16. Pensoso. Letter in response to N. P's letter in No. 214. No. 216, 4 August 1901.
17. P. Ts. 'Otvet G. Pensoso.' No. 272, 29 September 1901.
18. N. P. 'Dostoinaia pamiat' geroiam.' No. 272, 29 September 1901.
19. Pensoso. 'Po povodu otveta g. P. Ts.' No. 277, 4 October 1901.
20. Pensoso. 'Po povodu stat'i "Dostoinaia pamiat' geroiam" ' No. 278, 5 October 1901.
21. Kras-skaia, E. M. 'Po povodu zametki g. P. Ts. i N. P. v No. 272 gaz. *Askhabad.*' No. 280, 7 October 1901.
22. *** [Peterson] 'Po povodu stat'i o narodnom dome' (in reference to articles Nos. 348, 350, 351, 353, 354), No. 364, 30 December 1901.
23. _____. Letter to editor in reference to article in No. 364 1901; No. s, 2 January 1902.
24. Pensoso. 'Blazhennaia zhizh'.' No. 3. January 1902.
25. *** 'O svobode sovesti.' No. 8, 8 January 1902.
26. _____. 'Vopros o smysle i tseli.' No. 17, 17 January 1902.
27. Pensoso. 'Krugom da okolo.' No. 20, 20 January 1902.
28. *** Letter to editor. No. 45, 14 February 1902.

* 29. Y. [Fedorov]. 'Po povodu polemiki o "Blazhennoi zhizni" ' No. 45, 14 February 1902.
30. Pensoso. 'Svoboda na rozn'.' No. 47, 16 February 1902.
* 31. Y. 'Poetessa "vdumchivoi skorbi" '. No. 52, 20 February 1902.
32. G. R. 'Po povodu stat'i "O svobode sovesti" '. No. 52, 21 February 1902.
33. Z. Z. 'Otkrytoe pis'mo k avtoru stat'i 'O svobode sovesti" ' No. 52, 21 February 1902.
34. Pensoso. "Aga Negri i voskreshenie umershikh.' No. 52, 21 February 1902.
35. *** Letter to editor. No. 62, 3 March 1902.
* 36. Anonymous. [Fedorov] 'Po povodu statei g-na Pensoso "Blazhennaia zhizn' " i "Krugom da okolo" '. No. 62, 3 March 1902.
37. Pensoso. 'Avtoram statei o voskreshenii.' No. 65, 6 March 1902.
38. E. M. Kras-skaia. 'Esche po povodu polemiki mezhdu *** i Pensoso'. No. 67, 8 March 1902.
39. *** Letter to editor in response to Pensoso and Kras-skaia. No. 78, 19 March 1902.
* 40. Y. 'Poslednee slovo k g-nu "Pensoso" '. No. 78, 19 March 1902.
41. *** Letter to editor. No. 90, 31 March 1902.
* 42. Y. 'Polemika i voina, ili: o dvukh voinakh (vopros o vnutrennei i vneshnei rozni, ili svoboda na lozh' i na rozn', t. e. proekt umirotvoreniia, ili pokrasheniia polemiki i voiny).' No. 90, 31 March 1902.
43. G. R. 'Polemika po neobkhodimosti.' No. 92, 2 April 1902.
45. *** 'Esche o smysle i tseli'. No. 111, 21 April 1902.
46. Pensoso. 'Svoboda mneniia.' No. 121, 1 Maia 1902.
47. P. Ts. 'Razmyshleniia starogo mechtatelia.' No. 3, 3 January 1903.
48. Rubio. 'Kak sdelat'sia filosofom?' No. 5, 5 January 1903.
** 49. *** 'Ob obrashchenii orushiia, t. e. orudii istrebleniia v orudiia spaseniia.' Nos. 23, 24; 23, 24 January 1903.
50. N. P. 'M. Gork'kii, "Chitatel' " 3-ii tom 3-ego izdaniia t-va "Znam'e", str. 237-255 vkliuchitel'no.' Nos. 78, 87, 88; 19, 26, 27 March 1903.

* By Fedorov.
** Included in FOD.

BIBLIOGRAPHY

Much that Fedorov wrote and probably a good number of works about him remain to be discovered. Hence a definitive, comprehensive bibliography of works by and about Fedorov is not yet possible. Nevertheless, enough material does exist to justify a bibliography devoted exclusively to Fedorov and his thought. Background materials used for this book, and works treating subjects other than Fedorov, are referred to in the notes to the text and are not included in the present bibliography. Every item listed below has something to do with Fedorov.

In compiling this bibliography, (an earlier version of which was published in the April 1977 issue of the *Dartmouth College Library Bulletin*), I have found two previous lists of works by and about Fedorov particularly useful. The first appeared in *Vselenskoe Delo*, II, 1934, and the second in Taras Zakydolsky's dissertation, 1976. I have augmented these with materials discovered in the USSR in the summer of 1976 (see Appendix II). Hence the present bibliography is the most nearly comprehensive now available.

Many of the materials listed here are extremely rare. In some instances only one or two copies are known to exist. A few titles, listed in previous bibliographies, have not yet been located in any major library. And since many of the rarest items that have been located were printed on bad paper more than fifty years ago, they are too fragile to be photocopied or allowed out on interlibrary loan. For a list of all titles that have been located and copied, see my article, "Fedorov in Baker Library" in the April 1977 issue of the *Dartmouth College Library Bulletin*.

Fedorov archives are housed at the Museum of Czech Literature in Prague, and in the manuscript section of the Lenin Library in Moscow. Items contained in the Czech archive are listed in a brochure, *Fedoroviana Pragensia*, edited by M. Bradova and Dr. J. Louzil, and published by the museum, (Literarni archiv Narodniho muzea v Praze) in 1962. A description of the contents of the Fedorov archive at the Lenin Library may be found in *Zapiski otdela rukopisi Gosudarstvennoi biblioteki SSSR im. V. I. Lenina, Vol. 36*. Other materials of interest to Fedorov scholars may exist in the Dostoevskii, Tolstoi, Fet, Solov'ev, and Kozhevnikov archives housed at the Central State

Archive of Art and Literature (TsGALI) in Moscow. One hopes that future investigations of these archives will provide answers to a number of the questions which, in the present study, I have had to leave unanswered.

I. PRIMARY SOURCES

A. *Articles published during Fedorov's lifetime.*

No articles appeared under Fedorov's own name during his lifetime. But a number of articles written either by Fedorov himself or by friends (usually N. P. Peterson) eager to present Fedorov's ideas to the world were published, either anonymously or under pseudonyms or initials, and for the most part in obscure regional periodicals unavailable outside the USSR. By searching through one of these journals, *Askhabad*, for the period 1899-1903, I found many previously unlisted articles by and about Fedorov (see Appendix II). A careful search through other obscure periodicals in which Fedorov materials are known to have appeared, such as *Don* (Voronezh) or *Penzenskaia eparkhialniia vedomosti* (Penza), might result in the discovery of yet other titles never before included in a Fedorov bibliography. The following list, then, represents all that is known so far. The titles are listed chronologically, and items reprinted in FOD are so indicated.

'Vopros ob obmene izdanii Parizhem i Moskvoiu.' *MV*, No. 52 (22 February 1892), 2-3. Unsigned.

'K voprosu ob ustanovlenii postoiannago pravilnago nauchnoliteraturnago obmena mezhdu Frantsiiu i Rossiiu.' *RV*, No. 67 (9 March 1892), 3. Signed: D.

'V. N. Karazin i gospodstvo nad prirodoiu.' *RA*, 1892, No. 5, pp. 75-90. Unsigned.

'K 500-letnemu iubileiu prepodobnago Sergiia.' *MV*, No. 254 (13 September 1892), 2. Signed: Sergei.

'K reforme bibliotechnago dela.' *RV*, No. 283 (13 October 1892), 4. Signed: b.

'Postroika i osviashchenie novago zdaniia tserkovno-prikhodskoi shkoly v s. Mordovskom Kachim Gorodishchenskago Uezda.' *Penzenskiia eparkhial'niia vedomosti*, No. 20 (Penza, October 1892), 854-860; and No. 14 (1893), 549-552.

"Ob upravlenii silami prirody" *Penzenskie gubernskie vedomosti*, Nos. 130, 132 (Penza, 1892).

'Skazanie o postroenii obydennago khrama v Vologde "vo izbavlenie ot smertonosnyia iazvy." ' *Chteniia v imperatorskom obshchestve istorii i drevnosti Rossii pri Moskovskom Universitete*, CLXVI (Moscow, 1893), 1-21. [Fedorov collected and first published this legend from the people in *Vologodskiia eparkhiialniia vedomosti*, Nos. 16 & 17 (1879). The legend, with Fedorov's preface, was reprinted in *Chteniia*, as cited above, then later reprinted as a separate pamphlet. Fedorov's preface, but not the legend itself, appears in *FOD*, I, 650-655.]

'Vopros o Karazinskoi meteorologicheskoi stantsii v Moskve.' *Nauka i zhizn'*, No. 44 (Moscow, 1893). [Perhaps the same article as in *FOD*, I, 644-647.]

'K voprosu a pamiatnike V. N. Karazinu.' *Nauka i zhizn'*, Nos. 15-16 (Moscow, 1894). [Perhaps the same article as in *FOD*, I, 647-650.]

'Obydennyia tserkvy na Rusi.' *RA*, 1894, No. 11, pp. 448-53. Unsigned.

'Eshche ob istoricheskom znachenii tsarskago titula.' *RA*, 1895, No. 7, pp. 396-398. Unsigned [Reprinted in *FOD*, I, 353-355.]

"Chto takoe kartochka prilozhennaia k knige." *Don*, No. 119 (Voronezh, 1896).

'Dolg avtorov po otnosheniiu k publichnym bibliotekam.' *RV*, No. 224 (24 September 1896), 3. Signed: N.

'Dolg avtorskii i pravo muzeia biblioteka.' *Don*, No. 72 (Voronezh, 1897).

"Voronezhskii muzei v 1898 g." *Don*, No. 64 (Voronezh, 1898)

"31-ia godovshchina voronezhskogo okruzhnogo suda." *Don*, No. 139 (Voronezh, Dec. 17, 1898)

"K delu umirotvoreniia, vozbuzhdaemomu notoiu 12 Avgusta 1898 goda." *Don* (Voronezh, 1899)

'Razoruzhenie: kak orudie razrusheniia obratit' v orudie spaseniia.' *Novoe vremia*, No. 8129 (St. Petersburg, 14 October 1898), 2-3. Unsigned. [Reprinted in *Askh*. Nos. 154, 156, 1901, and in *FOD*, I, 565-668.]

'Neskol'ko predpolozhenii po povodu noiabr'skikh padaiushchikh zvezd.' *Askh.*, No. 298, 25 October 1899. Signed: N.

'Chemu nauchaet drevneishii khristianskii pamiatnik v Kitae.' *RA*, 1901, No. 4, pp. 631-637. Unsigned. [Reprinted in N. A. Setnitskii, 'Russkie mysliteli o Kitae: V. S. Solov'ev i N. F. Fedorov.' *IIuF*, III (1926) 223-229, Issued also as a separate pamphlet in 1926.]

'Otvet na vopros "Chto takoe Rossiia."' *Askh.*, No. 187, 6 July 1901. Unsigned. [Reprinted in *FOD*.]

'Samoderzhavie.' *Askh.*, Nos. 191, 192, 200, 202, 203; 10, 11, 19, 21, 22 July 1901. Unsigned. [Reprinted in *FOD*, I, 366-398.]

'Po povodu polemiki o "Blazhennoi zhizni."' *Askh.*, No. 45, 14 February 1902. Unsigned.

'Poetessa "vdumchivoi skorbi." *Askh.*, No. 51, 20 February 1902. Signed: Y.

'Po povodu statei g-na Pensoso "Blazhennaia zhizh' " i "Krugom da okolo." ' *Askh.*, No. 62, 3 March 1902. Unsigned.

'Poslednee slovo k g-nu "Pensoso." ' *Askh.*, No. 78, 19 March 1902. Signed: Y.

'Polemika i voina, ili: o dvukh voinakh (vopros o vnutrennei i vneshnei rozni, ili svoboda na lozh' i na rozn', t.e. proekt umirotvoreniia, ili pokrasheniia polemiki i voiny).' *Askh.*, No. 90, 31 March 1902. Signed: Y.

'Ob obrashchenii oruzhiia, t.e. orudii istrebleniia, v orudiia spaseniia.' *Askh.*, Nos. 23, 24; 23, 24 January 1903. Signed: *⁎*. [Reprinted in *FOD.*]

B. *Posthumous Publications*

1. *Collected Works* The first volume of the first edition of Fedorov's collected works, edited by Kozhevnikov and Peterson, appeared in 1906 in an edition of 480 copies. This volume contained most of Fedorov's major essays (for a translation of the table of contents of both volumes see Appendix I). The second volume appeared in 1913 in Moscow, and contains, in addition to some finished articles, a number of drafts, variations, and unfinished works. A planned third volume was to include letters and other materials that had not gone into the first two volumes. But the third volume as such has never appeared. The devaluation of the ruble caused the editors to postpone their plans to publish the third volume in 1916, and before they were able to find funds to cover the printing, the Revolution broke out, and within two years both editors were dead. Materials intended for the third volume were apparently passed on to N. A. Setnitskii and some of these were eventually published in Russian journals abroad. But many of the materials that Kozhevnikov and Peterson had not put into the first two volumes (essays on Wagner, Pushkin, Lermontov, Ibsen, Hauptmann, and Zola are among those mentioned by Peterson) were lost and have never reappeared. These lost works, and perhaps other materials intended for the third volume, are among the items that need to be looked for in the various Fedorov and Kozhevnikov archives. One hopes that these materials were among the precious papers that Solzhenitsyn tells us were not burned in the worst years of the purges.

In 1928, Setnitskii began to issue a second edition of Fedorov's works. The plan was to reprint both original volumes in twelve thin installments. But of the planned twelve, only three were issued, and thus the second edition contains only the first 247 of the 1200 pages printed in the first edition. The first issue of the second edition does, however, contain a valuable biography of Fedorov not included in the first edition.

In 1970, the original two-volume first edition was reprinted, with no deletions, and with the addition only of an English introduction by N. Zernov, in England. This reprint of the first edition is the text that I have used and referred to throughout this study.

First edition: *Filosofia obshchago dela: stat'i, mysli, i pis'ma Nikolaia Fedorovicha Fedorova.* Ed. V. A. Kozhevnikov and N. P. Peterson. Vol. I (Verny, 1906), Vol. II (Moscow, 1913) reprinted with an English preface by N. Zernov. Farnborough, Hants, England: Gregg International Publishers, 1970.

Second edition: * *Filosofiia obshchego dela: stat'i, mysli, i pis'ma Nikolaia Fedorovicha Fedorova.* 2nd edition. Issue 1, with a biographical essay by A. Ostromirov, Harbin, 1928; Issue 2, Harbin, 1928; Issue 3, Harbin, 1930. [Copies at Harvard University Library, Library of Congress, and elsewhere.]

2. *Selections Reprinted and Translated from FOD.* Between the attempted second edition of 1928-1930 and the Gregg reprint of 1970, selections from Fedorov's works appeared in three general anthologies of Russian thought, one in Russian, and two in English. These are:

Iz istorii russkoi filosofskoi mysli kontsa 19 i nachala 20 veka: Antologia. Ed. S. L. Frank. New York, Washington: Interlanguage Literary Associates, 1965, Pp. 51-61. [This selection is from *FOD,* I, 399-420, with omissions marked.]

Russian Philosophy, Ed. J. M. Edie, J. P. Scanlan, and M. B. Zeldin, with the collaboration of G. L. Kline. Chicago: Quadrangle Books, 1965. III, 16-54. [This translation, by Ashleigh E. Moorhouse and George L. Kline, is from *FOD,* I, 2-32, with some footnotes omitted, others shortened, paragraphing changed, and omissions marked.]

Ultimate Questions: An Anthology of Modern Russian Religious Thought. Ed. A. Schmemann. New York, Chicago, San Francisco: Holt, Rhinehart and Winston, 1965. Pp. 175-223. [This excerpt is taken not from a single continuous passage, but from many places in the first volume of *FOD.* Translated by Ashleigh E. Moorhouse.]

3. *Other Posthumous Publications.* No major works, but several interesting and important materials (most of biographical significance) have appeared in various journals since Fedorov's death. Two short articles appeared in the Symbolist journal *Vesy,* and in the No. 6 issue for 1906, Pasternak's death mask of Fedorov appears as a frontspiece, and a drawing of Fedorov on the balcony of the Museum, by M. Shesterkin, appears on the first page.

The first issue of *Vselenskoe Delo* published several valuable materials, the most important of which is Fedorov's letter to the editor of *Don* regarding Dostoevskii's letter to Peterson. This "preface" to Dostoevskii's letter was later quoted in part in Gornostaev's *Rai na zemle*, but is available in full outside the USSR only in *Vselenskoe Delo* I. Another important item on the list immediately below is the letter to Pobedonostsev. This letter, signed "N. Peterson" but attributed (perhaps mistakenly) by the editor to Fedorov, was written just after the assassination of Alexander II. The letter begins with a discussion of the moral chaos encouraged by university education and argues that if museums replaced universities acts of terror would never again happen. Then Peterson (or Fedorov) requests Pobedonostsev to look for and if possible return a manuscript sent to Dostoevskii late in 1880. This is the only indication we have that the manuscript begun as a reply to Dostoevskii's questions was actually sent to Dostoevskii. Whether Pobedonostsev found the manuscript among Dostoevskii's papers, and whether the manuscript was kept or returned to Peterson, or whether it still exists, is not known.

Other important materials published after Fedorov's death are those which Setnitskii sent to Berdiaev and Mirskii before returning to the Soviet Union in the early thirties. These materials, apparently intended originally for the third volume of Fedorov's works, appeared in the *émigré* journals *Versty, Put'*, the newspaper *Evraziia*, and the second issue of *Vselenskoe Delo*. With the exception of the short note "O pis'menakh" in *Vesy*, none of these materials appeared in *FOD*.

'Astronomiia i arkhitektura.' *Vesy*, No. 2 (Moscow, 1904), 20-24.

'O pis'menakh.' *Vesy*, No. 6 (Moscow, 1906), 1-5. [Included as part of a larger article in *FOD*, I, 23-25.]

'Pis'mo N. F. Fedorova k redaktoru gazety "Don" po povodu pis'ma F. M. Dostoevskago k N. P. Petersonu ob uchenii N. F. Fedorova.' *Vselenskoe delo*, I (Odessa, 1914), 24-30. [Fedorov's letter, and Dostoevskii's originally appeared in the Voronezh newspaper *Don*, No. 80, 1897.]

'Iz perepiski N. F. Fedorova.' *Vselenskoe delo*, I (Odessa, 1914), 97-99.

'Gramota Tsarei Ioanna i Petra Alekseevicha Kerenskomu Voevode Stolniku Ivanu Savinovichu Chubarovu.' *R.A.*, 1915, Nos. 11-12, pp. 282-295.

'Bytie krestnago syna.' *R.A.*, 1915, Nos. 11-12, pp. 296-303.

Letter of March 14, 1881, to K. P. Pobedonostsev. In *K. P. Pobedonostsev i ego korrespondenty: Pis'ma i zapiski*. Moscow, Petrograd, 1923, I, Half-Vol. 1, pp. 281-286.

'Iz perepiski N. F. Fedorova s V. A. Kozhevnikovym o Turkestane.' *Vsty.*, No. 3 (1928), 278-288.

'Iz tret'iago toma *Filosofii obshchago dela*.' *Pu.*, No. 10 (1928), 3-43.

'Iz posmertnykh rukopisei N. F. Fedorova.' *Pu.*, No. 18 (1929), 3-24.
'Pis'ma N. F. Fedorova k V. A. Kozhevnikovu.' *Evr.*, No. 24 (4 May 1929), 7.
'Chto takoe dobro.' *Pu.*, No. 40 (1933), 3-15.
'N. F. Fedorov: Iz perepiski s N. P. Petersonom i V. A. Kozhevnikovym.' *Vselenskoe Delo*, II (Riga, 1934), 149-155.

II. Secondary Sources

A. *Monographs and Lengthy Serialized Studies.* The first extensive commentaries on Fedorov were by Kozhevnikov and Peterson. Kozhevnikov's study, first published serially in *Russkii Arkhiv* and later reprinted as a separate monograph, offers valuable biographical information, and presents a systematic (but uncritical) overview of Fedorov's thought. The monograph version is a slightly enlarged version of the serialized study, and adds, as an appendix, Dostoevskii's letter to Peterson, Solov'ev's two letters to Fedorov, Fet's letter to Fedorov and Tolstoi's letter to Ivakin. All but the letter from Fet are available from other sources. Kozhevnikov apparently intended to write a biography of Fedorov, and so included only bits and pieces of biographical information in his initial study. Unfortunately, the intended biography has never appeared, and although the information and anecdotes included in Kozhevnikov's study provide most of what is now known about Fedorov's life, much of what we would like to know is missing.

Peterson's work, much less systematic, and much more polemical than Kozhevnikov's, also contains much valuable biographical information. But since his book is a collection of separate pieces rather than an integrated whole, the same points are made repeatedly. The eleven articles collected include: a comparison of Fedorov's idea of disarmament with William James' "moral equivalent of war," a contrast between Fedorov and Pisarev, and several polemical articles that set Fedorov's ideas against Tolstoi's.

The first major critiques of Fedorov's thought appeared just after the publication of the second volume of FOD. In a series of seven articles written between 1913 and 1916, and published in the theological journal *Bogoslovskii vestnik*, S. Golovanenko offers a systematic analysis of Fedorov's thought and concludes that Fedorov's project is a distortion of Christian doctrine. Berdiaev, in a single long essay written for *Russkaia mysl'* in 1915, also discusses Fedorov's thought at some length, rejects the scientific and materialistic side of Fedorov's project, but endorses his activism and considers Fedorov's interpretation of the apocalypse a stroke of genius.

The Fedorovian works by Setnitskii, Gornostaev, and others, published in Harbin in the late twenties and early thirties, are strongly partisan, but nevertheless have contributed a number of fresh insights to Fedorov studies. More objective discussions of Fedorov's thought have been attempted in recent doctoral dissertations. Grunwald's thesis offers a clear account of Fedorov's idea and makes interesting observations on Fedorov's relationship to contemporary and subsequent Russian thinkers. My dissertation addressed many of the same topics that I have treated in more detail in the present study, but was written without access to a number of sources that I have subsequently made use of, and contained a number of gaps, errors, and provisional conclusions that I have corrected and revised in the course of this study. Zakydalsky's dissertation represents a major contribution to Fedorov studies. He does not discuss most of the topics that I have focused on in this book, such as Fedorov's life, his relationship to other Russian thinkers, and secondary sides of the project of resurrection. Zakydalsky focuses exclusively on the idea of physical resurrection, analyzes it in detail from a philosopher's perspective, and presents a thorough and technical discussion of criteria for personal identity and of the question of the project's feasibility. His conclusions are that Fedorov's project of resurrection is best understood within the framework of reductive materialism, that recent theories of matter support Fedorov's conjectures, and that within even the strictest maerialist framework, the project of resurrection is theoretically feasible. Zakydalsky raises more objections, both theoretical and practical, than I have considered, and treats each objection with fairness and thoroughness. His work is the best systematic analysis and defense of the idea of physical resurrection yet attempted by a student of Fedorov.

The monographs and lengthy serialized studies on Fedorov that have appeared to dare, then, are, in chronological order:

Kozhevnikov, V. A. 'Nikolai Fedorovich Fedorov.' *RA.* (1904), No. 2, 315-325; No. 3, 390-401; No. 4, 545-554; No. 5, 5-26; No. 9, 106-124; No. 10, 225-261; 1905, No. 1, 180-200; No. 2, 333-365; No. 7, 417-470; 1906, No. 1, 63-102; No. 2, 260-301. [This work was later reprinted as a monograph: *Nikolai Fedorovich Fedorov: opyt izlozheniia ego ucheniia po izdannym i neizdannym proizvedeniiam, perepiske i lichnym besedam.* Moscow, 1908. Copy in Lenin Library, Moscow.]

Rozhkov, N. A. *Osnovy nauchnoi filosofii,* St. Petersburg, 1911.

Peterson, N. P. *N. F. Fedorov i ego kniga 'Filosofiia obshchego dela' v protivopolozhnost' ucheniiu L. N. Tolstogo . . . 'o neprotivlenii' i drugim ideiam nashego vremeni.* Verny, 1912.

Golovanenko, S. A review of *FOD, BV,* 1913, No. 12, pp. 832-844.

_____. 'Filosofiia smerti i voskresheniia.' *BV,* 1914, No. 4. pp. 664-688.

_____. 'Pravoslavie i kul't predkov.' *BV,* 1914, No. 5, pp. 83-109.

———————. 'Immanentizm i khristianskaia filosofiia.' *BV*, 1914, Nos. 7-8, pp. 569-592.

———————. 'Taina synovstva.' *BV*, 1915, No. 3, pp. 498-516.

———————. 'Proekt ili simvol'?' *BV*, 1915, No. 6, pp. 294-314.

———————. 'K suzhdeniiu o khristianstve N. F. Fedorova: polemika.' *BV*, 1916, No. 1, pp. 130-135.

Vselenskoe delo, I. Odessa, 1914.

Berdiaev, N. 'Religiia voskresheniia.' *Russkaia mysl'*, No. 367 (Moscow, 1915), 75-120.

Peterson. N. P. *Uchenie N. Fedorova o voskreshenii v istolkovanii Prof. S. N. Bulgakova*, Zaraisk, 1917.

Murav'ev, V. *Ovladenie vremenem*. Moscow, 1924.

Smertobozhnichestvo. Harbin, 1926.

Ostromirov, A [Pseudonym of N. A. Setnitskii.] *Nikolai Fedorovich Fedorov, 1828-1903-1928: Biografiia*. Issue I, Harbin, 1928. [The same essay appears as an introduction to the second edition of *FOD*.]

———————. *Nikolai Fedorovich Fedorov i sovremennost'*. Issue II, Harbin, 1928 [contains two essays: 'Proektivism i bor'ba so smert'iu and 'Bogoslovie obshchago dela']; Issue III, Harbin, 1932 [contains one essay: 'Organizatsiia mirovozdeistviia']; Issue IV, Harbin, 1933 [contains one essay: 'Ostrie mirovago krizisa'].

Gornostaev, A. K. [Pseudonym of Gorskii.] *Pered litsem smerti: L. N. Tolstoi i N. F. Fedorov. 1828-1903-1910-1т28*. Harbin, 1928.

L. N. Tolstoi i N. F. Fedorov. 1828-1903-1910-*1928*. Harbin, 1928.

———————. *Rai na zemle: k ideologii tvorchestva F. M. Dostoevskogo. F. M. Dostoevskii i N .F. Fedorov*. Harbin, 1929.

Setnitskii, N. A. *O konechnom ideale*. Harbin, 1932.

Vselenskoe Delo, II. Riga, 1934.

Grunwald, J. "N. F. Fedorov." Thesis, Diplôme études superieures, Université de Nancy, 1965. [Copy at Columbia University Library. Microfilm copy in Princeton University Library.]

Rapaglia, J. *The Religious Philosophy of Nikolay Fyodorovich Fyodorov*, M.A. Tesis, Columbia University. 1966. [Copy at Columbia University Library.]

Anonymous. *Otkroveniia Viktora Velskogo*. First appeared in *Feniks-66*, later reprinted in *GrF*, No. 75 (1970), 3-114.

Young, G. M. Jr. *The Philosopher of the Common Task: A Study of the Life and Thought of Nikolaj Fedorov.* Ph. D. Dissertation, Yale University, 1973.

Zakydalskii, Taras, N. F. *Fedorov's Philosophy of Physical Resurrection.* Ph.D. Dissertation, Bryn Mawr College. 1976.

B. *Articles on Fedorov and Books that Contain Information about Him.*

1. *Articles Published during Fedorov's Lifetime.* Since Fedorov himself was reluctant to publish his writings, Peterson, Kozhevnikov, and other friends first brought his ideas to public attention by sending summaries, or written versions of conversations, to the editors of newspapers and magazines. Sometimes, e.g. in the Askhabad series, the summaries provoked such lively controversy that Fedorov himself would join the debate. The list below contains both summaries of Fedorov's ideas by friends, and reactions to those ideas by writers who became aware of them. The titles are in chronological order.

Iu. B. [Iurii Bartenev.] 'Sviatoi Sergei Radonezhskii.' *RA,* 1892, No. 10, pp. 223-233.

_____, 'Tsarskii titul i koronovanie.' *RA,* 1895, No. 5, pp. 195-196.

V.A.K. [V. A. Kozhevnikov.] 'Mezhdunarodnaia blagodarnost'.' *RA,* 1896, No. 2, pp. 256-265.

Simonov, V. 'Voennye mysli o shtatskom dele.' *Novoe Vremia,* No. 8280 (St. Petersburg, 17 March 1899).

K-nev. [Probably Peterson.] 'Askhabadskii Muzei.' *Askh.,* No. 273, 30 September 1899.

Peterson, N. 'Razgovor so L. N. Tolstym.' *Askh.,* No. 285, 12 October 1899.

_____. 'K Istorii narodnogo obrazovaniia v Turkestanskom krae.' *Askh.,* Nos. 290, 303, 332; 17 October, 30 October, 28 November 1899.

Anonymous. [Peterson?] 'Gde byt' nauchnym s"ezdam v Turkestane.' *Askh.,* No. 295, 22 October 1890.

K-". 'Po povodu stat'i K. Sidorovicha: "K voprosu ob uchrezhdenii zakaspiskogo obshchestva liubitelei vostochnykh drevnostei" v No. 5 *Askhabad.' Askh.,* No. 9, 9 January 1901.

P. Ts. (Petr Iakovlevich Tsirkunov.) 'Po povodu stat'i "Razoruzhenie" ' *Askh.,* No. 170, 19 June 1901.

N. P. [Peterson.] 'K peresmotru sistemy nashego obrazovaniia.' *Askh.*, No. 186, 5 July 1901.

P. Ts. 'Zametki po povodu statei: "K peresmotru sistemy nashego obrazovaniia" i "Samoderzhavie."' *Askh.*, No. 199, 18 July 1901.

N. P. Letter in response to P. Ts's article in No. 199. *Askh.*, No. 203, 22 July 1901.

Sigma. 'Po povodu stat'i "Samoderzhavie"' *Uakaspiiskoe Obozrenie*, No. 164, (Askhabad, 26 July 1901).

Pensoso. 'Avtoru "Samoderzhaviia."' *Askh.*, No. 212, 31 July 1901.

N. P. Letter in response to Pensoso's article in No. 212. *Askh.*, No. 214, 2 August 1901.

Pensoso. Letter in response to N. P.'s letter in No. 214. *Askh.*, No. 216, 4 August 1901.

P. Ts. 'Otvet G. Pensoso.' *Askh.*, No. 272, 29 September 1901.

N. P. 'Dostoinaia pamiat' geroiam.' *Askh.*, No. 272, 29 September 1901.

Pensoso. 'Po povodu otveta g. P. Ts.' *Askh.*, No. 277, 4 October 1901.

Pensoso. 'Po povodu stat'i "Dostoinaia pamiat' geroiam."' *Askh.*, No. 278, 5 October 1901.

Kras-skaia, E. M. 'Po povodu zametki g. P. Ts. i N. P. v No. 272 gaz. Ashkhabad.' *Askh.*, No. 280, 7 October 1901.

⁂. [Peterson.] 'Po povodu statei o narodnom dome' (in reference to articles in Nos. 348, 350, 351, 353, 354). *Askh.*, No. 364 30 December 1901.

_____. Letter to editor in reference to article in No. 364, *Askh.*, No. 2, 2 January 1902.

Pensoso. 'Blazhennaia zhizn'.' *Askh.*, No. 3, 3 January 1902.

⁂. 'O svobode sovesti.' *Askh.*, No. 8, 8 January 1902.

_____. 'Vopros o smysli i tseli.' *Askh.*, No. 17, 17 January 1902.

Pensoso. 'Grugom da okolo.' *Askh.*, No, 20, 20 January 1902.

⁂. Letter to editor. *Askh.*, No. 45, 14 February 1902.

Pensoso. 'Svoboda na rozn'.' *Askh.*, No. 47, 16 February 1902.

G. R. 'Po povodu stat'i "O svobode sovesti" (*Askh.*, No. 8).' *Askh.*, No. 52, 21 February 1902.

Z. Z. 'Otkrytoe pis'mo k avtoru stat'i "O svobode sovesti." ' *Askh.*, No. 52, 21 February 1902.

Pensoso. 'Aga Negri i voskreshenie umershikh.' *Askh.*, No. 52, 21 February 1902.

***. Letter to editor. *Askh.*, No. 62, 3 March 1902.

Pensoso. 'Avtoram statei o voskreshenii..' *Askh.*, No. 65, 6 March 1902.

Kras-skaia, E. M. 'Eshche po povodu polemiki mezhdu *** i Pensoso.' *Askh.*, No. 67, 8 March 1902.

***. Letter to editor in response to Pensoso and Kras-skaia.' *Askh.*, No. 78, 19 March 1902.

—————. Letter to editor. *Askh.*, No. 90, 31 March 1902.

G. R. 'Polemika po neobkhodimosti.' *Askh.*, No. 92, 2 April 1902.

Pensoso. 'Svoboda na lozh'.' *Askh.*, No. 97, 7 April 1902.

***. 'Eshche o smysle i tseli.' *Askh.*, No. 111, 21 April 1902.

Pensoso. 'Svoboda mneniia.' *Askh.*, No. 121, 1 May 1902.

P. Ts. 'Razmyshleniia starogo mechtatelia.' *Askh.*, No. 3, 3 January 1903.

Rubio. 'Kak sdelat'sia filosofom?' *Askh.*, No. 5, 5 January 1903.

N. P. 'M. Gor'kii, "Chitatel' " 3-ii tom 3-ego izdaniia t-va "Znanie" str. 237-255 vkliuchitel'no.' *Askh.*, Nos. 78, 87, 88; 19, 26, 27 March 1903.

2. *Commentary since 1904*. Obituary notices appeared in the major Moscow newspapers immediately after Fedorov's death. Reviews of *FOD* began to appear soon after the publication of the first volume. Bulgakov's 1908 review described Fedorov as an 'enigmatic' thinker, a phrase which has been repeated in dozens of subsequent commentaries. Harsh critiques of Fedorov's ideas can be found in the articles by Florovskii and in the recent entries written for official Soviet reference works. But probably the best balanced general assessments of Fedorov's work are found in the aticles by Berdiaev, Losskii, Il'in, Pletnev, and Zenkovskii. Works are listed alphabetically by author. Anonymous articles are listed by title.

Alekseev, N. 'Priroda i chelovek v filosofskikh vozreniiakh russkoi literatury.' *GrE.*, No. 42 (1959), 187-204.

Altaiskii, K. 'Moskovskaia iunost' Tsiolkovskogo.' *Moskva*, No. 9 (Moscow, 1966), 176-192.

Arlazorov, M. *Tsiolkovskii.* Moscow, 1963. Pp. 25-26.

Arsenev, N. *Die russische Literatur der Neuzeit und Gegenwart in ihren geistigen Zusammenhangen.* Mainz, 1929. Pp. 358-363.

Bakushinskii, A. 'V puti k velikom iskusstve.' *Zhizn'.*, No. 3 (Moscow, 1922), 132-135.

Bartenev, S. P. 'Nikolai Fedorovich Fedorov: dva razgovora o voskreshenii mertvykh.' *RA.*, 1909, No. 1, pp. 119-122.

——————, *Dnevnik.* Unpublished, typed copy of 8 pp.

Bartenev, Iu. P. "Pamiati Nikolaia Fedorovicha Fedorova," *R.A.* No. 1 (1904) 191-92.

Belyi, A. (Pseud. of B. Bugaev.) 'Vospominanie o Bloke.' *Epopeia.*, No. 2 (Moscow-Berlin, September 1922), 119.

Berdiaev, N. 'Tri iubileia: L. Tolstoi, Gen. Ibsen, N. F. Fedorov.' *Pu.*, No. 11 1928, 88-94. [Translated into English as 'N. F. Fedorov,' *The Russian Review*, IX (New York, 1950), 124-130.]

——————. *The Meaning of the Creative Act.* Tr. D. A. Lowrie. London, 1956. Pp. 196, 336. [First published in Russian in 1914.]

——————, 'Russkaia religioznaia mysl' XIX-go veka.' *Sovremennye zapiski*, No. 42 (Paris, 1930), 309-343.

——————. 'Dva ponimaniia khristianstva.' *Pu.*, No. 36 (1932), 17-44.

——————. 'Chelovek i mashina.' *Pu.*, No. 38 (1933), 3-37.

——————, *Dream and Reality*, Tr. K. Lampert, New York, 1951, Pp. 233, 282, 286, 297.

——————. *The Russian Idea.* Tr. R. M. French. Boston, 1962. Pp. 208-212 and *passim.*

——————. Review of Setnitskii's *O konechnom ideale. Pu.*, No. 36 (1932), 93-95.

Billington, J. H. 'The Intelligentsia and the Religion of Humanity.' *American Historical Review*, LXV (Washington, 1959-1960), 814, 820.

Boranetskii, P. S. 'O novom zhiznennom ideale.' *Tret'ia Rossia*, N. 2 (Paris, 1932), 47-60.

——————. 'O iurodivykh chudachestvakh Fedorovstva i o zamysle preodoleniia smerti.' *Tret'ia Rossiia*, No. 8 (Paris, 1938), 72-124.

Brown, E. J. *Mayakovskii: A Poet in the Revolution.* Princeton, 1973. Pp. 122, 253-256.

Briusov, V. Ia. *Dnevniki, 1891-1910*. Moscow, 1927. P. 85.

Bulgakov, S. 'Zagadochnyi myslitel'.' *Moskovskii ezhenedel'nik* (Moscow, 5 December 1908). [Reprinted in: *Dva grada*. Moscow, 1911, II, 260-277.]

_____, *Svet nevechernii: sozertsaniia i umozreniia*. VTVG. Pp. 360-368. Reprinted. Westmead, Farnborough, Hants., England, 1971.

_____, 'Dusha sotsializma.' *Novyi grad*, No. 1 (Paris, 1931), 49-58.

_____. 'Ideia obshchago dela, zapis' po pamiati.' *Vestnik russkago studencheskago khristianskago dvizheniia* (Paris, 1934).

Bursov, B. 'Lichnost' Dostoevskogo.' *Zvezda*, No. 12 (Moscow, 1969), 85-172. [Reprinted in his *Lichnost' Dostoevskogo*. Leningrad, 1974. Pp. 7-79.]

Chkheidze, K. A. 'N. Fjodorovic Fjodorov' *Ruch Filosofisky*, XI, Nos. 3-4 (Prague, 1936), 112-115.

Chizhevskii, D. "Schiller und die *'Brüder Karamazov'*," *Zeitschrift*

_____, 'Tri knigi o russkoi filosofii.' *Novyi zhurnal*, No. 30 (New York, 1952), 279-287.

_____, *Hegel bei den Slaven. Bad Hamburg*, 1934. P. 355. Dyck, J. W. *Boris Pasternak*. New York, 1972. Pp. 149-150.

Chizhevskii, D. "Schiller und die *'Brüder Karamazov'*," *Zeitschrift fur Slavisch Philologie*, 6 (Leipzig, 1929), 1-42.

_____, "Shiller v Rossii," *Novyi zhurnal*, No. 45 (New York, 1956), 109-135.

Deiateli revoliutsionnago dvizheniia v Rossii. Biobibliograficheskii slovar'. Ed. V. Vilenskii-Sibiriakov, F. Kon', A. A. Shilov, B. P. Kuzmin, and V. I. Nevskii. Moscow, 1928. I, 428, 311.

Dostoevskii, F. M. Letter to N. P. Peterson, 24 March 1878. In *F. M. Dostoevskii. Pis'ma v chetyrekh tomakh*. Ed. A. S. Dolinin. Moscow, 1959, IV, 9-10. [This letter was first published in *Don*, No. 80 (Voronezh, 1879), then later reprinted in *RA*., No. 3 (1904), 402-403, in Kozhevnikov's monograph (see above, p. 78), and in *Vselenskoe delo*, I. It has been translated, with omissions, in J. Coulson, *Dostoevskii: A Self-Portrait*. New York, Oxford, 1962. Pp. 216-217.]

_____. *F. M. Dostoevskii: Mater'ialy i issledovanie*. Ed. by A. S. Dolinin. Leningrad, 1935. [Translated in *The Notebooks for 'The Brothers Karamazov.'* Ed. and tr. E. Wasiolek, Chicago, 1971.]

_____. 'Neizdannyi Dostoevskii: Zapisnye knizhki i tetradi 1860-1881.' In *LN*, LXXXIII (1971), 450, 452, 508-509.

Dyck, J. W. Boris Pasternak, New York, 1972, pp. 149-150.

"N. F. Fedorov: Nekrolog." *R.V.*, No. 346 (Dec. 17, 1903).

'N. F. Fedorov' *Izvestiia*, No. 300 (Moscow, 28 Dec. 1928), p. 3.

'Fedorov, Nikolai Fedorovich.' *Filosovskaia entsiklopediia.* Ed. F. V. Konstantinov. Moscow, 1970. V, 308-309.

'Fedorov, N. F.' *Istoria filosofii v SSSR.* Ed. V. E. Evgrafov. Moscow, 1968–. IV (1971), 57-64.

Fedotov G. 'Eskhatologiia i kul'tura.' *Novyi grad*, No. 13 (Paris, 1938), 45-56.

Florovskii, G. 'Proekt mnimago dela.' *Sovremennye zapiski*, No. 59 (Paris, 1935), 399-414. [Later reprinted in slightly condensed form in *Puti russkago bogosloviia.* Paris, 1937. Pp. 322-330.]

Fülop-Miller, R. *The Mind and Face of Bolshevism.* Tr. F. S. Flint and D. F. Tait. New York, 1929. Pp. 261-262.

"Fedorov, Nikolaj Fedorovic," *Enciclopedia Filosofica*, Ed. G. C. Sansoni. Florence, 1967, II, 1252-53.

G. G. 'Pamiati Nikolaia Fedorovicha.' *MV*, No. 334 (16 December 1903), 3.

Gessen, S. I. 'Nemetskoe izdanie neopublikovannykh rukopisei F. M. Dostoevskogo' *Sovremennye zapiski*, No. 39 (Paris, 1929), 502-515.

Ginken, A. 'Idealnyi bibliotekar': Nikolai Fedorovich Fedorov.' *Bibliotekar'*, No. 1 (Moscow, 1911), 13-26.

Gor'kii, M. [Pseudonym of A. Peshkov.] Letter to S. Grigor'ev, 15 March 1926; Letter to M. Prishvin, 17 October 1926; Letter to O. Forsh, 5 September 1926. In 'Gor'kii i sovetskie pisateli: Neizdannaia perepiska.' *LN*, *IXX* (1963), 134-136, 335, 591.

_____. 'Eshche o mekhanicheskikh grazhdanakh' and 'O zhenshchine.' In his *Sobranie sochinenii v 30 tomakh.* Moscow, 1953. XXIV, 447-455, and XXV, 154-166.

Gornostaev, A. K. [Pseud. of Gorskii.] 'Tiaga zemnaia.' *Vselenskoe delo*, I (Odessa, 1914), 140-207.

_____ "Fedorov N. F." *Izvestiia*, No. 300 (Dec. 28, 1928), p. 3.

Grunwald, J. "Fedorov et la Philosophie de l'Oeuvre Commune: I. L'Homme et son Destin." *Contacts*, No. 58 (Paris, 1967), 147-66.

———, "Fedorov: L'Homme et l'Oeuvre: II. Le Project Fedorovien." *Contacts,* No. 61 (Paris, 1968), 37-62.

———, "Fedorov: L'Homme et l'Oeuvre: III. Fedorov et Dostoievski." *Contacts,* Nos. 62-63 (Paris, 1968), 198-223.

Gusev, N. N. *Lev Nikolaevich Tolstoi: Mater'ialy k biografii s 1881 po 1885 god.* Moscow, 1970. Pp. 75-79.

Hare, R. *Portrait of Russian Personalities between Reform and Revolution.* London, 1959. Pp. 267-271.

Iakovenko, B. V., *Ocherki russkoi filosofiii.* Berlin, 1922. Pp. 93-94.

———, *Dejiny ruske' filosofie,* Prague, 1938. Pp. 19, 252, 343-346, 451, 452, 504.

Ianovskii, V. S. 'Obshchee delo'. *Novyi grad,* No. 13, (Paris, 1938), 172-174.

Il'in, V. N. 'O religioznom i filosofskom mirovozrenii N. F. Fedorova.' *Evraziiskii sbornik* (Prague, 1929), pp. 17-23.

Istoria gosudarstvennoi ordena Lenina Biblioteky SSSR im. V. I. Lenina za 100 let, 1862-1962. Ed. K. R. Kamenskaia, and E. V. Seglin. Moscow, 1962.

Ivakin, I. M. Letter to Tolstoi, 17 October 1891. *Vselenskoe delo,* II (Riga, 1934), 159.

———. 'Tolstoi v 1880-t gody. Zapiski I. M. Ivakina.' *LN.* LXIX, Bk. 2 (1961), 21-124.

Jakobson, R. O. 'O pokolenii rastrativshem svoikh poetov' in *Smert' Vladimira Maiakovskogo,* Berlin, 1931. Pp. 7-45.

Kiselev, A. 'Uchenie N. F. Fedorova v svete sovremennosti.' *GrF.* No. 81 (1971), 122-153.

——— "Nikolaj Fëdorov oggi" *Russia Cristiana,* No. 118, (Milan, 1971), pp. 7-28.

Kline, G. L. 'Religious Motifs in Russian Philosophy.' *Studies on the Soviet Union,* IX, No. 2 (Munich, 1969), 89-91.

Komarovich, V. 'Der Vatermord und Fiodoroffs Lehre von der "Fleischlichen Auferstehung." ' In *F. M. Dostoevski: Die Urgestalt der Bruder Karamasoff: Dostoevskis Quellen, Entwurfe und Fragmente, erläutert von Professor Dr. Sigm. Frend.* Munich, 1928, Pp. 3-58.

Koutaissoff, E. 'Some Futurological Aspects of Fedorov's *Philosophy of the Common Cause.*' *Russian Literature Triquarterly,* No. 12 (Ann Arbor, Spring 1975), 393-407.

Lazurskii, V. E. 'Dnevnik V. F. Lazurskogo.' *LN, XXXVII/ XXXVIII, L. N. Tolstoi,* Pt. 2 (1939), 443-509.

Levitskii, S. A. *Ocherk po istorii russkoi filosofii i obshchestvennoi mysli.* Frankfurt, 1968. Pp. 161-164.

Linnichenko, I. A. *Rechi i pominki.* Odessa, 1914. Pp. 311-319. [First published under the title 'Moi vstrechi s L. N. Tolstym.' *Odesskiia novosti,* (Odessa, 18 November 1913).]

Lord, R. 'Dostoevskii and N. F. Fedorov.' *The Slavonic and East European Review,* XL (London, 1961-1962), 408-430. [This essay was later expanded into a chapter in his *Dostoevskii: Essays and Perspectives.* Berkeley, 1970. Pp. 175-234.]

Losskii, N. O. *History of Russian Philosophy.* London, 1952. Pp. 75-80.

L'vov, V. 'Priamoe voskhozhdenie.' *Neva,* No. 2 (Moscow, 1966), 130-131.

Mandel'shtam, Nadezhda. *Mozart and Salieri.* Tr. Robert A. McLean. Ann Arbor, 1973. Pp. 18-23.

Mirskii, D. S. 'Some Remarks on Tolstoy.' *The London Mercury,* XX (London, June 1929), 167-175.

_____. 'Literatura o Tolstom.' *Evr.,* No. 1 (1928), 7.

_____. 'Nash Marksizm.' *Evr.,* No. 11 (2 February 1929), 3.

Mochul'skii, K. "The Final Years: The History of *The Brothers Karamazov.*' In his *Dostoevsky.* Princeton, 1967. Pp. 565-596. [This is a translation of the author's *Dostoevskii: Zhizn' i tvorchestvo.* Paris, 1947.]

_____. 'The Idea of Social Christianity in Russian Philosophy.' *St. Vladimir's Seminary Quarterly,* XII (Crestwood, N.Y., 1968), 157-160. [Tr. by T. E. Bird from an article in *Pravoslavnoe delo,* No. 1 (Paris, 1939), 45-61.]

_____, *Vladimir Solov'ev; Zhizn' i uchenie.* Paris, 1959. Pp. 153-156, 163, 205.

N. 'Nekrolog: Nikolai Fedorovich Fedorov.' *Vesy,* No. 1 (Moscow, 1904), 54.

Nekrasova, E. S. 'Pamiati N. F. Fedorova.' *RV,* No. 353 (24 December 1903), 4.

Nicholl, D. 'Fedorov.' Lecture on BBC, Radio 3, 17 November 1970. [Summary of lecture in *The Listener.* LXXXIV (London, 10 December 1970), 813.]

Pankratov, A. 'Filosof-pravednik.' *Novoe slovo*, No. 8 (St. Petersburg, 1913), 17-25.

Pasternak, L. O. 'Iz zapisok Leonida Pasternaka.' *Novyi zhurnal*, No. 77 (New York, 1964), 190-214.

Payne, R. *The Three Worlds of Boris Pasternak*. London, 1961. P. 140.

Peterson, N. P. 'Pis'mo N. Petersona k N. A. Chaevu o N. F. Fedorove, Aug. 16, 1874.' *RA*, 1915, No. 3, pp. 280-281. [Reprinted in *Vselenskoe delo*, II (Riga, 1934), 160-161.]

─────────── "Pravda o velikom pisatele zemli russkoi, gr. L. N. Tolstom." *Semirechenskie oblastnie vedomosti*, No. 3 (Novocherkask, 1908), 66-82.

─────────── "Pis'mo sviashchen. Grigoriia Petrova mitropolitu Antoniiu. Spb. 1908" *Turkestanskie eparkhialnie vedomosti*, d?

Peterson, N. P. "Iz zapisok byvshego uchitelia" *Mezhdunarodnyi Tolstovskii Almanakh*. Ed. P. Sergeenko. 2nd ed. Moscow, 1909, pp. 257-68.

───────────, "Moia perepiska s gr. L. N. Tolstym" *Turkestanskie eparkhialnie vedomosti*, No. 6 (1909), 94-120.

───────────, "K suzhdeniiu o khristianstve N. F. Fedorova: Polemika" *B.V.*, No. 1 (1916), pp. 119-30.

───────────. "Pozorno li naimenovanie, 'krestianin' i o messianizme" *Missionerskii sbornik*, Nos. 6-8 (Ryazan, 1916).

───────────, "Prikhod kak iuridicheskoe litso." *Missionerskii sbornik*, Nos. 1-2 (Ryazan, 1917).

───────────. 'Pis'mo k izdateliu *Russkogo Arkhiva*. Po povodu otzyva F. M. Dostoevskogo o N. F. Fedorove.' *RA*, 1904, No. 6, pp. 300-301.

───────────. 'Kak sozdat' natsionalnuiu shkolu.' *Missionerskii sbornik*, No. 1-2 (Ryazan, 1917).

───────────. 'Zametka po povodu stat'i kn. E. Trubetskogo—"Zhiznennaia zadacha Solov'eva i vsemirnyi krizis zhizneponimaniia"— v *Voprosakh filosofii i psikhologii*, Sent.-Okt. 1912.' In 'Polemika.' *VFP*, No. 118 (1913), 405-411.

───────────. 'Eshche po povodu statei S. A. Golovanenka o N. F. Fedorove.' *BV*, 1917, No. 1.

'Pis'ma iz Rossii.' *Evr.*, No. 3 (3 December 1928), 8.

'Pis'ma iz Rossii.' *Evr.*, No. 22 (20 April 1929), 6-7.

Pletnev, A. [Pletniow.] 'Grundlinien der philosophischen Lehre N. F. Fiodorows.' *Der Russische Gedanke: Festschrift N. O. Losskii.* Bonn, 1934. Pp. 133-140.

_____. 'N. F. Fedorov i F. M. Dostoevskii.' *Novyi zhurnal*, No. 50 (New York, September 1957), 220-246.

Pokrovskii, P. Ia. [Pseudonym of G. P. Georg'evskii.] 'Iz vospominanii o Nikolae Fedoroviche.' *MV*, Nos. 23-26 (23-26 January 1904), 4-5, 4-5, 5, 4.

_____ Letter to Countess S. A. Tolstoi, April 24, 1911. *Novoe vremia*, No. 12684 (St. Petersburg, July 6, 1911), p. 1.

_____, "L. N. Tolstoi i N. F. Fedorov: Iz lichnikh vospominanii." Manuscript in the Lenin Library.

Piatidesiatiletie Rumiantsovskago Muzeia v Moskve, 1862-1912. *Istoricheskii ocherk.* Moscow, 1913.

Pokushenie Karakozova. Ed. M. M. Klevenskii and K. G. Kotel'nikov. 2 vols. Moscow, 1928-1930.

'Pokushenie Karakozova 4 aprelia 1866 g:,' Ed. A. Shilov. *Krasnyi Arkhiv*, No. 17 (Moscow, 1926), 91-137.

'Put' Evraziistva.' *Evr.*, No. 8 (12 January 1920), 1.

Romanovskii, N. *Kniga i zhizn'.* Moscow, 1950. [Copy in the Lenin Library, Moscow.]

Saltykov, A. 'Pervyi illustrator Maiakovskogo.' *Tvorchestvo*, No. 12 (Moscow 1965), 15.

Scheibert, P. 'Der Übermensch in der russische Revolution.' In *Der Übermensch*. Ed. E. Benz. Stuttgart, 1961, Pp. 179-196.

Schultze, B. *Russische Denker: Ihre Stellung zu Christus, Kirche, und Papsttum.* Vienna, 1950. Pp. 199-210.

Setnitskii, N. A. 'Kapitalisticheskii stroi v izobrazhenii N. F. Fedorova.' *IIuF*, III (1926), 9-25. [Reprnted as a separate pamphlet of 17 pp. in Harbin, 1926, and later in *Vsty.*, No. 3 (1928), 250-277.]

_____. 'Russkie mysliteli o Kitae: V. S. Solov'ev i N. F. Fedorov.' *IIuF*, III (1926), 191-222. [Reprinted as a separate pamphlet of 39 pp. in Harbin, 1926.]

_____. 'Eksploatatsiia.' *IIuF*, v (1920), 215-257. [Reprinted as 45 pp. pamphlet in Harbin, 1928.]

_____. 'O konechnom ideale.' *IIuF*, VII (1920), 191-256. [Reprinted as pamphlet of 65 pp. in Harbin, 1929, and later included in the author's book of the same title.]

Sezeman, V. Review of Murav'ev's *Ovladenie vremeni*. *Vsty.*, No. 3 (Paris, 1928), 172-176.

Shenrok, V. I. 'Pamiati N. F. Fedorova i A. E. Viktorova.' *Istoricheskii vestnik*, No. 2 (St. Petersburg, 1904), 663-670.

Shestov, L. [Pseudonym of Shvartsman.] *Umozrenie i otkrovenie*. Paris, 1964. Pp. 127-130.

Shklovskii, V. *Zhili-byli*. Moscow, 1964. P. 448.

───────. 'Kosmonavtika ot A do Ia.' *Literaturnaia gazeta*, No. 15 (Moscow, 7 April 1971), 13.

Smirnov, A. 'Dva filosofa.' *Golos rabochego* (Noginsk, 21 November 1940).

───────, 'Nikolai Fedorovich Fedorov.' *Znamia kommunizma* (Noginsk, 19 November 1959).

Solov'ev, V. S. 'Pis'ma N. F. Fedorovu.' In his *Sobranie sochinenii: Pis'ma i prilozhenie*. Ed. E. L. Radlov. St. Petersburg, 1909. II, 345-347. [Both letters first appeared in Kozhevnikov's monograph (see p. 78).]

───────. Letter to N. N. Strakhov, 1881. In his *Sobranie sochinenii: Pis'ma i prilozhenie*. I, 12.

───────, Letter to K. Leont'ev. Undated. *Vselenskoe delo*, II (Riga, 1934), 147-148.

Strakhov, N. N. Letter to L. N. Tolstoi, 19 October 1881. *Perepiska L. N. Tolstogo s N. N. Strakhovym. 1870-1894*. St. Petersburg, 1914. Pp. 284-285.

Stremooukhoff, D. *Vladimir Soloviev et son Oeuvre messianique*. Paris, 1935 Pp. 121, 122, 138, 173.

Tolstoi, I. L. *Tolstoi, My Father: Reminiscences*. Tr. A. Dunnigan. Chicago, 1971. Pp. 185-186.

Tolstoi, L. N. 'Dnevniki.' In his *Polnoe sobranie sochinenii*. Moscow-Leningrad, 1928-1958. XLIX (1952), 58, 73, 89, 90; L (1952), 23, 33, 65, 72.

───────. 'Pis'ma.' In his *Polnoe sobranie sochinenii*. LXIII (1934), 81; LXVI (1953), 85; LXVIII (1954), 247; LXXVIII (1956), 48; LXXXII (1956), 179-180; LXXXIII (1938), 314.

Tolstoi, S. I. *Ocherki bylago*. 2nd edition. Moscow, 1956. P. 116.

Trepka, A. *Wizjoner Kosmosu Konstanty Ciolkowski*. Katowice, 1974. Pp. 56-70.

Tr ov, N. P. 'Zametki po povodu mater'ialov k *Brat'iam Karamazovym.*' *Vselenskoe delo,* II (Riga, 1934), 169-175.

Trubetskoi, E. 'Zhiznennaia zadacha Solov'eva i vsemirnyi krizis zhizniponimaniia.' *VFP,* No. 114 (September-October 1912), 224-287. [Reprinted as a chapter in his *Mirosozertsanie Vl. S. Solov'eva.* Moscow, 1913, I. 35-93.]

_____. 'Polemika: Neskol'ko slov o Solov'eve i Fedorove.' *VFP,* No. 118 (May-June, 1913), 412-426.

Ustrialov, N. V. 'O filosofii N. F. Fedorova v svete sovremennosti.' *Vselenskoe delo,* II (Riga, 1934), 162-166. [Reprinted in his *Nashe Vremia.* Shanghai, 1934. Pp. 197-202.]

_____. *Rossia: u okna vagona.* Harbin, 1926. P. 46.

Utechin, S. V. 'Bolsheviks and their Allies after 1917: The Ideological Pattern.' *Soviet Studies,* X (Oxford, 1958/1959), 113-135.

Wiles, P. 'On Physical Immortality.' *Survey,* No. 56, 57 (London, 1965), 125-143, 142-161.

Young, G. M., Jr. 'Fyodorov in Baker Library.' *Dartmouth College Library Bulletin,* XVI (NS), No. 2 (Hanover, N.H., April 1976), 54-61.

_____ "Fyodorov in Baker Library: II. The Bibliography." Dartmouth College Library Bulletin, XVII (NS), No. 2 (Hanover, N. H., April, 1977), 74-88.

Zabelin, I. M. 'Chelovechestvo—dlia chego ono?' *Moskva,* No. 8 (Moscow, 1966), 172-186, and No. 5 (1968), 147-161. [Reprinted in *Chelovew i chelovechestvo.* Moscow, 1970. Pp. 129-261.]

_____. *Fizicheskaia geografiia i nauka budushchego.* 2nd edition. Moscow, 1970. P. 152. [1st edition, 1963.]

Zenkovskii, V. V. *Istoriia russkoi filosofii.* Paris, 1950. II 131-147. [English edition: *A History of Russian Philosophy.* Tr. G. L. Kline, New York, 1953. II, 588-604.]

Zernov, N., *The Russian Religious Renaissance of the Twentieth Century.* New York, 1963, Pp. 292-293.

Abbreviations are used for the following titles frequently referred to:

Askh. Askhabad. (Ashkhabad)
BV. Bogoslovskii vestnik. (Moscow)
Evr. Evraziia; ezhenedel'nik po voprosam kul'tury i politiki. (Paris)

FOD. Filosofiia obshchago dela. (Farnborough, 1970) see pp. 76-77.
GrE. Grani. (Frankfurt-am-Main).
IIuF. Harbin. Iuridicheskii Facul'tet. *Izvestiia.* (Harbin)
LN. Literaturnoe nasledstvo. (Moscow)
MV. Moskovskiia vedomosti. (Moscow)
Pu. Put'. Organ russkoi religioznoi mysli. (Paris)
RA. Russkii arkhiv; istoriko-literaturnyi sbornik. (Moscow)
RV. Russkiia vedomosti. (Moscow)
Vsty. Versty. (Paris)
VFP. Voprosy filosofii i psikhologii. (Moscow)

INDEX OF NAMES

Akhmatova, A. A., 9, 181, 190
Aksakov, K. S., 172
Aleksandrov, V. 222
Alekseev, V., 61
Alexander the Great, 130
Alexander II, 26, 153-158
Altaiskii, K., 205, 210
Amvrosii, Father, 207
Aristotle, 170
Bakhmetov, P., 222
Bakushinskii, A., 225
Baratynskii, E. A., 170
Barlow, G., 152
Bartenev, P. B., 207
Bartenev, P. I., 26
Bax, E. B., 152
Belyi, A., 9, 176, 180, 190, 203, 225
Belinskii, V. G., 158, 170, 220, 221
Berdiaev, N. A., 9, 79, 109, 168, 172, 176, 181, 187, 194, 195, 204, 205, 216, 220, 221, 226
Berlin, I., 71, 215
Biese, F., 152
Billington, J., 217, 220, 225
Blok, A. A., 170, 175, 176, 190, 191, 225
Blumenbach, J., 161, 220
Bondarev, T. M., 152
Boranetskii, P. S., 110, 218
Boris and Gleb, Saints, 137
Brasol, B., 210
Brikhnichev, I., 222
Briusov, V. Ia., 9, 28, 180, 190, 222, 225
Brodskii, I. A., 170
Brown, E. J., 193, 225
Büchner, L., 23, 163
Bulgakov, S. N., 9, 78, 172, 181, 204, 214, 216, 221
Bursov, B., 41, 212
Calvin, C. S., 222

Carnegie, A., 152
Catherine II, 17, 153, 154
Chaadaev, P. Ia., 59, 168-172, 177-179, 221
Chaev, N. A., 209
Chekhov, A. P., 28, 219
Chekrygin, V. N., 193-195, 225-226
Chernogub, N. N., 36, 64
Chernyshevskii, N. G., 23, 154, 156-158, 160, 162, 163, 170, 208, 209, 220
Chizhevskii, D., 164, 218, 220
Chkheidze, K. A., 187, 203, 222, 224
Christoff, P., 218, 221
Chuev, S., 222
Chulkov, N. P., 206
Comte, A., 23, 86, 217
Copernicus, N., 104, 234
Coulson, J., 204
Crisanius, Iu., 169, 220, 221
Danilevskii, N. Ia., 133
Dante, 14, 134, 135, 206, 215, 225
Darmesteter, J., 217
Darwin, C., 23, 151, 163
Descartes, R., 79, 87, 98
Dewey, J., 92
Dobroliubov, N. A., 23, 156, 157
Dokuchaev, V. V., 163
Dolinin, A. S., 203, 210
Dostoevskii, F. M., 8, 11, 26, 28, 36, 37-52, 53, 78, 89, 93, 109, 133, 140, 167, 170, 175, 178, 186, 196, 202-205, 210-212, 215, 221, 224, 227, 238
Duddington, N., 213
Dzhavrov, Z. D., 238
Edie, J. M., 201, 213, 221
Einstein, A., 187, 193, 224
Empson, W., 217

Ermolov, 26
Evgrafov, V. E., 205
Fedotov, G. P., 220
Fennell, J., 218
Fet, A. A., 8, 202, 204
Fichte, J. G., 87
Florenskii, P. A., 181, 196, 222
Florovskii, G. V., 116, 117, 181, 205, 219, 222
Forsh, O. D., 185, 223
Fourier, F. M. C., 86, 217
Frank, S. L., 54, 181, 213
Freud, S., 187, 211
Fülop-Miller, R., 185, 223
Gagarin, I. A., 17, 206
Gagarin, I. S., 17, 206
Gagarin, P. I., 17-20, 206, 207
Georgievskii, G. P., 215
Gershenson, M. O., 170, 221
Gezhelinskii, G. G., 222
de Gobineau, A., 161, 220
Gogol', N. V., 50, 170, 175, 209, 221
Golovanenko, S., 91, 205, 219
Goncharov, I. A., 84
Gor'kii, M., 185, 203, 219, 223, 237
Gornostaev, A. K., 41, 52, 69, 186, 205, 211, 213-215, 222-224
Grigor'ev, S., 185
Grimm, J. I. C., 161, 220
Grunwald, J., 206
Gusev, N. N., 61, 65, 67, 214, 215
Hamann, J. G., 232
de Harlez, C., 217
Headlam, A. C., 152
Hegel, G. W. F., 79, 143, 164, 165, 232
Herodotus, 131
Herzen, A. I., 86, 157, 173, 174
Homer, 131
Ibsen, H., 204
Il'in, V. N., 188
Iurasov, 26
Ivakin, I. M., 64, 65, 214, 222

Ivan IV, 127, 140, 170, 218, 221
Ivanitskii, P., 223
Ivanov, A. A., 194
Ivanov, V. I., 170, 191, 221
Jacobi, F. H., 89, 90, 232
Jakobson, R. O., 192, 225
James, H., 11
James, W., 92, 207
Jones, W., 220
Kalinin, M. I., 189
Kant, E., 79, 80, 88, 90, 152, 232, 233
Karakozov, D. V., 26, 157, 202, 208, 209, 219
Karazin, V. N., 78, 230, 235
Karnaukhova, M. G., 209
Katkov, M. N., 208
Kemeny, J. G., 216
Khlebnikov, V. V., 9, 180, 190
Khomiakov, A. S., 133, 137, 170, 172, 174, 177, 178, 217
Kireevskii, I. V., 133, 170, 172, 178, 221, 233
Kiselev, A., 190, 205, 225
Klevenskii, M. M., 209
Kline, G. L., 190, 201, 205, 213, 221, 225, 226
Kliuchevskii, V. O., 28
Komarovich, V. L., 41, 211, 212, 222
Kononov, D. S., 222
Konstantinov, F. V., 205
Kotelnikov, K. G., 209
Koutaissoff, E., 206, 223
Kozhevnikov, V. A., 7, 8, 20, 21, 29, 31, 35, 36, 72, 74, 75, 77-79, 86, 89, 180, 201-203, 209, 210, 216, 217, 219, 222, 228, 237-239, 242, 243
Kraiskii, A., 191, 192
Krasin, L. B., 184
Kras-skaia, E. M., 241, 244, 245
Kropotkin, P. A., 17
Kruchenykh, A. E., 191
Kurbskii, A. M., 127, 170, 218, 221
Kuznetsova, V., 182, 222

INDEX OF NAMES

Lavrov, P. L., 190
Lazurskii, V. F., 13, 66, 206, 215
Leibniz, G. W., 233
Lenin, V. I., 28, 176, 184, 189
Leont'ev, K. N., 170, 222
Linnichenko, I. A., 29, 64, 65, 209, 214, 215
Lord, R., 41-44, 79, 206, 211, 216
Losskii, N. O., 108, 109, 181, 205, 218, 219, 223
Lotze, R. H., 234
Luchitskii, P., 222
L'vov, V., 210
McLean, R. A., 225
Magarshak, D., 212
Maiakovskii, V. V., 9, 180, 192-195, 222, 225, 226
Malevich, K. S., 191, 192
Malthus, T. R., 104
Mamin-Sibiriak, D. N., 28
Mandelshtam, N. Ia., 190, 225
Mandelshtam, O. E., 190, 225
Manovskii, R., 222
Marx, K., 138, 151, 152, 158, 165, 166, 176, 179, 181, 189, 204, 235
Matthewson, R., 208
Matiushin, M., 191
Mechnikov, I. I., 163, 221
Mendeleev, D. I., 28, 163
Metalnikov, S. I., 221
Mill, J. S., 23
Mirskii, D. S., 8, 187, 188, 189, 204
Moleschott, J., 163
Moser, C. A., 208, 220
Murav'ev, M. N., 208
Murav'ev, N. M., 188
Murav'ev, V. N., 187, 188, 222, 224
Negri, A., 242
Nesmelov, A., 222
Nestor, 110
Nicholas I, 156

Nietzsche, F., 79, 88, 151, 166, 232, 233
Novotny, 187
Odoevskii, A. I., 168
Orlov, V. F., 61, 63
Pankratov, A., 222
Pasternak, B. L., 9, 180
Pasternak, L. O., 74, 75, 216
Pavlov, I. P., 163
Pavlov, P. V., 220
Peirce, C. S., 92
"Pensoso," 240, 242, 244, 245
Peresvetov, V., 219
Peter I, 223
Peterson, N. P., 7, 8, 20, 24-27, 36, 38, 40, 52-54, 61, 68, 72, 77-79, 93, 155, 180, 181, 201-203, 207-210, 212-215, 219, 222, 227, 228, 232, 237-242, 245
Philotheus, 142, 168
Pisarev, D. I., 23, 156-160, 162, 220
Plato, 79, 152, 170
Platonov, A., 190
Plekhanov, G. V., 165, 174
Pletnev, R., 41, 43-47, 206, 211
Pokrovskii, M. N., 222
Prishvin, M., 185, 223
Pushkin, A. S., 17, 85, 110, 158, 163, 185, 193, 204, 215, 217, 220
Rask, R. C., 161, 220
Raeff, M., 221
Rees, H., 214
Repin, I. E., 63
Ritschl, A., 233
Riurik, 17
Rozanov, V. V., 170
"Rubio," 241
Rumiantsev, N. P., 27
Saltykov, A., 226
Samarin, Iu. F., 152, 170, 172
Scanlan, J. P., 201, 213, 221
Schiller, F., 42, 163
Schmemann, A., 175, 201, 221
Schopenhauer, A., 88, 232, 233

Scriabin, A. N., 9, 180, 190, 191
Sechenov, I. M., 163
Sedunov, Iu., 223
Semenova, K., 17, 206
Semenova, N., 206
Sergius, Saint, 230
Setnitskii, N. A., (Ostromirov, A.), 7, 8, 27, 28, 75, 184-187, 203, 204, 207, 210, 220, 222-224
Shilov, A., 209
Shklovskii, V. B., 33, 34, 196, 210
Shmankevich, B., 222
Sezeman, V., 224
Shakespeare, W., 19, 163
Shenrok, V. I., 209, 210
Shestov, L. I., 170, 186, 205, 223
Sidorovich, K., 240
Simmons, E. J., 214, 215
Siuteev, 63
Socrates, 87
Solov'ev, V. S., 8, 11, 28, 36, 38, 40, 41, 43, 47, 50, 52-60, 72, 74, 78, 89, 98, 108, 112, 167, 170, 174, 178, 179, 181, 186, 190, 191, 202, 204, 205, 213, 214, 218, 219, 222, 224, 229, 233
Solzhenitsyn, A. I., 9, 170, 184, 205, 223, 226
Spengler, O., 133
Stalin, I. V., 9, 140, 181, 183, 204, 223
Starkov, A., 207
Stirner, M., 88
Stokham, A. B., 70
Storzhenko, N. I., 65, 209
Strakhov, N. N., 68, 215, 219
Timiriazev, K. A., 28
Tiutchev, F. I., 170
Tolstoi, L. N., 8, 11, 13, 17, 18, 24, 26, 28, 34, 36, 41, 50, 53, 57, 60-71, 74, 140, 145, 152, 167, 170, 175, 180, 181, 186, 195, 204, 205, 207, 209, 214, 215, 221-224, 236, 239
Troitskii, I. E., 66
Trotskii, L. D., 137, 188
Trubetskoi, E. N., 52, 213
Trubetskoi, N. S., 188
Tsiolkovskii, K. E., 9, 31-34, 168, 195, 196, 204, 207, 210
Tsirkunov, P., 240, 242, 244, 245
Turgenev, I. S., 71, 117, 154, 157, 163
Uspenskii, G., 152
Ustrialov, N. V., 8, 185, 204, 222, 223
Utechin, S. V., 182, 205, 223
Valuiev, 158
Velskii, V., 226
Venevitinov, M. I., 209
Veresaev, V. V., 28, 152
Vereshchagin, N., 152
Vernadskii, G., 188, 189
Vernadskii, V. I., 9, 181, 183, 195, 223
Viktorov, A. E., 210
Vladimir, Saint, 145
Vodovozova, E. N., 219, 220
Voeikov, A. I., 152
Vogt, K., 163
Volynskii, A. L., 9, 204
Voronov, 221
Wagner, R., 233
Wasiolek, E., 212
Wiles, P., 176, 205, 221
Yeats, W. B., 221
Zabelin, I. M., 196, 226
Zabolotskii, N. A., 9, 180, 190
Zagibalov, 26
Zakydalsky, T., 41, 95, 96, 203, 206, 209, 212, 213, 214, 217, 218, 224, 247
Zamiatin, E. I., 144
Zeldin, M.-B., 201, 213, 221
Zenkovskii, V. V., 78, 168, 171, 179, 202, 205, 214, 220, 221
Zenkovsky, S., 218
Zernov, N. M., 228
Zhukovskii, V. A., 207
Zouboff, P. P., 213